Shared Governance in Higher Education

Shared Governance in Higher Education

Demands, Transitions, Transformations

VOLUME 1

Edited by

Sharon F. Cramer

Preface by

Peter L.K. Knuepfer

Introduction by

Tina Good

Published by State University of New York Press, Albany

© 2017 State University of New York

For information, contact State University of New York Press, Albany, NY
www.sunypress.edu

Production, Ryan Morris
Marketing, Kate R. Seburyamo

Library of Congress Cataloging-in-Publication Data

Names: Cramer, Sharon F., editor.
Title: Shared governance in higher education : demands, transitions,
    transformations / edited by Sharon F. Cramer ; preface by Peter L.K.
    Knuepfer ; introduction by Tina Good.
Description: Albany : State University of New York Press, [2017] | Includes
    bibliographical references and index. Contents: Volume 1 —
Identifiers: LCCN 2016031462 (print) | LCCN 2016047976 (ebook) | ISBN
    9781438464275 (hardcover : alk. paper) | ISBN 9781438464268 (pbk.
    alk. paper) | ISBN 9781438464282 (e-book)
Subjects: LCSH: Education, Higher—United States—Administration. | Teacher
    participation in administration—United States. | Student participation in
    administration—United States.
Classification: LCC LB2341.S44779 2017 (print) | LCC LB2341 (ebook) | DDC
    378.1/01—dc23
LC record available at https://lccn.loc.gov/2016031462

10 9 8 7 6 5 4 3 2 1

Contents

Part II.
Broad-Based Shared Governance Explorations and Solutions

Preface

Peter L. K. Knuepfer

The first SUNY Voices Shared Governance conference, "Shared Governance for Institutions of Higher Education in the 21st Century: Beyond Stereotypes" was held in Albany, New York, on April 23 and 24, 2014. More than 150 registrants, from campuses throughout the State University of New York and City University of New York as well as a number of other institutions, attended and participated in plenary and concurrent sessions that explored a broad range of topics around shared governance. The conference opened with remarks from SUNY Board of Trustees Chairman H. Carl McCall and SUNY Chancellor Nancy Zimpher about SUNY's commitment to shared governance. In addition to the two keynote addresses that Dr. Tina Good summarizes in her introduction, nineteen papers and panels were presented at the conference, and this volume contains fifteen papers that grew out of these conference presentations.

The conference included some general overviews of shared governance, especially viewed through a faculty lens, with a group of case studies that illustrate how shared governance structures and processes have led to successful outcomes, whereas in other cases a lack of effective shared governance has led to less robust results. Again, those foci are well represented by the papers contained in this volume.

The first group of papers explores a range of aspects regarding the interactions of different stakeholders in shared governance. The first three papers by Bruce Simon, T. John McCune, and Rob Deemer from SUNY Fredonia describe the ways in which they have leveraged modern technology and their own bylaws revisions to foster a greater degree of collaboration across all campus governance constituencies, including faculty (and the faculty-professional staff union), students, and administrators. Their papers highlight the processes developed at Fredonia that led to the campus being awarded the first SUNY Voices Shared Governance Award, in recognition of the collaborative structure that has evolved on the campus. The award, presented to Deemer and his colleagues by Chairman McCall, is aimed at recognizing effective engagement of campus constituencies— administrators, faculty, staff, students, governing board members—on a particular topic or general campus structure that addresses issues and policies that affect the SUNY campus. The award, which continues to be offered, honors a campus rather than an individual or single constituency.

The next set of papers explores the integration of students in shared governance, highlighting experiences from both the State University of New York and the City University of New York. Minna Barrett and Duncan Quarless explore the myriad pressures on shared governance that exist in the 21st-century university, and particularly those for a public university system committed to open access. In their review of the changing nature of shared governance, they consider approaches that can encourage faculty and students to participate—and continue to participate—in meaningful shared governance. Daniel Ryan provides an overview of faculty-student partnerships, viewed in particular from his experience at the University at Albany. The companion papers by Síocháin Hughes and by Oluwadamisi Atanda and Emily Sohmer Tai explore the relationships that have evolved at the City University of New York to more effectively engage student governance leaders in working with other governance bodies and limit the disconnects between student governance leaders and other governance constituencies while at the same time enhancing the educational opportunities that shared governance offers to students. The two papers examine the issue from perspectives not usually obtained: faculty, Office of Veterans Services, graduate student, and artist.

The next set of papers explores a number of structural aspects of shared governance. Sharon Cramer and Rochelle Mozlin identify "holes" in shared governance structures. They then offer "systemness" as a way to close them, exploring how taking advantage of the breadth of a university system can operate at both campus and system levels. Quarless and Barrett, in a second co-authored paper, recognize that existing governance structures on campuses may not always be adequate to address particular issues. They argue that the use of task forces, properly formulated, can be a useful response to these special circumstances. They caution that task forces need to be clearly defined, with proper attention to identifying appropriate expertise and to identifying to whom the task force will make recommendations; that the role of the task force within the shared governance structure of the academic unit needs to be clearly defined; and that the task force should operate in as open and transparent a manner as possible, depending on the nature of the issues to be addressed.

The next two papers summarize key aspects of two major initiatives within the SUNY System—seamless transfer (described by Elizabeth L. Bringsjord and co-authors) and Open SUNY (discussed by Tina Good). The two papers are good companions to explore how different structures were developed and employed to tackle system-wide initiatives. As Good argues, the ability of a range of constituencies to work together in new ways not only provides the opportunity to accomplish complicated objectives, but also strengthens and expands the sharing of governance.

The next three papers explore challenges that have been faced in the evolution of shared governance on individual campuses. Kelley Donaghy describes the challenges that have been faced at the College of Environmental Science and Forestry in moving shared governance forward, and offers pragmatic recommendations for individuals new to governance leadership roles. Noelle Chaddock and Beth Hinderliter explore the impediments that restrict and block engagement in shared governance of faculty who bring diversity, especially race, ethnicity, gender, and sexual orientation. They argue that recognizing barriers is essential to moving into more engaged, and diverse, governance. Sallie Cuffee and co-authors explore the challenges that have been faced at Medgar Evers College, City University of New York, in maintaining effective shared governance through times of administrative turnover and other campus turmoil.

In the final paper, Norman Goodman provides a perspective on two questions I posed to the panelists at the final session of the conference. He suggests that the most important message from the conference was the need to develop strategies to engage and retain faculty and students with administrators to work together to address issues facing individual campuses or systems, but with a shared recognition of expected actions and the timeframes necessary to identify and implement them. He argues that the future of shared governance requires fostering trust and mutual respect among participants in order for governance to be effective in the modern university. His final point is that faculty, staff, and students need to appreciate that their efforts can be effective at shaping and implementing campus policies and programs, a position that has certainly manifested itself on many campuses in recent months.

In closing, I want to thank the people who made both the conference and this volume possible. Tina Good, then President of the Faculty Council of Community Colleges, chaired the planning committee, with close cooperation from me and Tremayne Price, then President of the SUNY Student Assembly. We are indebted to Lori Mould and Robert

Drumm representing the SUNY Student Assembly; Christine Fogal and Jarrod Cone representing the community college faculty; Sharon Cramer from the State-operated SUNY campuses; Cynthia Demarest representing the New York Community College Trustees; and David Belsky from SUNY System Administration. We were ably assisted by Bryant Barksdale (graduate student intern), Carol Donato, Cherí Burnham, and Lisa Kelsey (the three assistants to the SUNY faculty and student governance organizations). We all extend a special thank you to Sharon Cramer, who stepped forward to bring this volume to a successful conclusion by assuming the editorial duties as it became clear that the rest of us could not. Without her dedication, and the assistance of Donna Dixon and the staff at SUNY Press, this volume would not have materialized.

Introduction

Tina Good

In April 2014, the State University of New York (SUNY) hosted its first academic conference on shared governance. At a time when the Association of American University Professors (AAUP) was predicting the demise of shared governance and ceasing to host its own national conference on shared governance, the SUNY-wide faculty and student governance bodies joined with Chancellor Nancy Zimpher and SUNY System Administration to bring together faculty, students, provosts, business officers, presidents, council members, and trustees from the two public higher education systems within the state of New York (SUNY and the City University of New York—CUNY) to discuss how and why to share governance in the 21st century. Just as the AAUP was pulling back on its efforts to serve as a shared governance resource, SUNY, through its strategic planning initiative known as SUNY Voices, declared its commitment to shared governance as a fundamental tenet of higher education within a democracy.

The SUNY Voices conference—"Shared Governance for Institutions of Higher Education in the 21st Century: Beyond the Stereotypes"—was a culminating event that focused on how processes and structures of shared governance could stay flexible enough to meet the rapid pace of initiatives being introduced to or demanded of our colleges and universities without compromising fundamental principles of shared governance. The conference was framed by two keynote speakers: Rick Legon, President of the Association of Governing Boards (AGB), and Benjamin Ginsberg, author of *The Fall of the Faculty: The Rise of the All-Administrative University and Why It Matters*. While Legon suggested the necessity for establishing trust within a shared governance system that included trustees, presidents, faculty, and students, Ginsberg suggested that governance of colleges and universities should be minimally shared. Instead, he suggested that the faculty should be the primary governing body of the institution. While Legon suggested that a system of shared governance built on trust would lead to effective and innovative colleges and universities, Ginsberg suggested that such trust was unachievable because of the rise of administrative power in colleges and universities. Such division of thought served to motivate panelists to offer practical solutions to preserving and strengthening shared governance at our institutions, the fundamental mission of the SUNY Voices initiative.

SUNY Voices was a result of "The Power of SUNY Strategic Plan," which was launched by the SUNY Board of Trustees and Chancellor Nancy Zimpher in April 2010. While The Power of SUNY Plan is best known for its aspirational goals (the six big ideas), a lesser known function of the plan was to strengthen the infrastructure of SUNY, itself. Chancellor Zimpher and the leaders of the Faculty Council of Community Colleges, the Student Assembly, and the University Faculty Senate agreed that maintaining and strengthening shared governance throughout SUNY was a crucial element of SUNY's infrastructure and deserved strategic planning attention. Consequently, funding was allocated to strengthening shared governance through the SUNY Voices initiative, which has provided for campus workshops, structured collaboration with constituency groups, surveys and survey analysis, training institutes for campus governance leaders, an annual conference, publications, and a SUNY Shared Governance Award, the first of which was presented at this conference to SUNY Fredonia.

Presented with their award by the Chairman of the Board and the Chancellor, SUNY Fredonia launched the first SUNY Voices conference on shared governance. The theme of the conference declared our intention to continually work toward building and maintaining sustainable shared governance systems within higher education in general, and SUNY in particular.That celebration and intention continues with the publication of this book, which excerpts and further develops the concepts of shared governance discussed at this seminal conference.

Editor's Note

Anchovies and Governance

Sharon F. Cramer

At the 2014 SUNY Voices Shared Governance Conference, someone asked me what it was about shared governance (and, actually, governance in general) that seemed to be so foreign to many people. My gut response was, "Governance is like anchovies—it is something people either love or hate." And while a bit of an overstatement, since governance is completely dismissed by some, I have found the simile to be consistently true during the last few years. Fortunately, while serving as editor of this volume, I have come to know people who care as deeply about governance as they do about anchovies. Some authors I have come to know only through their writings; others I have known for years but had never read their work. All rose to the challenge of translating their SUNY Voices Conference presentations into chapters. Together, we have forged this book. Working with each of the authors has been a humbling privilege.

As you will find when you take a look at our chapters, authors come from all across New York—SUNY, FCCC, and CUNY. And those of you who are deeply enmeshed in governance challenges will find authors whose experience in many ways parallels your own. Shared governance members and leaders have reflected on the paths they followed to advance their governance goals: Some explain what they did that worked, whereas others consider alternatives that might have led to more successful results.

What I can promise you is that you will feel the passion each author has for the work done to address the unique governance complexities that faced them. Intellect partnered with heart to yield solutions, as well as to raise further questions about what is needed to ensure shared governance's vitality on our SUNY campuses. You will find here a feast for the mind, as well as prompts for discussions on your own campus about the ways you and your campus colleagues can foster shared governance. Get ready for a hearty meal—hope you like anchovies!

Acknowledgments

Gratitude is extended to the authors of this volume, who mined their own experiences, not only to present at the first SUNY Voices shared governance conference, but when composing their chapters. Their efforts enable others to learn. Their patience with the timeline and editorial process is much appreciated. Thanks are extended to the leaders who enabled SUNY Voices and this volume to come into being: President Pete Knuepfer (UFS), President Tina Good (Past President, FCCC), Past President Ken O'Brien (UFS), and SUNY Chancellor Nancy Zimpher—without their commitment to shared governance, New York State's public higher education system would be the poorer. As always, Carol Donato's skills and dedication to excellence improved many aspects of this volume from start to finish. Our editors at SUNY Press, Donna Dixon and Ryan Morris, made what can be a cumbersome process much easier, for which I am extremely thankful. Last, my late husband, Leslie R. Morris was the founding editor of the *Journal of Interlibrary Loan, Document Delivery & Electronic Reserve.* Although he died before I began my editorial work on this volume, he was a remembered role model for me, in the care and discipline that informed all his work with authors and their manuscripts.

Part I

Shared Governance Stakeholders

1

Improving Shared Governance through Bylaws, Technology, and Collaboration

Rob Deemer, T. John McCune, and Bruce Simon

The State University of New York at Fredonia was awarded the first SUNY Shared Governance Award in 2014. This chapter explores practices implemented by governance leaders at Fredonia that have had positive results. Bruce Simon focuses on bylaws, John McCune on technology, and Rob Deemer on collaboration among participants in shared governance activities. Through our commitment to developing comprehensive and flexible bylaws, innovative technology, and collaborative processes and relationships, we hope not only to continue to address the myriad issues inherent in the workings of a liberal arts comprehensive four-year institution, but also to provide others with a model for shared governance that is both effective and sustainable.

Introduction

Rob Deemer, T. John McCune, and Bruce Simon

What does it mean and what does it take to improve shared governance in academia? At the State University of New York at Fredonia, recipient of the first SUNY Shared Governance Award in 2014, we have been living with and working through this question (and many others that follow from it) for many years. To set the stage for our exploration of how we developed our distinctive approach to sharing governance, we open with a snapshot of our university and its governance constituency.

Fredonia is a master's-level public regional university with over 4,600 undergraduate and graduate students, over 260 full-time faculty and librarians, over 180 part-time faculty, over 200 professional staff, and 27 management-confidential administrators within four major divisions. Our University Senate currently has 60 seats, including representatives from each of our 23 departments and interdisciplinary studies as well as college-wide and university-wide at-large positions, five positions reserved for contingent faculty, four positions reserved for professional staff from each of our divisions, one graduate student representative, and six undergraduate student representatives from our Student Association. In addition, the senate has almost 20 *ex officio* members including the five senate officers who comprise its executive committee, our president, vice presidents of each division, all of the deans, and many of the directors of major offices within the university. Our campus governance leader is elected yearly and can run again for up to four consecutive years as senate chairperson. According to university policy, senate officers and standing committee chairs are compensated by either stipends or by course releases.

What structural and technological aspects of our shared governance system could fairly easily be replicated at or customized to other institutions? What personal and interpersonal aspects, while they may be more challenging to reproduce, are just as important to learn from and perhaps strive for? In what follows, Bruce Simon focuses on the review, revision, and ratification of bylaws as an ongoing effort to upgrade Fredonia's framework for institutional communication and decision-making, T. John McCune surveys several innovations in the use of technology during and between University Senate meetings, and Rob Deemer explains the strong commitment to collaboration among those who participate in shared governance activities, including administrative leaders. We presented early versions of each section at the 2014 SUNY Voices Shared Governance conference.

We hope that you find our accounts of our ongoing efforts to share governance useful for your campus or organization. We encourage you to consider which of our improvements might be adaptable for, to, and in light of your specific conditions and cultures, histories and missions, and people and relationships.

I.
Improving Shared Governance through Bylaws Review, Revision, and Ratification

Bruce Simon

Why Bylaws? An Autobiographical Opening

Among my highest governance priorities at Fredonia for much of the last decade has been working with others to improve our *Faculty and*

University Senate Bylaws. Why? What good can this project, and the repeated review, revision, and ratification of bylaws it entails, possibly do? I will seek to answer both questions in what follows, but let's linger for a moment on the more incredulous, dismissive, or skeptical questions that my first sentence might inspire.

Those who are familiar with or contribute to the voluminous body of scholarship on higher education leadership, management, and governance might well ask: Why prioritize bylaws? Shouldn't governance leaders among the academic faculty focus instead on substantive issues? Wouldn't it make sense to prioritize problem solving and trust building, thereby cultivating a culture in which shared governance is valued? Why should we squander time, effort, and good will wrangling among ourselves and with administrative leaders over procedural and structural matters? Shouldn't everyone involved in shared governance be results oriented? What can changing bylaws really do to counter the view that shared governance is necessarily inefficient and ineffective?[1]

I wouldn't have had very good answers to any of these questions when I first began paying attention to bylaws in the mid-2000s, for two main reasons. First, my own research focused on other aspects of academia, from controversies over the state and standing of the humanities and liberal arts ("political correctness" and beyond) to the casualization, corporatization, and globalization of universities ("fiscal correctness" and beyond). I simply wasn't aware of the burst of new work on governance in the late 1990s and early 2000s as I was getting my own academic career off the ground. Second, that very career trajectory put me in positions in which I was interacting extensively with fellow graduate student and faculty activists, most of whom tended to value union organizing over shared governance.[2] Bylaws were the furthest thing from my mind for most of my time as an assistant professor—and, frankly, I was skeptical that anything substantive could be accomplished through shared governance channels.

So what changed? As I became more involved in both union and governance leadership, and contributed to strategic planning, assessment, and accreditation endeavors, I gained experience and perspective that enabled me to reflect on the strengths and limitations of various means for faculty to gain influence and exert leverage at Fredonia. Perhaps the most important turning point came when the longstanding chair of the Planning and Budget Advisory Committee (PBAC) announced his retirement. Faced with the imminent prospect of the loss of his leadership, his understanding of the budget process, his institutional memory, and—most important—the informal understandings and communication styles he and our then-president had developed over years, the committee members all decided we would need to rethink the role of PBAC and reset our relationship with the president and campus community. We knew we wanted PBAC as a body to become better informed, more proactive, better synchronized with administrative decision-making schedules so as to influence decisions still in process, and more focused on strategic planning. So we researched planning and budget committees nationwide, particularly ones we knew of through our networks that had good reputations and institutional clout, searching for common elements in their structures, responsibilities, and functions that could help us reach or improve on our goals. We engaged chairs, deans, and vice presidents in extensive discussions to better understand administrative rhythms, workflows, and relationships during the Fredonia budgeting process, as well as attitudes toward them and ideas for improving them. This research informed our revision of the committee's policies and procedures manual: it enabled us to focus on codifying our expectations for information sharing through documents and meetings, clarifying the responsibilities and expanding the functions of the committee, and, in so doing, ensuring that the president and the senate leadership understood and supported the new PBAC.[3]

One crucial lesson I took from this process was that revisiting a committee's policies and procedures, some of which were part of the *Faculty and University Senate Bylaws* (and hence needed Senate approval, faculty ratification, and the president's signature to go into effect, as they affected consultation between the president and the faculty), could influence culture and climate. Not only did these revisions facilitate team building within PBAC and help identify and rethink assumptions about expectations for its work, but they also helped enhance working relationships between faculty and administrative leaders, build trust between us, and set an example to the campus in the midst of a major generational transfer of authority within Fredonia's faculty. Most important, perhaps, they informed candidates for an open Vice President for Academic Affairs position—not to mention search committee members and the members of the campus community who met with candidates—of Fredonia's changing values, priorities, and goals.

As the then-new VPAA's appointment and my election as Chair of PBAC occurred almost concurrently, we became natural allies and worked to keep PBAC in the decision-making loop on such substantive matters as a major strategic planning initiative and a new memorandum of understanding between the SUNY System Administration and Fredonia. Looking back, the good consequences that followed from our reboot of PBAC led me to start trusting my intuition that too-strict divisions between structure and culture, procedural and substantive, and process and results are a conceptual error, that a both/and approach to these pairs can be more effective than an either/or, and indeed that an institution can achieve better, faster, and more sustainable results by focusing first on the first part of these binary oppositions.

Even as a newly tenured chair of a major committee of the faculty at Fredonia, however, there was still much I did not understand.

- What relationship did PBAC have with the University Senate and its executive committee?

- Why did our then-president want it to be an advisory committee and not a standing committee? Which should it be?

- How much and in what ways was I supposed to coordinate PBAC's work with other committees?

- Why didn't key policy documents at Fredonia—PBAC's policies and procedures manual, the Fredonia *Bylaws*, the *Faculty Handbook*—offer more guidance to new leaders?

The opportunity to become a Fulbright Visiting Lecturer in American Studies in Fukuoka, Japan, for an academic year meant that I wouldn't have time to pursue such questions for a while, either pragmatically via action at Fredonia or conceptually via research. But, after I returned to Fredonia, was elected Vice Chair of the Senate in 2008, and cycled into the Chair position in 2009, I could no longer avoid larger questions about what governance is, what it is for, and how it ought to work. Bylaws revision became the key means to sort through these questions, as well as the complicated and difficult issues they raise, both for myself and with others who had a stake in the success of university-wide shared governance at Fredonia.

Even as the 21st century's first decade was coming to a close, however, I was too involved in the actual practice of shared governance to devote much time to scholarship on it. Fortunately, SUNY's statewide University Faculty Senate provided a plethora of support and information, through publications of its Governance Committee, meetings of campus governance leaders at every UFS plenary session, and the generosity of UFS leaders. The Governance Committee's *Governance Handbook* became my guide as I pored through AAUP's "Statement on Government of Colleges and Universities" and "On the Relationship of Faculty Governance to

Academic Freedom," as well as the Middle States Commission on Higher Education's *Characteristics of Excellence in Higher Education.* Analyzing the relations between these and other key governance documents helped me as I puzzled and stumbled through a variety of ambiguities and interpretive conundrums in Fredonia's *Bylaws*, not to mention unintended consequences, emergent developments, and outmoded arrangements, all of which raised previously unforeseen or unsettled issues. Talking through all of this with my colleagues on the senate executive committee (on which I served off and on between 2008 and 2014), exploring options and rationales with my SUNY governance gurus, and working out solutions in concert with faculty and administrative leaders at Fredonia were invaluable steps along the path toward improving Fredonia's *Bylaws*.[4] What kept us moving down that path was a shared commitment to frank airing of disagreements. While we preferred that these difficult conversations take place in private, we accepted that, at times, it would become necessary to carry out our debates in public. Without these ongoing dialogues, we would not have made what progress we did. To explicate that progress, and better answer my opening questions, I'll shift from autobiographical to theoretical and metaphorical modes of writing before concluding with a couple of case studies and some open questions.

Why Bylaws Matter: Theory and Simile

Every set of bylaws, no matter how seemingly dry, arcane, or limited to technical or procedural matters, enacts not only a theory of shared governance but indeed a vision of how the organization constituted by it ought to work. Bylaws emerge from a complex and specific institutional history and culture and exemplify the explicit and implicit choices made by a variety of individuals and groups within it over time. Those choices are made in the context of, and in response to, particular conditions, structures, and relationships within the organization, so that revisions to the bylaws can be both the result and cause of changes in the organization. Hence, bylaws are and will always remain a work in progress. Their content will, and should, respond to, among other things, incoming leaders' philosophies, personalities, and projects; new readings of the intended and unintended consequences of specific provisions; emerging situations that expose a crucial ambiguity or gap in existing provisions; shifting attitudes, perspectives, interests, roles, and alliances among the members of the organization; and changing legislative, demographic, and financial circumstances affecting the organization.

Due to their inherent volatility and institution-specificity, Fredonia's *Bylaws* don't necessarily provide a blueprint for those of any other college or university, but understanding how and why they've come to take the shape they now have can be useful to those considering whether and how to go about revising their own guiding policies and procedures regarding institutional communication and decision making. Our *Bylaws* enjoin the president and the delegated representatives of the faculty to reach procedural agreement for every kind of decision where consultation with or input from the faculty is warranted. In our experience at Fredonia, the least productive conflicts usually result from either a lack of initial agreement over what kind of shared governance activity is necessary for a given decision, or a failure to determine in advance who should legitimately be involved in the process leading up to it. We've found that the better we front-load the process (by specifying who shall participate in what ways at which stages of what kind of decision-making or recommendation-generating process at which level of the institution), the more likely we will achieve satisfactory results. By limiting the odds and scope of procedural conflicts, the Fredonia *Bylaws* are designed to enable all of us to focus on substantive matters.

And this is a recursive process. Anything that diminishes trust or threatens working relationships provides an opportunity to reexamine bylaws and consider whether there may be any procedural or structural dimensions to the problem. When there are, bylaws revision can help focus faculty members' and administrative leaders' attention on analyzing and evaluating the challenges and opportunities facing the university; exchanging, considering, and evaluating views on how to meet them; carefully identifying the grounds for goals, decisions, and actions; and developing a clear understanding of who plays what role when and what those roles entail as goals are being set, decisions are being made, and actions are being taken.[5]

Let's shift from theory to simile to help flesh out these abstractions. Try thinking of Fredonia's *Bylaws* as the university-wide shared governance analogue to the *Agreement between United University Professions and the State of New York*. Just as system-wide contract negotiations mobilize UUP leaders in Albany and members across New York State (first to prepare to send representatives to the bargaining table with the Governor's team and later to ratify the results of those negotiations), so, too, do bylaws revisions and ratifications demand of the faculty and its officially delegated representatives at Fredonia that they enter into high-level discussions with their administrative counterparts. This may be a courtesy for bylaws revisions that are purely about the internal workings of the Senate, as these require only the approval of the Senate and the ratification of the faculty to be enacted. But, for any bylaws revisions that affect consultation between the faculty and the president of the university, the process by which the senate executive committee and the president and her designee(s) reach agreement on what language to propose to the Senate (as well as on any revisions to it discussed by the Senate) is as close to negotiations as it is possible to get in a shared governance environment. Similarly, the president's signature enacting bylaws revisions that affect consultation are as close to a legally binding agreement as is possible outside a contractual realm. In this sense, both the *Agreement* and the *Bylaws* are the product of academic faculty and professional staff members and leaders first organizing and then interacting with administrative leaders, just as they both are platforms for further organizing and interactions that go beyond the formal revision of documents.

One major difference between the *Bylaws* and the *Agreement* prompts another simile that may also help convey the significance and stakes of bylaws review, revision, and ratification. Because, within SUNY, the president is a member of the faculty and the *Bylaws* establish a framework for all other policymaking by the faculty, our *Bylaws* are much like a constitution for the Fredonia faculty. Consider that a constitution's primary function is to provide a framework within which disagreements can be aired, examined, debated, and eventually resolved. The only consensus a constitution need presume is a shared commitment to resolving disagreements within the framework established by it, including the means for amending it. In the same way that all branches of the U.S. federal government are subject to the U.S. Constitution, and that state laws must be consistent with it, so, too, the Fredonia president and her designees (~ [equivalent to] the executive branch), the University Senate (~the legislative branch), and any other official governance bodies, like standing committees, affiliate committees, and academic departments at Fredonia (~the states), are all subject to the Fredonia *Bylaws*. The analogy isn't perfect, of course—for instance, we have no clear analog to the U.S. Supreme Court—but it helps convey the high stakes of bylaws review, revision, and ratification. With those stakes in mind, our *Bylaws* err on the side of over-specificity; our goal is to provide everyone involved with as clear a picture as possible of how the overall system is supposed to work.[6] By thus embedding institutional history within our "founding" document, we provide a framework within which experienced members' institutional memory can most helpfully orient new members of the faculty, whether academic faculty, professional staff, or administration, to the meaning, practice, and significance of shared governance at Fredonia.

Another way of understanding the functional significance of well-conceived structures is to turn to an "operating system" simile. To the extent that bylaws function in a way similar to an operating system in a computer, they allow the parts of the computer (~the university) to work together, act as an intermediary between hardware (~the people and resources of the university) and programs (~the functions of those people and resources), and provide a platform for application software (~the range of things universities do). In essence, an operating system (~bylaws) needs to be working for users (~administration, academic faculty, professional staff, students) to make the computer (~university) do anything. Bylaws allow the orchestration of a variety of concurrent decision-making processes essential to the operation of the university.

To put a spotlight on the stakes of that orchestration, let's start with the observation that bylaws, like cars, need to be inspected, tuned up periodically, and sometimes even overhauled so that their drivers can use them to get somewhere safely and speedily. Our process of revising our vehicle, Fredonia's *Bylaws*, has helped faculty and administrators to better trust the vehicle, and also each other, as we travel our academic road together.

In fact, the key feature enshrined and instituted in the current Fredonia *Bylaws* is that nobody occupies the driver's seat permanently. This idea may seem strange to those who understand governance only through a corporate, bureaucratic, or legal lens. In one sense, they are correct that the campus president will ultimately take the wheel when it comes time to make and implement a given decision. But all governance leaders at Fredonia, both academic and administrative, reject the view that since everything that bubbles through shared governance processes is ultimately advisory to the president—that is, is at heart a recommendation to the president—the activities of official governance bodies must therefore be either a rubber stamp or roadblock for decisions the president already has made. At Fredonia, we've put the principle of shared governance through repeated stress-testing (and avoided crash-testing thus far). We can point to numerous kinds of situations in which the president has freely given up the driver's seat:

- through ensuring that designated drivers (whether the Provost, Deans, Chairs, or Directors) seek appropriate input or feedback on administrative matters within their decision-making purview;

- through delegating recommendation-generating authority either to administrative task forces or senate affiliate committees for other decisions that are purely administrative;

- through seeking formal recommendations from the faculty on policy recommendations originally made by administrative task forces or affiliate committees when such consultation (which we define as the highest level of shared governance activity at Fredonia) is warranted or required;

- through working with the senate executive committee to constitute and charge joint task forces for certain decisions that will ultimately require formal consultation with the faculty;

- through turning the wheel over to the senate executive committee to charge a Senate standing committee to develop or respond to a proposal, or to bring a proposal to the Senate, on a matter that will ultimately require formal consultation between the faculty and the president; and

- through responding to faculty initiation of such consultation (most often through Senate recommendation, but sometimes via standing committee or department proposal).

In each of these types of cases, the president has acted on the recognition that other individuals and groups must often take the wheel—or take turns taking the wheel—during the drive toward a decision.

Furthermore, since each decision requires its own car to complete its journey, we need many different drivers on the shared governance road at any given time. This suggests that effective shared governance is most crucial when things really get humming and everyone needs traffic to keep moving smoothly: when bottlenecks, traffic jams, and pile-ups are the biggest danger. Really good bylaws, then, can establish a robust highway system for multiple kinds of shared governance activities at many levels within the university. Although there are unavoidable costs involved in maintaining and improving both the roads and the rules of the road, we have found at Fredonia that both are well worth the investment.

Moving from cars and roads to rails can also help dramatize why strong bylaws matter—and why the process of strengthening bylaws can have electrifying effects if leaders are willing to take risks together. Governance leaders from the faculty and administration couldn't joke about "living on the third rail," as we sometimes do at Fredonia, without a strong degree of confidence in the definitions, agreements, and procedures regarding institutional communication and decision making established by our *Bylaws*. Because we have laid the groundwork through bylaws review, revision, and ratification, we feel grounded enough that the risk of burnout or power failure is small enough to justify taking on major initiatives. Developing an online system for collecting and sharing student perceptions of learning and revising our general education program are much easier said than done, but we did both in the last few years. Next on the agenda—having brought administrative, faculty, and union leaders together over the last two years to decide how to reboot Fredonia's *University Handbook*—is to keep the many policy review/revision trains on track and on schedule during their journeys toward approval and implementation.

Making Bylaws Matter: Closing Case Studies, Open Questions

Neither the theories nor the similes laid out in the preceding section emerged from anyone's head fully formed. Rather, they slowly took shape over time, as faculty and administrative leaders worked through multiple waves of bylaws review, revision, and ratification. One wave that transformed Fredonia's *Bylaws* entailed reconceptualizing administrative review and developing clearer definitions of and agreements on fundamental concepts such as "Faculty," "Voting Faculty," "shared governance," and "consultation." A later wave further developed these definitions and processes and clarified roles and relations between executive, standing, and affiliate committees, different kinds of task forces, and academic departments. The most recent wave developed rules for electronic quorum and voting and fine-tuned Senate membership and representation requirements. There's a story—actually, many stories—behind every one of these waves.[7] In this final section, I would like to focus on one from the second wave and one from what I predict will be the next.

Some of our most difficult conversations over bylaws revision came in the first year of our current president's administration, when senate executive committee leaders went back and forth with the Interim Provost at the time over terms, issues, and procedures, sometimes sharply. It was an exhausting, and often frustrating, process for all involved, partly because it took us so long to realize we were using the same words (such as "consultation") with different meanings. Certain concepts and contexts were familiar to each of us from our own metacognitive frameworks, resulting in our inadvertently coming at issues with radically different assumptions. As a result, we often differed on what models were most appropriate to university-wide shared governance.[8] Still, none of us walked away from those difficult conversations, and over time we got better at hearing, understanding, and responding to each other's concerns, interests, and ideas.

That level of persistence, patience, and charity on all our parts was not easy to sustain, but it was well worth whatever pain we endured from repeated decisions not to end the conversation, because when we had finished our work we had put together the most significant and comprehensive set of changes to the Fredonia *Bylaws* of the 21st century to date. Our revisions formalized and institutionalized our mutual understanding that shared governance is a system for institutional communication and decision making; that different kinds of decisions require different kinds of decision-making processes; that the president and the senate executive committee must begin by reaching agreement on the proper decision-making process for each decision; and that that agreement must be conveyed through specific charges from the president and/or chairperson to the appropriate committee or task force. These second-wave revisions didn't just stand up to scrutiny during the senate approval and faculty ratification process. They also helped end a longstanding impasse over online course evaluations (through the efforts of a joint task force that included both critics and proponents of going online) and deeply informed the search for a new Provost (by signaling to candidates, search committee members, and the campus community the kinds of values, relationships, and communication and decision-making processes that matter most at Fredonia).

The moral I take from this story is that friction and noise can be signs that the system is working (because communication is frank and open) *and* symptoms of where it can work better (through conflict resolution and problem-solving processes) at one and the same time. Staying focused on procedural and structural solutions can help increase the odds that the heat produces light and that signals emerge from the noise.[9] In hindsight, and quite improbably, Fredonia ended up forging a working prototype made of materials we welded together in creative configurations derived from organizations often understood to be at an impasse over the meaning and value of shared governance, most notably the American Association of University Professors (AAUP) and the Association of Governing Boards of Universities and Colleges (AGB).[10] If we could accidentally bridge that gap, anyone can do it.

My second story is still in process and is likely to put these lessons to the test. It concerns the faculty's decision to formally acknowledge in the Fredonia *Bylaws* that SUNY Board of Trustees *Policies* mandate recognizing academic departments and department personnel committees as official faculty-delegated bodies for certain types of consultation, including the selection of department chairs by the former and the appointment, reappointment, and promotion of academic faculty in a department by the latter. The Fredonia *Bylaws* establish three preconditions for these kinds of "limited and specific" delegation of "consultative authority" by the faculty (II.6):

- departments must establish their "own voting eligibility rules, means for academic staff participation in decision-making processes, and other policies and procedures by developing and approving its own written bylaws, handbook, and/or policy manual";

- these departmental documents must be "consistent with and subject to these bylaws, current university policies, the *Policies*, the laws of the State of New York, and the current *Agreement* between UUP and the State of New York"; and

- the departments must share their documents "with the Governance Officer and with new hires during the first week of their appointment to the academic staff."

However, even years after this second-wave revision to the *Bylaws*, it's pretty clear that a good number of departments have not satisfied all three conditions.

Without a strong push from the senate executive committee—which in recent years has understandably prioritized matters such as general education and *University Handbook* revision—some academic departments have not documented or updated their internal governance policies, procedures, structures, and systems, while others have done so in ways that have raised serious and thorny questions about department-level shared governance and its relations to university-wide shared governance:

- Which kinds of communication and decision-making processes within departments should be determined only at the department level? What ground rules, if any, should apply to all departments? And by what process should any university-wide rules for departmental shared governance be established?[11]

- What should happen if a department cannot or will not develop its own policies and procedures on matters that are clearly departmental prerogatives? Should the department be penalized, as the *Bylaws* imply, and if so, how and by whom? If it is penalized, who should do the work the department is no longer authorized to do, and who should appoint or elect the people to do that work? Should the *Bylaws* be changed to clarify these matters? Should defaults be developed through the *University Handbook* that would take effect if departments do not develop their own policies by a certain date?

- Who ought to participate in what ways at which stages of what kind of department-level decision-making or recommendation-generating process? How do we sort through the differences in faculty appointment types, professional obligations, workloads, time in the department, areas of expertise among department faculty, and the wide range of decision types facing departments to arrive at equitable, efficient, and effective internal governance structures and voting systems for departments?

- To what extent and in what ways, if any, should the Fredonia *Bylaws* serve as a model for departments? To what extent and in what ways, if any, should recommendations from professional associations like AAUP be adopted or adapted for department-level shared governance?

- Since academic departments are also part of the administrative chain, how do we clearly differentiate administrative from governance matters? How do we clarify the duties and responsibilities of department chairs (given that their simultaneous roles as president's designee and department governance leader) so that decisions that require consultation with the faculty are distinguished from those that facilitate input-seeking from the chair?

As a newly elected and appointed department chairperson, I have begun working with my colleagues in the English department through a consideration of these questions as we figure out how to revise our department handbook to clearly distinguish departmental bylaws from a departmental policies and procedures manual. Since I have also recently started my term as Fredonia's voting representative on the SUNY University Faculty Senate and hence have returned to the Fredonia University Senate's Executive Committee, I expect to be in the thick of exploring and better articulating relationships between department-, university-, and system-level governance for years to come.

Perhaps one moral to this story may turn out to be that past performance does not guarantee future results. Another might be that past successes can create future problems. Given the potential for disagreements between academic faculty members, both within and across departments, as well as turf battles between different kinds of officially delegated representative bodies of the faculty, I wouldn't be surprised if further upgrading the Fredonia *Bylaws*, the *University Handbook*, and department handbooks proves to be an even more difficult task than any we have yet accomplished. Yet I remain confident we will do more than avoid being swamped by this next wave of bylaws revision at Fredonia and within SUNY. If we can learn to ride the next wave as successfully as we have previous ones, we will be able to offer further proof that bylaws review, revision, and ratification are crucial tools for strengthening shared governance at any level within a college or university and across a state university system.

II.
Improving Shared Governance through a Focus on Technology

T. John McCune

Background

Over the last 3 years, the University Senate at the State University of New York at Fredonia has focused on integrating technology into governance. While the overall goal has been to foster collaboration, specific projects have included online voting and assessing feedback. Technologies included the use of student response systems, online voting tools, and Google Apps for Education for online deliberation. During the process, literature and research were reviewed to determine and assess potential benefits. In addition, lessons have been learned regarding the relationship between technology and the governance process. Here I review the work that has been done at Fredonia and how the use of technology has been adopted. I also identify further challenges and opportunities for further work.

Throughout, elements of the Technology Acceptance Model (TAM) will be used as a paradigm to illustrate and analyze the perceived usefulness and ease of use of technology. TAM serves as a model for understanding how users of technology make sense of technology (Davis, Bagozzi, & Warshaw, 1989). The members of the senate at Fredonia are a multi-generational sample: Members include individuals with a wide range of experience and comfort with technology, from undergraduate students to professors who have worked in higher education for several decades. Aligned with the principle of shared governance, the technology must be able to facilitate a collaborative and inclusive process for all participants.

Although users may acknowledge the purpose of using technology within the governance process, adoption challenges can exist due to lack of trust, technology being perceived as difficult to use, and lack of a strategy on how to encourage participation and collaboration. An additional concern in using technology in governance is often not rooted in the technology but rather is based in the surrounding politics: these non-technical aspects then affect the ability to fully utilize the potential of the technology (Oblak, 2003). Here I will review multiple governance uses of technologies at Fredonia, including student response systems, electronic voting, and online deliberation in advance of electronic voting.

Electronic Voting

Voting over the Internet can be accessible and convenient, and offers a method for potentially increasing voter participation (Simons & Jones, 2012). However, voting over the Internet can also raise concerns about accuracy, privacy, and reliability (Merighi & Ravaioli, 2009). Through explicit consideration of these concerns, and after testing a variety of electronic voting options, the senate selected a product that met the needs of the campus. Subsequently, electronic voting has been used to conduct a number of polls, as well as election of senators, ratification of bylaws, voting on resolutions, and a variety of other purposes.

Within shared governance, trust is essential to facilitate collaboration. Trust of technology is a primary concern about electronic voting (Carter & Belanger, 2012). When attempting to foster trust in the use of electronic voting over the Internet, many factors must be considered (Volkamer, Oliver, & Dubuis, 2011):

> *Transparency.* When little information is available on the process of governance and electronic voting, trust can diminish. Both the purpose and process for using electronic voting must be consistently explained. All involved must have confidence in the transparency of the process.

Evaluating the system according to international standards. Electronic voting must adhere to widely adopted security standards to ensure that voting can be done in a secure and reliable manner.

Implementing separation of duty. When duties for electronic voting are separated across multiple groups, the ability to modify election results is reduced, and trust can be fostered.

Enabling verifiability. Verification of votes can be achieved, with the poll administrator and poll participants being able to access results directly from the voting server once the poll has concluded.

Enabling vote updating for the correction of errors. To reduce the impact of votes cast in error, online voting systems should permit individuals to re-cast their votes to ensure that their vote has been cast correctly.

Enabling vote updating to reduce potential for coercion. To reduce the likelihood of individuals being coerced to vote against their will, systems should permit voters to update their votes so they can recast their votes in a private and secure manner to limit external influence.

Test elections. Through conducting test elections, the online voting process can be experienced prior to the time of an actual vote. This can reduce doubt, thereby increasing trust in the system.

Allowing independent implementation of voting client software. If there is distrust in software, the selection of an independent alternative can foster trust.

After the elements related to trust are understood, they can be applied to analyze potential electronic voting solutions. Elements related to fostering participation should then be considered, leading to the development of an electronic voting strategy. As per, Vlachokyriakos, Dunphy, Taylor, Comber, and Olivier, (2014), additional criteria that can aid in the encouragement of participation of electronic voting on the Internet include the following:

Eligibility. An analysis must be done to determine the criteria for identifying who is eligible to participate in each poll. If ineligible participants are sent voting information for electronic polls, the poll will not be perceived as valid.

Fairness. Electronic voting must ensure that only one vote per person is permitted. Communications must be sent to participants to assure them that the system permits each voter to cast only a single vote.

Secrecy. Anonymous voting may have the potential to increase participation, as individual records are not linked to the choices made via the votes of specific participants.

Expression. The ability for poll participants to express themselves to other poll participants permits an interactive voting process in which voters may wish to recast their votes. After receiving new or further information on a voting item, poll participants may reconsider their positions and votes based on communication with others.

After considerations regarding the creation of strategies for building trust and participation, electronic voting systems must be evaluated for use (and perceived ease of usability) by a diverse range of voters. Voters with different skill sets and experiences should be sought to participate in the evaluation process. By testing, and ultimately selecting, systems that are designed with usability in mind, it may be possible to achieve both a higher level of confidence in the system and greater voter participation (Bederson, Lee, Sherman, Herrnson, & Niemi, 2003). However, there must also be a focus on having integrity in an online voting system to ensure reasonable security; security must be balanced with convenience and perceived usability (Simons & Jones, 2012; Wang & Leung, 2005).

When evaluating electronic voting options for use at Fredonia, three key criteria were identified: building trust, encouraging participation, and evaluating usability. These criteria were explicitly used when assessing potential electronic voting options. Based on an application of the criteria, the Condorcet Internet Voting Service, an online voting tool developed at Cornell (Myers, n.d.), was identified as a test electronic voting platform, with a pilot starting in 2012. In assessing the areas identified for building trust, the only area not permitted is the ability for enabling the updating of votes. The primary benefits of being able to update votes is so that votes can be changed if new information is presented and to reduce the potential impact of voting coercion. Further, when assessing the criteria Vlachokyriakos and colleagues (2014) identified for encouraging participation (as listed above), only the *expression* element is limited, because votes cannot be updated with the Condorcet Internet Voting Service.

Based on the pilot assessment, during the 2013–2014 academic year, the senate approved the use of the Condorcet Internet Voting Service for electronic voting, with the understanding that almost all areas could be covered to foster participation and to facilitate trust. The factors that have been most appreciated and perceived as useful by senate members at Fredonia include the ability to have a transparent and anonymous process for voting, whereby only eligible voters are permitted to cast a single vote, using a unique voter key issued to each voter. With the unique key sent to the email address for each participant, voters are unable to submit more than a single vote for each poll.

With the adoption of electronic voting, the Fredonia Senate Executive Committee found it necessary to monitor the number of votes received for polls so that reminders of participation could be sent to poll participants. In the pilot electronic polls, when reminders were not planned and continually provided, poll participation was low. Through the continued use of electronic voting, poll participants have become more comfortable with the tool. Combined with continued reminders, adoption of the use of electronic voting continues to increase.

Student Response Systems

Student response systems—commonly called "clickers"—have been incorporated into many forms of classroom instruction. They have a variety of uses, such as fostering collaboration through the creation of an interactive dynamic. Their use helps to make participants aware of the perceptions of others (Sanserverino, 2010). For senate meetings at Fredonia, the anticipated benefits included the ability to tabulate attendance and votes in a shorter amount of time and the ability to hold anonymous votes during meetings.

Prior to the uses of student response systems at senate meetings, votes were conducted at meetings in traditional ways (e.g., senators raising their hands). When using these methods, all attending the meetings could observe how each senator voted. With nontenured faculty and contingent faculty taking part in the meetings, perceived concerns were identified: Those who did not have tenure or a permanent appointment could feel a sense of anxiety when voting on matters that could be perceived as controversial.

When using student response systems for polling, anxiety can be reduced, while the speed of the vote may also improve attention for the participants (Sun, 2014). Unsolicited comments received from junior faculty members at Fredonia reinforced the findings that using student response systems for voting helped create a perceived positive effect by reducing voting anxiety.

The flow of senate meetings has improved through the use of student response systems. The voting via the student response systems has required significantly less time than other voting methods previously used to tabulate results; saved meeting time has been used to address other agenda items (Murphy, Fletcher, & Haston, 2010). With the use of the technology, processes have significantly increased the ability during meetings to amend statements and proposals, and to reduce the time required for processing motions. With initial training provided to the senators and Executive Committee by vendors, and the straightforward design of the products, the perceived ease of use and usefulness has resulted in a high level of usability.

The overall impact of using student response systems has been extremely positive. For voting items including a General Education curriculum revision, the creation of policies for sabbaticals, online course evaluations, and many others, the impact of using student response systems was confirmed in improving the flow of meetings and increasing their efficiency. Continued received feedback from junior faculty consistently reaffirms the need and importance for the tools for anonymous voting. Without the anonymity that the tool permits, participation from those without tenure or permanent appointment might be affected significantly.

Online Deliberation

With online deliberation being shown as effective in encouraging participation in governance (Min, 2007), it is important to create a strategy to plan how online deliberation can take place within the context of campus governance. The use of technology within governance permits for the engagement with participants outside of the physical rooms where governance meetings take place, moving from that synchronous environment to asynchronous communication. In addition, broader engagement and consultation can take place in governance actions through the ability to engage in online deliberation and voting during break periods, such as summer, when calling a synchronous face-to-face meeting of the senate might not be feasible. However, in fostering an online open and interactive environment that is politically open and engaging, the process must be clear and deliberate.

During the 2013–2014 academic year, the Fredonia Senate approved and adopted the use of Google Apps for Education to serve as the platform for online deliberation. With the use of collaborative technology, success can be predicted and influenced by a widespread adoption of the technology by peers, as well as compatibility with existing systems and practices (Cheung & Vogel, 2013). For these reasons, the use of Google Groups was perceived as a valuable platform for online deliberation, with a perceived high level of usefulness and relative ease of use. As Fredonia is a Google Apps for Education campus, many faculty, staff, and students were already familiar with the use of Google Apps.

At the conclusion of the 2013–2014 academic year, Google Groups were used for online deliberation. The initial governance items that were processed through online deliberation included departmental name changes, an academic calendar proposal vote, committee member slates, and an upper-level requirement policy change. During the process, although not previously planned, the role of an online facilitator was assumed by the Chairperson of University Senate. For most Google Groups, an individual takes on this role, which is similar to the role of an online instructor. The online facilitator's presence is viewed by most as essential to positively influence and guide interactions and deliberations in online forums (Oliviera, Tinoca, & Pereira, 2011). In the governance context, the Chairperson's role as facilitator, offering guidance of interactions, was viewed as necessary for online deliberation to successfully take place. The actions were perceived as very similar to an online instructor.

The experiment with online deliberation was a big success. As a result of online deliberation, four electronic votes were successfully conducted during the summer of 2014, with one item being tabled for the first meeting of the 2014 fall semester.

During Fredonia's use of online deliberation, the only challenge has been with facilitating the process through asynchronous computer-mediated communication, where participants in the process may view and respond to communications at different dates and times. Although online incivility can pose a challenge to online deliberation when participants create polarizing arguments through value predispositions (Anderson, Brossard, Scheufele, Xenos, & Ladwig, 2014), this has not presented a challenge yet with the online deliberation process at Fredonia.

Through the use of online deliberation, Fredonia successfully extended governance into times of the year that enabled consultation with the body of the Fredonia University Senate to take place, where this might not have been feasible previously. With break periods during and between traditional academic semesters being about 20 weeks throughout the year, and with many changes not being limited to the traditional academic semesters, the use of online deliberation is necessary to ensure that shared governance can take place.

Implications and Recommendations

The use of technology in the governance process in higher education must be done with a careful focus on how to implement change. When planning the integration of technology within governance, key areas need to be addressed, including how the technology enables trust, how easy the technology is to use, and how collaboration and participation are encouraged. If intentional planning does not take place, the technology may not be considered useful and risks not being accepted and adopted. When done effectively, the use of technology to facilitate governance can promote an increased collective intelligence in an organization through engaging constituent groups in discussions, promoting the management of knowledge, and performing tasks that aid in innovation (Grasso & Convertino, 2012).

As use of technology has increased at Fredonia, the need for the Governance Officer to be able to assist with technology has also increased. The duties of the Governance Officer include the need to design, revise or replace, and test an electronic system for deliberation of and voting on motions between any two senate meetings. See the appendix for a full description of these duties. Because it has these duties, the Governance Office must have a certain degree of knowledge and expertise with electronic voting and online deliberation. Hoke (2010) stressed that expertise is essential to provide assurance in the integrity and security of data. In the future, the role of the Governance Officer, as a member of a governance organization having knowledge of information assurance practices, may become more common. This could enable more people to understand the role of technology in fostering both trust and participation in governance.

Using technology for the University Senate at Fredonia has also served to help educate faculty and staff on available technology, and on how it can be used in the classroom and for governance. With clickers being found to help foster active learning and promote higher student achievement (Blasco-Arcas, Buil, Hernandez-Ortega, & Sese, 2013), there are benefits to raising awareness of, and experience with, the technology through the governance process. This might have the byproduct of extending these collaboration practices into the classroom.

Further research in the area of acceptance of technology in campus governance would be beneficial by examining the impact on segmented participant samples. With a multi-generational group participating in campus governance through computer-mediated communication, digital natives and immigrants may hold different perceptions about technology. Research could be conducted with regard to acceptance variables related to perceived usefulness and ease of use, especially in instances involving asynchronous and synchronous communication modalities.

As computer-mediated communication in governance evolves, an exploration of perceived inclusiveness regarding the use of technology is relevant. Examples include the channel of communication preferred, such as a young adult preferring to communicate via text message or social media, and an older adult preferring an email message. If one communication channel is prioritized over another, and any group feels they are a secondary audience, this might affect participation.

The use of technology in governance at Fredonia has been positive in both results and perception. Through planning the use of technology in addressing concerns and needs to build trust, and utilizing easy-to-use technology, the goals of increasing participation in governance and fostering collaboration have been achieved at Fredonia. The role of governance at Fredonia has transformed to embrace technology to improve collaboration, engagement, and effectiveness in communication.

III.
Improving Shared Governance through Collaboration

Rob Deemer

Over the last 3 years, Fredonia has experienced an influx of new campus leaders. Our President, Provost, and Vice President for Academic Affairs; Vice President for Finance and Administration; Vice President for Engagement and Economic Development; Associate Provost for Curriculum, Assessment, and Academic Support; Associate Provost for Graduate Studies, Sponsored Programs, and Faculty Development; and our Dean of the newly formed College of Visual and Performing Arts all began their tenures since the summer of 2012. In addition, my own tenure as the Chairperson of our University Senate started in the summer of 2012 and will continue through the spring of 2016.

This fortuitous confluence has given Fredonia a rare opportunity to formulate strong relationships among faculty and administrative governance leaders from the outset of our tenures. This was necessary for many reasons, not the least of which was a number of high-profile campus initiatives that loomed before us. Some of these initiatives had been approved by the senate but were in need of implementation, while others had yet to be created, proposed, and approved. For example, implementations including a new strategic plan, a new set of baccalaureate goals, a rebranding initiative, an online student course evaluation policy, and a comprehensive internationalization plan, along with developments including revision of our mission statement, our general education program, and our *University Handbook* were all awaiting our attention. In many ways, it was the need to successfully address and complete these initiatives that created the high priority to engage our administrative and faculty governance leaders in searching for the best way to work together. In what follows I will explore the results of that search—namely, the admission, evolution, and execution of a collaborative concept of shared governance.

In the University of Iowa's AAUP 2007 document "What is Shared Governance Anyway?" the implementation of shared governance is described as having two possible concepts (Schotz, 2007). The "shareholder" version places the president and administration at the top of the "power pyramid" with the remainder of the constituents being allowed to provide input equally before decisions are made (almost always by a single executive administrator). This is in sharp contrast to the "classic" (or "delegative") version, which is described as emanating from the AAUP's 1966 "Statement on Government of College and Universities," whereby power and authority for decision making is delegated to the relevant administration and faculty members, based on areas of expertise. In both cases, the focus is on the question of *with whom* the decision-making authority and responsibility resides.

An argument could be made, however, that simply designating which individual or group *owns* the authority and responsibility does not go far enough to be effective. Both constructs (as described by the AAUP document) seem to assume that the faculty has (or, in the case of the "classic" version, should have) little to no overt influence over the decisions being made by the administration. Either concept presupposes a one-size-fits-all structure that could easily engender an overly divisive or overly apathetic governance environment.

Initially, I considered suggesting that collaboration between faculty governance and administration could consider a third version along with the "shareholder" and "classic" approaches. However, there are a number of reasons why collaboration may indeed transcend either "shareholder" or "classic" approaches, including our insight that meaningful shared governance has more to do with process and intention than ownership of authority/responsibility. On further reflection, I realized that, in addition to the intangible collaborative relationships that form within such a governance culture, we do have a number of examples of "joint" procedures that cannot be described as anything other than collaborative in structure. To that end, an analysis of our governance practices here at Fredonia should demonstrate the viability of incorporating all three concepts of shared governance—stakeholder, delegative, and collaborative—within a single governance structure.

Let me illustrate our way of collaborating. An example of a "stakeholder" model is seen in the budget process that has been adopted by our Academic Affairs division. It incorporates several interlaced layers of input to our provost: department chairs, deans, our Planning and Budget Committee[1] and our Provost's Council[2] all review the budget before the provost brings the division's budget proposal to the President's Cabinet. At that time, the provost, vice presidents, and the president negotiate the final budget for the university. In this model, while final budget decisions are always made by one or a handful of administrators, this occurs only after substantial input from across the campus has been sought and considered.

Alternatively, a prominent example of the "classic" model of shared governance at our institution would be that of our process of general education revision. A 3-year revision process, entirely driven and overseen by faculty governance, saw many iterations of a plan evolve. What began as an initial proposal from a revision subcommittee eventually became the final approved proposal. Administration provided feedback and suggestions in the same way many other constituencies did, but they did not impose any ultimatums or impede the process; while there were numerous comments along the way about the risk of the initiative never coming to fruition, ultimately everyone conceded that the governance process was the right way to go.

While either of these models can be effective, and might even be essential within its own area of focus, governance at Fredonia transcends the limitations these models contain. For example, when I began work as the Chairperson of the University Senate in 2012, there had been several calls for an overhaul of the methods by which task forces were formed; too often, they were formed in an *ad hoc* nature by the president or one of the vice presidents, with little or no consultation with faculty governance. The negative sides of this situation became apparent when major initiatives were brought to the senate floor with little to no prior communication with the Senate Executive Committee or appropriate standing committees. As a result, an important part of restructuring Fredonia's *Faculty and University Senate Bylaws* was the inclusion of language describing a joint process of forming task forces between the president (or designee) and the campus governance leader (or Senate Executive Committee). That language reads as follows:

ARTICLE VI: AD HOC COMMITTEES OF THE FACULTY

Section 2: Task Forces

a. Task Force Types and Activities

2. The Executive Committee and the President may also jointly submit for senate approval the size, composition, function, membership, and charge of a joint task force. These task forces shall submit their reports and/or proposals simultaneously to the Executive Committee and to the president.

This mechanism for formal collaboration between administrative and faculty governance has been very helpful. Most recently, in December of 2014, several undergraduate students came to our senate meeting and submitted a request for the establishment of a task force to develop a "preferred name" policy, because of the difficulty that transgendered students had in changing their first names within the campus systems. After the senate voted unanimously to support the policy request, President Horvath and I discussed what the size and composition of the task force should be and jointly created a charge for the group. We discussed membership of the task force in terms of what areas from campus should be represented, the various specializations that would be needed for the endeavor, and who might be appropriate to serve. Once we agreed on an initial list, I contacted the various members of our faculty, professional staff, and student body to request their service on the task force. Once everyone agreed to take part, they met with the president and me to accept and discuss their charge, and the task force members began to do their work. At every point in the process, both publicly and privately, the formation and organization of this task force was a truly shared responsibility of both the president and the campus governance leader.

I have been asked by colleagues why I have prioritized collaboration so heavily in my work as senate chairperson. I always answer this question in the same way, clarifying that it has a lot to do with my own background and discipline. Since 2007, I have been the head of the Music

Composition studio within the School of Music at Fredonia. Much of my experience as a composer has been in a collaborative environment. While most of my interactions with performers and conductors have been collaborative in nature, I have also worked extensively with individuals outside my discipline, including filmmakers, theater directors, choreographers, and poets. There are a number of challenges to interdisciplinary collaboration in a creative format. Making art on one's own is almost always difficult in its own right, but when two or more creative artists work together, their combined differences in language, expectations, and assumptions can easily overwhelm any chance for effective communication and collaboration. Similar challenges can also be found when academic faculty and administrators work together to achieve shared goals. In order to overcome the challenges inherent in a collaboration, all involved parties must be aware of how (and be willing) to actively take part in the underlying processes that occur.

Chris Ansell and Alison Gash describe a five-part cyclical process in their *Journal of Public Administration Research and Theory* article "Collaborative Governance in Theory and Practice" that neatly encapsulates the elements needed for effective collaboration: communication, trust, commitment, understanding, and outcomes (Ansell & Gash, 2007). Their research was based on findings from case studies about collaboration among various civic governance groups, but the overall concepts hew nicely to the processes involved in academic collaborative governance. One important point to remember is that these elements are nonlinear; in addition to their being cyclical, they are also concurrent—you need strong communication in order to elicit trust, but you need that trust to consider the communication to be a necessary part of the relationship.

It is difficult to overstate how important communication is within shared governance; the entire endeavor relies on it. If open and frank communication lines do not exist between administrators, governance leaders, and the general campus population, all of the other elements of the collaborative process will be difficult, if not impossible, to achieve. At Fredonia, we have a multi-tiered communication culture that works well enough so that when any communication breakdown occurs, it is promptly recognized and addressed, without assigning blame. Face-to-face interactions are common, held in the form of standing meetings every month between the campus governance leader and president, provost, and associate provost. These meetings are conversational and candid, and provide both participants the opportunity to ask important questions, and provide answers when possible. The second tier of communication would include three committee-level meetings with the Senate Executive Committee, Standing Committee chairs, and the Provost's Council. A special second-tier communication piece is our Campus Initiatives Roundtable. This was formed three years ago, when it was deemed necessary to have each of the task forces and implementation teams communicating with one another. This group, which is convened by the Senate Chairperson, meets twice monthly, once on their own and once with the President's Cabinet. The last tier would include conveying information with and through the University at our monthly meetings, and communicating directly with all of the campus community through monthly email updates sent to all faculty, professional staff, and administrators by the Senate Chairperson. Finally, underpinning all of these officially scheduled meetings are the less formal interactions: hallway conversations, spontaneous discussions over lunch, and the occasional text message or Facebook chat. These informal connections do allow for efficient communication to occur, but they also encourage stronger, more trusting relationships among the various individuals and factions.

Building and maintaining trust between individuals and constituencies is another imperative element of the collaborative process. Ansell and Gash state that

> [t]he lack of trust among stakeholders is a common starting point for collaborative governance. The literature strongly suggests that the collaborative process is not merely about negotiation but also about building trust among stakeholders. In fact, when there has been a prehistory of antagonism among stakeholders, we found that trust building often becomes the most prominent aspect of the early collaborative process and can be quite difficult to cultivate. (558)

One of the major challenges over the past three years has been the building of trust between the new administration and much of the faculty. While, over time, both open communication lines and consistency in vision have helped to strengthen the establishment of that sense of trust, it is still a work in progress. This creates a particularly difficult situation for the campus governance leader and Senate Executive Committee, who need to foster a close and effective working relationship with the members of the administration, and concurrently maintain their independence. Senate executives must find a way to convey information to the faculty at large while at the same time not being perceived as "collaborators" in the pejorative sense (a comment that we on the Senate Executive Committee have heard more than once).

As our communication lines and trust have improved over time, so has the commitment to shared governance in general, as well as the processes that it brings forth. Convincing both administrators and faculty members to believe in the shared governance system is a constant concern, since if either party loses commitment to the process, the entire shared governance system could grind to a halt or disappear altogether. More than once the campus has come to terms with accepting a policy or issue, recognizing that members of no single cohort got what they wanted; however, all involved were able to agree to the compromise for the sake of the institution. Such endeavors as convincing an entire campus to commit to a truly "shared" governance framework take years to complete (or at least they have for us), and as with the trust element, this is a work in progress.

Over time, all sides have begun to realize that they all "own" the governance at Fredonia—in different ways, at different times, and within different contexts. This burgeoning realization of the true strength of our shared governance system has coincided with an understanding of the issues that face the institution, and of the methods and strategies that the campus can (and should) use to address those issues. The first major step toward this understanding of the issues was the revision of our mission statement and the creation of a strategic plan and set of baccalaureate goals. We were able to accomplish both of these goals in a collaborative way. With these concepts as a foundation, everything else that we have had to deal with[3] has been addressed with them in mind.

A major concept of Ansell and Gash's is to focus on intermediate outcomes (or "small wins") in order to nurture the trust, commitment, and understanding needed to bring those outcomes to completion. Looking back at the list of campus initiatives that Fredonia's shared governance has dealt with over the past 3 years, intermediate outcomes were indeed focused on throughout each initiative by necessity, since the larger outcomes (i.e., the approval of an entire initiative) were not possible unless those smaller "wins" were achieved first. The small wins—such as the approval of a mission statement for the General Education program which helped to set the terms for the discussions that followed—that slowly accrued throughout each initiative's deliberation process were indeed useful to slowly build the perception (and the reality) that a collaborative shared governance system was successfully accomplishing a growing number of initiatives. All could see that faculty governance and administration were working together; this helped to foster confidence in some of the larger issues that the campus has addressed, and continues to face.

It is worth noting that no matter how collaborative a faculty governance body chooses to be, there is a preponderance of responsibility on the shoulders of the president (and the campus administrators) to ensure that an authentically collaborative relationship is fostered. Our University Senate is both large and diverse, but in the end it has an advisory role; the president is within her right to take any and all senate-approved policies or initiatives and choose not to follow those recommendations. That being said, we have been lucky to have a president and a provost to whom collaboration comes naturally. It is hoped that the structures and processes we have worked hard to form over the past several years will continue to grow and mature.

Conclusion

Rob Deemer, T. John McCune, and Bruce Simon

Sharing, at any level, is difficult. When one is asked to share something, there is a perception that something is being lost, be that broad power or sole authority, the ownership of important information, or all of the chips and salsa. The reaction to this perceived "loss," which can range anywhere from contentment that the greater good has been served to slight irritation to outright refusal, can be greatly influenced by the underlying perceptions of both the ownership of that which is being shared and the reasons why sharing is necessary in the first place.

So many aspects of an institution of higher education, including budget and strategic planning, academic policies, curriculum, and personnel, will and should be affected by the level and quality of shared governance that exists between the institution's administration and faculty. Issues arise, however, when there are discrepancies as to where the ownership of governance resides and/or why shared governance is necessary within an institution. At Fredonia, the faculty and administration have worked diligently to ensure that there are as few discrepancies in our governance mechanisms as possible. The sense of ownership of authority and responsibility—which dictates who is sharing governance to begin with—has evolved over time so that all of the primary partners continually work to understand not only how the various governance processes and procedures work, but why they need to work the way they do. Similarly, we have striven to provide ourselves with strong rationales as to the necessity for effective shared governance and continue to use those rationales as the foundation on which we are able to work together. Through our commitment to developing comprehensive and flexible bylaws, innovative technology, and collaborative processes and relationships, we hope not only to continue to address the myriad issues inherent in the workings of a liberal arts comprehensive 4-year institution, but also to provide others with a model for institutional communication and decision making that is both effective and sustainable.

It's not surprising that the concepts of shared governance and consultation are so elusive and so difficult to implement at many of our institutions; they take an immense amount of hard work and understanding on the parts of a number of interested groups that are rarely in sync with each other. We hope that the example we at Fredonia are setting is indeed a positive one and that, through our efforts, others may find opportunities for improvement at their own institutions.

Acknowledgments

Rob Deemer, T. John McCune, and Bruce Simon respectfully recognize President Virginia Horvath and Provost Terry Brown for their strong embrace of shared governance and gratefully acknowledge Sharon Cramer for her leadership and collaboration at every stage of this project. In addition, Bruce Simon thanks Mike Davis, Robert Simon, and Jeffrey Tucker for their thoughtful suggestions on multiple drafts of his essay.

Appendix

Governance Officer Duties from the University Senate Bylaws

The Governance Officer shall be elected by the senate during a meeting in May for a 1-year term, and shall be allowed to stand for reelection in following years without any term limit, on the same schedule as the Vice Chairperson and Faculty Secretary. Candidates for the position may be nominated at any time prior to the election by any member of senate or by the Executive Committee. The Governance Officer shall assume office on July 1.

The Governance Officer shall:

1. Review the operations of these bylaws and propose amendments of these bylaws to the Executive Committee.

2. Prepare slates of candidates and conduct elections for at-large senators, the University Faculty Senator, the University Faculty Senator Alternate, the faculty representatives to the Faculty Student Association, and representatives on various standing committees.

3. Notify all candidates and the campus of election results.

4. Regularly review the responsibilities and actions, or lack thereof, of senate standing committees and propose changes to the Executive Committee.

5. Declare, under certain circumstances and after appropriate review, a standing committee member's seat vacant and order a replacement.

6. Design, revise or replace, and test an electronic system for deliberation of and voting on motions between any two senate meetings.

Notes

I. Improving Shared Governance through Bylaws Review, Revision, and Ratification

1. These questions are my own attempt to distill the issues engaged by the multiple contributors to Ehrenberg (2004), Tierney (2004), Tierney and Lechuga (2004), Tierney (2006), and Bastedo (2012). See also Gayle, Tewarie, and White (2003), Hendrickson, Lane, Harris, and Dorman (2013), and Gerber (2014) for useful overviews.

2. See, for instance, Rhoades (1998), Newfield (2008), and Bousquet (2008), who in my view are cited far too rarely in scholarship on governance. During the late 1990s and early 2000s, even as the seismic shifts occasioned by the public break between the Association of Governing Boards of Universities and Colleges (AGB) and the American Association of University Professors (AAUP) were in their most active phase, I covered and contributed to academic unionism by serving as co-General Editor of *Workplace: A*

Journal for Academic Labor and as a chapter officer and statewide delegate in SUNY's faculty and professionals union United University Professions (UUP).

3. If we had found Schuster, Smith, Corak, and Yamada (1994) at the time, this process would have been even more efficient and effective.

4. Special thanks to Rob Deemer, Dale Tuggy, Andy Cullison, T. John McCune, Brian Masciadrelli, President Dennis Hefner, President (and former Vice President for Academic Affairs) Virginia Horvath, Vice President for Engagement and Economic Development (and former Interim Provost) Kevin Kearns, Provost Terry Brown, Sharon Cramer, Dennis Showers, and Ken O'Brien. Each played crucial roles at different stages of the bylaws review and revision process at Fredonia, whether from off campus or just across the hall. It would take too long to list all their contributions, and even longer to share their back stories.

5. We have extended this principle to the review of other documents that guide institutional decision making and policy making at Fredonia, such as department handbooks, committee policies and procedures manuals, and the *University Handbook*.

6. Of course, peculiarities inherent in being a campus in a state university system that includes a statewide union that represents all faculty and professionals in the system strain the "constitution" simile. For one thing, the SUNY Policies of the Board of Trustees might be better compared to the U.S. Constitution, while the Fredonia Bylaws might be better compared to a state constitution. Everything we do has to be consistent with the Policies, as well as with the system-wide policies and procedures approved by the statewide University Faculty Senate and signed by the Chancellor. For another, the current Agreement, which focuses on terms and conditions of employment and establishes what is subject to negotiation rather than consultation, sets bounds on what the system- or campus-level shared governance processes can achieve. When UUP asserts its exclusive right to bargain on behalf of the faculty and professionals it represents, the most any governance body can seek to do is advise both labor and management on that matter. By the same token, unless management agrees to negotiate with UUP on any matter other than terms and conditions of employment, the union can only advise official governance bodies and suggest policies that governance leaders might use to initiate consultation.

7. The first wave was largely the result of work by Tuggy, Hefner, and me. The second wave was led by Deemer and Horvath, but Kearns, Cullison, and I played our roles. The third wave was a Deemer/McCune/Simon collaboration. Right now, Deemer, Horvath, Brown, Masciadrelli, and I are among those trying to surf the next wave.

8. In hindsight, taking the time to read and discuss major scholarly studies of shared governance at the start of the process might have helped us recognize and bridge these gaps more quickly.

9.   Similar points have been made very recently by Bahls (2014, pp. 43–45, 55, 86–88, 91–95) and Bowen and Tobin (2015, pp. 92–98, 147–150, 201–212).
10. For analyses of and responses to the AAUP-AGB divergence, see Duderstadt and Womack (2003); Gayle, Tewarie, and White (2003); Tierney (2004); Tierney and Lechuga (2004); Esterberg and Wooding (2012); Hendrickson, Lane, Harris, and Dorman (2013); Gerber (2014); Bahls (2014); and Bowen and Tobin (2015). In my view, governance researchers need to pay more attention to the AGB's shift in emphasis since around 2010. Do the Fredonia Bylaws hint at a possible convergence between AAUP and AGB?
11. One way these questions have recently been answered was through negotiations between administrative and UUP chapter leaders, myself included, over Fredonia's *Handbook on Appointment, Reappointment, and Promotion* (*HARP*). The result of dozens of hours of bargaining during Spring 2015 over terms and conditions of employment for contingent faculty at Fredonia, the new *HARP* establishes both a coherent and comprehensive array of ranks and titles and fair and consistent systems for appointing, reappointing, evaluating, and awarding faculty members whose appointment types make them ineligible for tenure at Fredonia. The *HARP* should be read in the context of arguments by Berube and Ruth (2015) for the development of peer review and due process procedures for contingent faculty. The *HARP* provides further evidence that the revision, review, and ratification of documents that establish constitutive rules for a university and its faculty will never stop having ripple effects. Some of those ripples might extend to the system, state, and nation.

III. Improving Shared Governance through Collaboration

1.   This group is composed entirely of faculty and professional staff.
2.   This group includes the campus governance leader.
3.   For example, we faced a drop in enrollments, a serious budget situation, and the revision of our General Education curriculum, to name just a few.

References

American Association of University Professors (2012). *The inclusion in governance of faculty members holding contingent appointments.* Retrieved from http://www.aaup.org/report/governance-inclusion

American Association of University Professors (1994). *On the relationship of faculty governance to academic freedom.* Retrieved from http://www.aaup.org/report/relationship-faculty-governance-academic-freedom

American Association of University Professors (1966). *Statement on government of colleges and universities* (1966). Retrieved from http://www.aaup.org/report/statement-government-colleges-and-universities

Anderson, A., Brossard, D., Scheufele, D., Xenos, M., & Ladwig, P. (2014). The "Nasty Effect": Online incivility and risk perceptions of emerging technologies. *Journal of Computer-Mediated Communication, 19*(3).

Ansell, C., & Gash, A. (2007). Collaborative governance in theory and practice. *Journal of Public Administration Research and Theory, 18,* 543–571.

Bederson, B., Lee, B., Sherman, R., Herrnson, P., & Niemi, R. (2003). Electronic voting system usability issues. *Proceedings of the SIGCHI Conference on Human Factors in Computing Systems,* 145–152. Fort Lauderdale, FL.

Blasco-Arcas, L., Buil, I., Hernandez-Ortega, B., & Sese, F. (2013). Using clickers in class. The role of interactivity, active collaborative learning and engagement in learning performance. *Computers & Education, 62,* 102–110.

Board of Trustees. State University of New York. (2014). *Policies of the Board of Trustees.* Retrieved from http://www.suny.edu/media/suny/content-assets/documents/boardoftrustees/SUNY-BOT-Policies-June2014.pdf

Bousquet, M. (2008). *How the university works: Higher education and the low-wage nation.* New York: New York University Press.

Carter, L., & Belanger, F. (2012). Internet voting and political participation: An empirical comparison of technological and political factors. *The DATA BASE for Advances in Information Systems, 43*(3), 26–46.

Cheung, R., & Vogel, D. (2013). Predicting user acceptance of collaborative technologies: An extension of the technology acceptance model for e-learning. *Computers & Education, 63* (April 2013), 160–175.

Davis, F., Bagozzi, R., & Warshaw, R. (1989). User acceptance of computer technology: A comparison of two theoretical models. *Management Science, 35*(1), 982–1003.

Deemer, R., & Simon, B. (2014). Shared governance at Fredonia. *Faculty Senate Bulletin,* (Fall/Winter 2014), 14–16.

Duderstadt, J., & Womack, F. (2003). *Beyond the crossroads: The future of the public university in America.* Baltimore, MD: Johns Hopkins University Press.

Ehrenberg, R. (Ed.), (2004). *Governing academia.* Ithaca, NY: Cornell University Press.

Esterberg, K. & Wooding, J. (2012). *Divided conversations: Identities, leadership, and change in public higher education.* Nashville, TN: Vanderbilt University Press.

Faculty and University Senate Bylaws. (2015). The State University of New York at Fredonia. Retrieved from https://docs.google.com/document/d/1wn2L4A7y_psBTk7AqRq4E2FDNJVw7oT_cbkd7V_kH3k/edit?usp=sharing

Gerber, L. (2014). *The rise and decline of faculty governance: Professionalization and the modern American university.* Baltimore, MD: Johns Hopkins University Press.

Governance Committee. (2013). *Governance handbook.* University Faculty Senate, State University of New York.

Grasso, A., & Convertino, G. (2012). Collective intelligence in organizations: Tools and studies. *Computer Supported Cooperative Work, 21,* 357–369.

Handbook on Appointment, Reappointment, and Promotion. (2015). University handbook, The State University of New York at Fredonia.

Hendrickson, R., Lane, J., Harris, J., & Dorman, R. (2013). *Academic leadership and governance of higher education: A guide for trustees, leaders, and aspiring leaders or two- and four-year institutions.* Sterling, VA: Stylus.

Hoke, C. (2010). Internet voting: Structural governance principles for election cyber security in democratic nation. *Proceedings of the 2010 Workshop on Governance, Technology, Information and Policies,* 61–70. Austin, TX.

Merighi, F., & Ravaioli, S. (2009). U-Vote: A convenient on-line e-voting system. *Proceedings of the 5th Annual Workshop on Cyber Security and Information Intelligence Research: Cyber Security and Information Intelligence Challenges and Strategies.* Oak Ridge, TN.

Middle States Commission on Higher Education. (2011). *Characteristics of excellence in higher education.* 12th ed. Retrieved from https://www.msche.org/publications/CHX-2011-WEB.pdf

Min, S. (2007). Online vs. face-to-face deliberation: Effects on civic engagement. *Journal of Computer-Mediated Communication, 12*(4), 1369–1387.

Murphy, T., Fletcher, K., & Haston, A. (2010). Supporting clickers on campus and the faculty who use them. *Proceedings of the 38th Annual ACM SIGUCCS Fall Conference: Navigation and Discovery,* 79–83. Norfolk, VA.

Myers, A. (n.d.). *Condorcet internet voting service.* Retrieved from http://civs.cs.cornell.edu

Newfield, C. (2008). *Unmaking the public university: The forty-year assault on the middle class.* Cambridge, MA: Harvard University Press.

Oblak, T. (2003). Boundaries of interactive public engagement: Political institutions and citizens in new political platforms. *Journal of Computer-Mediated Communication, 8*(3).

Oliveira, I., Tinoca, L., & Pereira, A. (2011). Online group work patterns: How to promote a successful collaboration. *Computers & Education, 57* (August), 1348–1357.

Rhoades, G. (1998). *Managed professionals: Unionized faculty and restructuring academic labor.* Albany, NY: State University of New York Press.

Sanserverino, M. (2010). Pedagogy that clicks: "Clickers" in the CSC classroom. *Proceedings of the 15th Western Canadian Conference on Computing Education.* Kelowna, Canada.

Schotz, G. (2007). What is shared governance anyway? Retrieved from http://www.uiowa.edu/~aaupweb/shared_gov.pdf

Schuster, J.H., Smith, D.G., Corak, K.A., & Yamada, M.M. (1994). *Strategic governance: How to make big decisions better.* Phoenix, AZ: American Council on Education, Series on Higher Education, Oryx Press.

Simons, B., & Jones, D. (2012). Internet voting in the U.S. *Communications of the ACM, 55*(10), 68–77.

Sun, J. (2014). Influence of polling technologies on student engagement: An analysis of student motivation, academic performance, and brainwave data. *Computers & Education, 72,* 80–89.

Tierney, W. (Ed.). (2004). *Competing conceptions of academic governance: Negotiating the perfect storm.* Baltimore, MD: Johns Hopkins University Press.

Tierney, W. (Ed.). (2006). *Governance and the public good.* Albany: State University of New York Press.

Tierney, W., & Lechuga, V. (Eds.). (2004). *Restructuring shared governance in higher education.* New Directions for Higher Education, Number 127. San Francisco: Jossey-Bass.

United University Professions. (2013). *Agreement between United University Professions and the State of New York, July 2, 2011–July 1, 2016.* Retrieved from http://uupinfo.org/negotiations/Contract2011to2016webSECUREv6.pdf

Vlachokyriakos, V., Dunphy, P., Taylor, N., Comber, R., & Olivier, P. (2014). BallotShare: An exploration of the design space for digital voting in the workplace. *Computers in Human Behavior, 41,* 433–443.

Volkamer, M., Oliver, S., & E., Dubuis. (2011). Measures to establish trust in Internet voting. *Proceedings of the 5th International Conference on Theory and Practice of Electronic Governance.* Tallinn, Estonia.

Wang, C., & Leung, H. (2005). A secure voter-resolved approval voting protocol over Internet. *Proceedings of the 7th International Conference on Electronic Commerce.* Xi' an, China.

2

Engaging and Keeping Faculty and Students in Governance

Minna S. Barrett and Duncan Quarless

What value should we assign to the work of designing and delivering the curriculum in the modern American university? Does it matter what mechanisms are institutionalized to accomplish the ongoing tasks required to deliver comprehensive, demanding, and effective programs to students? What is the role of representative governance and shared responsibility among constituents? What is the intended purpose of sharing authority in designing and delivering the foundational products of higher education? Has the value and authority of faculty engagement in the process of decision making changed over the last half century? If so, what are the impacts of such a transformation on higher educational quality and values? Should students be encouraged to participate in service outside of the classroom that affects the design of their studies and other factors relevant to their educational and social experiences while attending university? What external and internal pressures shape the current values and choices of faculty and students and exert influence on the quality and efficacy of shared governance decision making?

The authors review the challenges facing the mechanisms of shared governance in the modern American university. They support the role of representative shared governance and provide a review of published voices that argue for its maintenance, defend its underlying intent, and provide "best-practice" approaches that promote its effective functioning for administrators, faculty, and students.

Introduction

How do we keep faculty and students engaged in the time-consuming work of shared decision making? This can be particularly challenging

if campus administrations channel the work into outcomes that reinforce the interests of administrative decisions. Faculty and students are
particularly alert to shared decision making that seeks to run counter
to their own best interests. How do administrative, faculty, and college-
wide community "rewards" influence how faculty and students decide
to "spend" their professional and educational development energies and
time? The actual "rewards" have declined over time, since state funding
has been declining proportionally to costs. With campus and systems
administrative budgets growing, and academic budgets flat for more than
a decade, engaging faculty and students in governance is necessary, yet
not necessarily simple.

On many campuses, the pressure to publish takes precedence over
teaching and serving, despite declarations that excellence in learning,
serving, and professional development are all valued expectations for
advancement in the public academy. As faculty members advance, many
express feeling increased pressure to avoid the time-consuming work of
governance, particularly as they attain tenure and are no longer "forced"
to engage in service. Others voice the discouragement they feel from the
lack of valance their voices yield in administrative decisions, on campus,
or in statewide systems. While others continue to value, contribute to and
support shared governance, others simply considered governance a waste
of their time and are happy to be free of the yoke of service.

Students have different obstacles to participation in governance.
Recent years have seen an increase in the number of students both attending classes and working a substantial number of hours weekly. Work may
be taken on either because students feel increased pressure to focus on
gaining career skills, because they are worried about higher amounts of
loan debt, or to support one's self or families. These students may not be
willing or able to apportion time to governance—an "extra-curricular"
activity—despite research that shows they could derive important skills
via participation in governance. Although such activities might help shape
their futures, they remain a low priority for many students.

What types of education, incentives, and supports sustain faculty and
student involvement in the work of shared governance? This chapter gives
voice to (1) foundational issues related to some of the pressures we face
as members of the professoriate, (2) the benefits students may gain from
taking time to engage in governance, and (3) factors that help to promote,
maintain, and make use of shared governance.

Perspective

The role of constituents in the formation of policy and operation of a college has been part of the academic landscape since the operation of the Academy, in both ancient Greece and Europe. In the United States, the American Association of University Professors (AAUP) has been advocating for meaningful faculty participation since 1916. The organization issued its first statement on the matter in 1920, but it is the oft-quoted 1966 *Statement on Government of Colleges and Universities* that is the cornerstone of all that follows regarding shared governance. The *Statement* was jointly formulated with the American Council on Education (ACE) and the Association of Governing Boards of Universities and Colleges (AGB). The *Statement* intended to guide the complex work of the U.S. University by (1) acknowledging the need for constituent authorities, (2) highlighting the need to align processes and outcomes in decision making across decision-making units, and (3) recognizing the expertise of faculty over all matters academic and that influence academic design and delivery. To that end, the *Statement* emphasizes the values of joint responsibility, mutual interest, and the central role of transparent operation and communication:

> This statement is a call to mutual understanding regarding the government of colleges and universities. Understanding, based on community of interest and producing joint effort . . . The variety and complexity of the tasks performed by institutions of higher education produce an inescapable interdependence among governing board, administration, faculty, students, and others. The relationship calls for adequate communication among these components, and full opportunity for appropriate joint planning and effort. (Section 1: Introduction)

Anyone who has participated in an accreditation review of a college campus will have experience with the "Standards" that address the roles and quality of shared governance functions. There is scrutiny by outside evaluators as to how campus constituents work together to assess the strengths and weaknesses of the delivery of its specific and general educational missions. At the least, a campus must (1) outline processes and procedures of decision making and (2) present an assessment of the efficacy of those mechanisms.

Attention to such standards does not guarantee positive valuation or transparency of governance mechanisms. However, inclusion of such should signal to campus constituents that shared governance is valued and that there exist best-practice expectations. If an accreditation review is transparent and inclusive, a fair process should offer (1) reinforcement and acknowledgment to members of campuses that meet best-practice guidelines and (2) specific recommendations for campus operations that do not while (3) spelling out expected methods or steps for improvement for those noted by the deadline of a future interim review.

No matter the outcome, the inclusion of a governance standard indicates that the role of shared governance across the American Academy is *expected* and, in principle, *required to meet specific qualities and best practices* on campuses and across a system. Since shared governance has valence in accreditation, obstacles to it should be of concern to all constituents whose voices are intended to be given authority via its appropriate exercise.

Universities in the United States are complex, with many various demands placed on faculties. The Academy is intended to (1) promote the search for knowledge and communicate it and its value to peers and students, (2) translate its findings, benefits, and functions to broader audiences, and (3) engage in processes that allow its members to design and initiate effective decisions while upholding values and procedures that ensure integrity and quality. Locating all of the difficulties of, and potentialities for, shared governance in this chapter is unrealistic. Herein are highlighted some basic issues to consider in designing and evaluating participation by faculty and students in shared governance.

Administrative Growth, Faculty Losses, and Governance Impacts

Growth of Contingent Faculty and Administrative Budgets. Review of the budgets of campuses nationwide over the last 15 years indicates that administrative budgets and professional nonacademic staff have increased dramatically over this period, by 228%, while academic salaries and budgets have essentially remained flat since 2000 (Desrochers, 2012). The ratio of part-time (contingent) to full-time faculty in classrooms has increased dramatically as well, doubling to 51.2% (Kezar & Maxey, 2014). Much of the "beyond the classroom" value (which is where governance work is lodged) of full-time faculty is lost when contingent faculty become central to delivery. Tuition is rising, while proportional allocation of state budgets to the full costs of running public colleges and universities continues to decline.

In his book, *The Fall of the Faculty: The Rise of the All Administrative University and Why it Matters* (2011), Benjamin Ginsberg, David Bernstein Professor of Political Science at Johns Hopkins University, writes that faculty across the sectors of colleges and universities throughout the United States have been losing ground in their salary growth, their academic funding, and their authority to design curriculum that ensures the quality of the education they deliver. Full-time faculty are being terminated or retiring and being replaced with adjunct (contingent) faculty.

Ginsberg explains that along with the budget shift, a power shift has taken place. Faculty control of the design, delivery, and assessment of the curriculum has moved out of the jurisdiction of faculties and is dictated more and more by administrators who are often not academically qualified. Ginsberg presents a myriad of examples across private elite universities and public colleges and universities that make the point that universities are more and more bureaucratized and corporatized, as example after example highlights ways in which faculty experience, excellence, and the liberal arts are undermined. Included on the list of attempts to limit liberal education are the 1999 SUNY Board of Trustees' actions with regard to General Education in the SUNY system, through which trustees mandated a new system-wide general education curriculum "without so much as consulting the SUNY Faculty" (p. 10).

Tension exists regarding how to best provide meaningful inclusion for decisions about new or transformed mandates. Differences of opinion exist among members of SUNY leadership, state political leadership, and SUNY faculty. In many cases, administrators exercise a boundary-centered engagement mechanism, creating the "structure and particulars" of change, the processes for faculty inclusion, and the time frame for actualizing the outcomes and expectations of the style of, and time limits for, faculty commentary. Faculty members prefer and best practices include engagement from the outset and input into all aspects of the processes and outcomes. This pattern of tension is not unique to the SUNY system. Such tension constitutes an ever-transforming challenge as membership and leadership of constituents change hands and as the pressures of economic and social conditions and forces shape access and values.

Ginsberg notes that when those of us now senior in the professoriate were acquiring undergraduate and graduate educations, the administrators who argued over (and served to administer) the educational and research missions of the campus were drawn from the faculty. Few of them trained to be professional college administrators. Once culled almost exclusively from the faculty and loyal to it, they understood and typically valued the traditional mechanisms and functions of the faculty and the academy. He concludes that as public funds wither, more and more professional administrators are increasingly loyal to boards, councils, and fundraising.

Administrators' pressures direct or dictate to faculty, matters that were once the purview of the faculty—namely, educational programs and curricular decision making. Actions are often accomplished by ignoring the required governance mechanisms granted to faculty by policy and tradition. Ginsberg posits that the current trend toward professional, vocational, and career-driven education (and away from liberal education) is part of this redirection. Across the United States, administrators have successfully argued to reduce the requirements of liberal education, and from that outcome they have reduced the critical value of the examination of the social experimentation and societal values that are occasioned by a coherent study of liberal curricula (Gerber, 2001; Ginsberg, 2011). Preparation for citizenship via general education in the liberal arts is part of the social capital that derives from higher education (Colby et al., 2003). Truncating it short sells civic education and decision-making skills.

This is certainly the case in SUNY, where general education has been reduced to about half of the expectation of the baccalaureate requirements in the 1960s through the 1990s. Laboratory science requirements have been reduced dramatically from a full year of lab science to one semester, math reduced to a less-demanding base level, language from two years of course work or its equivalent to one semester, and the standards for acquiring specific types of liberal course distributions have been nearly eradicated. Meanwhile little has been added to prepare current students for their roles as citizens and workers in their communities. According to Ginsberg (2011), education that encourages an understanding of the context in which a profession or major is imbedded is now seen as less relevant, so long as students meet a narrowing standard of general knowledge.

Ginsberg argues that an increasing reliance on vocational and professional training and the declining importance of critical thinking and foundational academic skills are occasioned, fundamentally, by the expansion of higher education administrators. He charges that most of them neither hold academic qualifications nor have the requisite academic experience that prior administrators had. He sees most of them as detached from the fundamental mission(s) of the university: to learn, to search, and to serve. Instead, their mission is "to manage." Both the redirection of academic focus and the reduction in the number of full-time faculty make it more difficult for Faculty (as the constituency closest to research and student intellectual growth) to engage in the service tasks required to maintain the academic quality of the university's mission. With reduced control of the academic process, and a lack of reward for shared governance, faculty rights that have been guaranteed by policy and tradition for decades are being undermined.

The impact of this expansion in administrative authority, Ginsberg concludes, is the erosion of quality education, particularly in the undergraduate curriculum. Rather than encouraging students to experiment with and develop interests and commitments to a lifelong obligation to responsible adulthood in a complex society and providing a working understanding of mechanisms of democratic institutions, the mission of the university is transformed by the drive for "efficiency," narrow curricular feifdoms, curricular control, and reification of administrative management. The result is an undermining of technical and social knowledge intended to innovate social progress, which, admittedly, sometimes challenges the status quo.

From research on hiring and employment patterns in higher education, Scott Carlson's (February 5, 2014) review of findings from the Delta Cost Project, "Labor Intensive or Labor Expensive: Changing Staffing and Compensation Patterns in Higher Education," highlights the concerns of its authors Desroschers and Kirshstein, (2014). The data indict that "the average number of full-time faculty and staff per administrator declined by roughly 40 percent, in most types of four-year colleges and universities between 1990 and 2012, and averages 2.5 or fewer faculty and staff per administrator" (p. 3). Full-time faculty members lost ground to part-time instructors, who now numerically comprise half of the instructional staff at most types of colleges, particularly at public master's and bachelor's institutions (Desrochers & Kirshstein, 2014) although they may not necessarily be responsible for teaching half of the courses offered at the institution.

Some pundits and politicians outside of the Academy argue that the rising cost of instructional salaries explains the rise in tuition and other costs at public colleges and universities. Consider the 2014 and 2015 attacks on public service and teaching lodged by Scott Walker, Governor of Wisconsin. His demand was to minimize labor expenses. He didn't call for a reduction *in administrative costs* in the public university. In New York State, Governor Andrew Cuomo removed dollars from the 2015–2016 SUNY budget to cover a small raise of 2% in salaries that he negotiated in "good faith" with the union that represents faculty and professional staff. Prior to that decision, Governor Cuomo decided to deduct income directly from faculty paychecks to cover the state's budget deficit. He promised to return that "loan" he deducted from all members of the University teaching and professional staff. In 2016, he returned some of it, while shorting those initially docked 2 days pay. After persistent protest from students, faculty, staff, and administrators (united), the New York State legislature restored some of the funding to cover the salary increase, but not all of it. The remainder will be borne by campuses, some of which are not equipped to do so. Who negotiates a raise with his/her employees and then refuses to fund the raise?

The data from the *Delta Cost Project Report* show that faculty salaries were "essentially flat" from 2000 through 2012, with no evidence of the savings that would have been expected from the shift to part-time faculty (Desrochers & Kirshstein, 2014). Private research campuses fared the best, while public community colleges fared the worst, losing both full- and part-time faculty while increasing professional staff. Carlson (2014) concludes that: "expansion in wages and salaries derives not from instruction, institutional support, or academic support, but from student services, which can include athletics, admissions, psychological counseling, and career counseling, among other activities. Nearly every type of college had increases in that area, with little growth, and some declines, in other areas" (Carlson, 2014; *Chronicle* online, February 5, 2014).

Professional staffs serving in student services, and who coordinate co-curricular functions, provide a variety of supports to students. However, these staff members cannot and do not design (and neither may nor can they deliver) the curricular requirements that make a university education what *it should be*. In most cases, they do not have the academic skills of full-time faculty when tutoring or designing specific academic tasks and expectations for study in and out of the classroom (Kezar & Maxey, 2014; Umbach & Wawrzynski, 2005).

While a professional's service on some committees of shared decision making provides important perspective on the social or emotional needs of students, staff without rank, and contingent faculty, administration should not be speaking to the foundational mission of the Academy; non-foundational issues should not receive more attention and resources than the educational mission. As such, neither professional staff nor part-time faculty can, nor should they, replace the ranked faculty. As their numbers increase and as the number of full-time faculty remains flat or decreases, the implications for faculty engagement in shared governance should be obvious, as described here by Carson:

The external demands on colleges and universities are greater than ever before. Government regulations regarding hiring, safety, student aid, athletics, and performance have created a layer of bureaucracy that is new and enduring. External demand has come in the form of unfunded mandates from system administrators (who themselves have been multiplying in number). Over the past 15 years in SUNY, those mandates have related to general education, assessment, seamless transfer, and teacher education, just to name a few. Each campus must meet each directive with a plan for implementation, an actual implementation, metrics for assessment, and then a review. These mandates have increased the bureaucratic workload, and campuses have responded by hiring more administrators and professional staff just to keep up or by turning faculty into administrators and as an aside, charging their department academic side budgets for maintaining their salaries, even when the majority of what they do is administrative. Other demands in the form of accreditation are also met at the expense of scholars in the classroom. (2014, p. 17)

Administrative Recognition of the Value of Shared Governance. According to national surveys, board members and administrators generally report that the faculty role in shared governance is productive. However, in settings in which there are barriers to productive shared governance, the authors of a majority of studies agree that there is a need for governance training and experience for both managers and faculty. The most consistent recommendation from such studies is for more effective communication, especially from college presidents in support of the need for (and value of) shared governance. The president who encourages and supports joint decision making and transparency has an institution that functions more effectively and supports student learning and faculty advancement (Bahls, 2014). Bahls explains that presidents are needed who communicate and who, in practice, honor the value of the shared governance processes consistently and clearly to all constituents.

In his comprehensive overview of the modern American University system, Derek Bok (2013), former President of Harvard University, assesses the notable strengths and challenges of the current status and state of higher education in the United States. His book appropriately reifies the seminal value of the university system, underscoring its central role in the production of both human capital and the critical knowledge on which modern societies and economies rest heavily. He argues that the university maintains its capacity to accomplish such contributions through its fundamental values of professional autonomy, peer review, freedom of thought and expression, and the disinterested discovery and communication of knowledge. In favor of maintaining this orientation of social value, Bok urges the university to remain free from commercial influences. Bok further notes that the values that support such progress are not served if managed by hierarchies of authority; rather, they are advanced by free discourse and peer review. He supports the entry of faculties and students into shared governance and, like Bahls, places responsibility for successful shared governance on a welcoming and supportive expectation from administrators—especially to acknowledge the expertise of its faculty and the central role of ranked faculty in the work of the university.

The Faculty Common. In order to increase the number of full-time faculty as suggested by Kezar and Maxey (2014), and to actively advocate for a return to higher proportional support for public higher education from the state, more of us need to engage the organizational structures in shared governance and our professional unions. How else can we advance the interests and fulfill the needs of the public academy? It is an illusion to think that we operate in an ivory tower apart from the forces that influence funding, student preparation, and access to resources. The belief that our primary task is to attend to our own silos—our own interests, departments, schools, labs, or classrooms—might be enticing, but it doesn't serve our collective best interests and is not a rational approach to long-term sustainability. The public university is shaped by and depends on a range of resources and outside influences that have little to do with the search for truth, the transfer of pure knowledge, or the development of critical thinking.

We won't need to plan for succession governance if there aren't enough of us who can, who do, who will take on the challenges of shared governance because shared governance will, essentially, cease to exist. Those who operate in the "silo" model and who claim the privilege to ignore collective responsibility for the system that houses us choose to undermine the hard work of colleagues who contribute to the development of the whole. Those who eschew the frustrations of collective debate and expert exchange about the welfare of our campuses and university missions undermine colleagues who do struggle with governance. Colleagues who deny the value and eschew the work of sharing governance do so either by (1) ignoring or demeaning an obligation to participate or (2) engaging in decision-making processes intended to violate representative governance mechanisms (Quarless & Barrett, 2015). The entitlement of the silo, the demeaning of the engaged, and the undermining of the representative systems weaken faculty capacity to make critical decisions about our work. What do these approaches to faculty engagement mean for the "community of scholars" intended to construct and to maintain the "Academy"?

But convincing fellow faculty who do not engage in the work of shared governance that such work is necessary for maintaining academic quality and that their input is important and necessary remains a challenge. In his review of Bok's *Higher Education in America,* Morrill (2013) isn't optimistic about the issues Bok raises to explain the values and difficulties of shared governance. For Morrill, efficacy of faculty decision making is inhibited by low engagement; there is a need to find effective ways to get faculty engaged in strategic decision making and academic leadership. He sees faculty as needing to take more responsibility for the common curriculum, student learning, and "the good of the whole organization."

Institutional missions rely on individual achievements *and* the quality of the whole, not merely on the sum of the individual parts. While Morrill (2013) rightfully highlights the responsibility and obligations of faculties to this decision making, it is also the case that if there is little institutional incentive and little communication that engagement is *expected and valuable,* some colleagues will always find it easy to remove themselves from such service.

Contingent faculty. Relying on significant numbers of contingent faculty in the classroom ensures that fewer and fewer of those who are tasked with designing and delivering the curriculum, and assuring standards for permanent appointment and promotion, will be available to engage in these necessary tasks. Highly trained, specialized contingent faculty can and should play an important role in helping to expand access to subspecialties for which very few are trained, or to support a full schedule of options when an underfunded or small faculty cannot.

However, when as a general measure, contingent faculty members are hired to lower academic costs across an institution, to teach upward of half or more of the sections of required courses, to teach general education or introductory courses because there aren't enough full-time faculty members to meet student demand, or so qualified faculty don't have to carry those courses, it is students and the active, committed, full-time engaged faculty who lose out; so, too, does the quality of the institution (Ginsberg, 2011). Students lose contact with ranked faculty, some of whom find it advantageous to be separated from educational obligations to take their turn at delivering introductory courses or common core sections.

Levels of preparation. If it were true that those with master's-level training are as prepared for teaching as are credentialed faculty with full-time
continuing appointments, why would any department hire credentialed
faculty to design and deliver the courses necessary to prepare students?
In disciplines for which a master's-level education or direct experience is
sufficient for advancement in the academy, requisite contingent faculty
might be equivalent in capacity. In cases when a doctorate is the expectation for continuing appointment, allowing other than doctoral-level lectur-
ers into classrooms to meet financial pressures or to cover for increased
enrollments is a practice that compromises the preparation and skilled
engagement that research on student success has demonstrated to support
retention, persistence, and completion (Ginsberg, 2011; Kezar & Maxey,
2014; Umback & Wawrzynski, 2009).

Silo and star faculty. Faculty who make few commitments to their home
campuses to little more than meeting their classes or engaging predominantly in their research might not feel the impact of the budgetary and
staffing trends outlined herein; but those serving on representative committees, spending long hours advising students, and mentoring independent study and individualized research and service projects likely will. As
just noted, the research on student retention, persistence, and completion
shows that faculty engagement (in and outside of the classroom) positively
affects retention and completion.

While a collection of "star" faculty heightens the reputation of an
institution, and typically enhances the resources of a campus, the balance between the number of "special" members of the faculty free from
the demands to which other professional academics attend is critical.
Such balance might be sector sensitive. However, as the number of "star"
faculty increases at each level, so do demands on other members of the
faculty—to serve, mentor, and advise. It may not be a division of labor
that is so much at issue, but the differential valuation of efforts extended
to the various and different necessary tasks of the academy. The stars are
well rewarded and acknowledged, while the "servers" are minimized as
less valuable to the reputation of the campus, and are thus less valued
by the institution.

The silo and star systems allow administrative staff to design and
maintain a reward scheme that minimizes the role and value of those
who engage in the less glamorous shared burdens. This can eventually

lead to outcomes that reduce campus-wide commitments to missions and values or erode standards and quality. For example, some or all of the following may occur: (1) a reduced commitment to educational access for students *across* socioeconomic class; (2) a lack of commitment to ensuring diversity across faculties, staff, and students; (3) an acceptance of lowered or differential standards across departments for hiring, retention and promotion, and student performance; and (4) a lack of concern about the removal of critical thinking or interdisciplinary approaches to teaching from learning outcomes.

According to Ginsberg, withdrawal from engaging in the processes, values, and standards of representative governance compromises the quality and the educational missions of the Academy (2011). A lack of commitment to the general welfare of the Academy has resulted in a lack of protection of liberal arts education, the values of citizenship, and the understanding of critical analysis of current social conditions and needs intended to be gained from the study of liberal education. Tending only one's own garden can jeopardize disciplines or programs that might not have the luxury, flexibility, or independence occasioned by external funding or expansive growth. As a result, it might be impossible for such programs to remain viable, and available to students. The consequence of such reductions might thereby compromise contents that help shape citizens with humane values and critical sensibilities. Is a curriculum that manufactures students only as "units of skill" to satisfy a system of production that operates independent of the role of a democratically prepared citizenry the goal of baccalaureate level education? Ginsberg (2011), Colby and colleagues (2005), and Gerber (2001), among many other voices, argue that it should not be so.

Declining per-student allocations to academic delivery within state budgets. Proportional declines in per-student allocations to academic delivery are destructive to maintaining the consistency and quality of degree-granting institutions of public higher education. When M. Barrett was a student at a newly developing state university, public higher education was funded by the state budget at about 75% of the operating costs (plus funds for development and maintenance). The governor, at that time, lauded public higher education in that state and urged children of the state to attend the public institution he fought to expand. Today, the same system receives about 25% of its operating costs from the state (with additional funds for maintenance and development) while students and their families carry significantly more of the burden. Support for public higher education is further challenged on the instructional side, as a larger proportion of the allocation is now devoted to administrative rather than to academic costs. No wonder many departments draw consistently on a contingent faculty that can't deliver the tutoring and advising, and other forms of student support, that are shown to encourage retention, persistence, and completion.

Proportionally less state support for public higher education undermines the capacity for universities' critical role in the development of social capital. This situation pressures publically funded campuses to rely on low-wage contingent faculty and to make difficult decisions about deferring maintenance of facilities necessary to deliver a quality education. The increased costs to individual families makes public higher education less accessible via increased tuition and more financially overwhelming for students via increasing levels of loan debt.

Withdrawal from engaging in the one mechanism that gave faculty a significant role in decision making about the product they deliver and the administrative trend in some institutions to deflect, defer, and deny that authority have consequences that significantly affect faculty, students, and quality of education and its costs

Students and the Value of and Obstacles to Engagement in Shared Governance

What students gain by participating in shared governance. Currently, students in U.S. colleges and universities are very different from those of even 20 years ago. A much larger proportion than in the past are older, part-time, and from ethnic/racial/socio-economic minority groups. In 2000, students aged 25 years and older comprised about 40% of total college enrollment and nearly one-quarter of full-time enrollments. Over one-quarter of all college students were ethnic minorities, up from 16% in 1980, with the greatest increases over the last decade among Latino students, who are likely to surpass African American enrollments in the next few years (Trowler & Trowler, 2010).

For students struggling with transition (e.g., foreign students, low-income students, newly arrived or first-generation immigrant populations, first generation to college, older students), engagement in governance and co-curricular activities that increase a student's involvement with other students, faculty, and staff members strongly correlates with positive educational outcomes. Engagement in campus affairs facilitates a sense of belonging and a positive student identity (Cabrera et al., 1999; Carini et al., 2006; Cruce et al., 2006; Kuh, 2003, 2005). Investment increases a sense of ownership and responsibility to achievement and offers opportunities for mentorship and closer connections with faculty and staff who can transfer skills and engage in problem solving, intentionally and by social modeling.

Will students who have off-campus obligations be able to commit to the work required of shared governance? As tuition increases and loan programs require larger commitments from students, will greater numbers choose or be forced to work while attending college, and of necessity to forfeit some of the benefits that derive from stretching oneself by taking responsibility for one's peer and institutional communities outside of the classroom? Will students from immigrant communities and from low-income neighborhoods assess shared governance as worthwhile while they work to attain the skills they need to gain entry to a professional workforce? What do researchers have to add to our understanding of what students gain from engaging in shared governance? What mechanisms or rewards help to encourage student efforts to provide their input into academic decision making? If research supports that faculty contact in and out of classrooms increases students' academic performance or persistence to complete, then student engagement in shared governance should be of value to students who get involved and supported by faculty.

The benefits of engagement across student types are well documented. In a review of studies of student engagement and student success, Kuh (2009) concluded that "virtually every report . . . emphasized to varying degrees the important link between student engagement and desired outcomes of college" (p. 684). Bensimon (2009), concludes:

> . . . productive engagement is an important means by which students develop feelings about their peers, professors and institutions that give them a sense of connectedness, affiliation, and belonging, while simultaneously offering rich opportunities for learning and development. (pp. xxii–xxiii)

Support for Kuh's (2009) and Bensimon's (2009) conclusions comes from a review of findings from 200 research studies on the impacts of engaging students academically and in governance prepared by Trowler and Trowler (2010). These findings report positive effects of student engagement and the positive impact faculty has on students with whom they share the process of solving college-wide issues. They note that "high performing" colleges and universities that graduate higher proportions of students typically engage in best practices for encouraging and including students in shared governance. Their summary review concludes that while students are shown to benefit from engagement as student representatives, many institutions benefit as well. Other studies show that society benefits. Trowler and Trowler explain that student engagement helps institutions understand changing student needs since students who serve on functional committees have opportunities to speak directly about their needs and experiences (2010). Similarly, student engagement brings attention to problems in units, sectors, or departments that might otherwise go unattended.

Individual students gain increased agency and contact with decision makers, and may also receive mentoring and opportunities to develop leadership skills. In institutions where faculty, staff, and administrators help shape, encourage, and reward effective student participation, students have better retention rates.

Engagement gives students more time with faculty and staff and more tools for staying in school and completing their studies. Students who are engaged enjoy greater gains in academic outcomes than students who are not. The relation between engagement and student academic success is particularly notable for at-risk student groups. "Studies have revealed the compensatory effect of engagement—meaning that those students who are least prepared academically—benefit more from engagement than those who are most prepared, in terms of effects on grades and persistence" (Trowler & Trowler, 2010, p. 11).

Shared governance has more than just a democratizing effect on students. Those who engage receive more attention and mentoring. They gain skills in leadership. They learn to communicate, organize, and advocate for their peers in settings where authority *must* be part of the solution. They learn to negotiate with "power" and to address both the positive and negative impacts of hierarchical and democratic decision making. As a result, they are likely to bring more than just academic skills into their future career paths. Students who engage in governance learn how to engage a community, enlist others, and work collectively to solve problems that cannot be solved by one person and to work for solutions that benefit an entire community. They learn how to go back to constituents to assess needs, to organize, and to advocate for solutions to dysfunctional mechanisms and policies and to distinguish effective strategies. They learn how to manage others, provide leadership in work settings, and bring disparate views together, thus gaining proficiency in all-important skills for success in the modern world. Since engagement appears to have academic benefits, encouraging student involvement in decision making is a best practice.

Institutional values and successful student involvement. All students are not equal; thus they benefit from their engagements in different ways. Institutions also vary in their effectiveness to engage students, to use student input wisely and effectively, and to help students find value in their educational experiences. Kezar (2005) lists the following critical best practices of institutions that are labeled by the National Survey of Student Engagement (NSSE) as "best performing." These institutions

- develop a shared understanding of institutional mission and philosophy,

- use celebrations to engage the campus community in conversations about student success,

- advocate for shared governance,

- ensure that students have a prominent voice in campus governance,

- alter structures to encourage cross-function activities focused on student success,

- tighten the philosophical and operational links between academic and student affairs, and

- empower and support staff leadership. (Kezar, 2005, pp. 2–4; emphasis added)

Kezar also suggests the following questions to consider in the design of the institutional contexts and cultures that encourage student engagement and promote and direct effective learning outcomes.

- Do campus leaders have a common view of the institution's mission, vision, and philosophy?

- How is community celebrated and fostered?

- Is collaboration and distributed leadership modeled through shared governance?

- What mechanisms are available to involve students in campus governance?

- Are cross-functional activities focused on student success encouraged and supported?

- Are collaborative efforts between academic and student affairs encouraged? (Kezar, 2005, p. 4; emphasis added)

Finally, Magdola (2005, pp. 2–4) summarizes the following best practices of successful student leaders:

- Understand and embrace their organization's mission, history, and culture.

- Collaboration is essential.

- Improve group performance by doing less, better.

- Focus on creating win-win scenarios for the organizational members and the students they serve.

- Strengthen the organization by strengthening its members.

- Celebrate important events, transitions, and passages.

Critiques of some of the conclusions drawn from the research on student benefits of such engagement are introduced by Bensimon (2007) and by Harper and Quaye, (2009). They question the efficacy of specific survey instruments and raise concerns about generalizing the outcomes and assuming the value of engagement across all student groups. They challenge the content of some items on survey instruments such as the National Survey of Student Engagement (NSSE) and the Australasian Survey of Student Engagement (AUSSE). They suggest that these instruments include assessment factors based on activities more likely to appeal to traditional college students, students from higher-income communities, majority and nonimmigrant student groups, and those who proceeded directly from high school to college.

However, data from these same instruments show that students coming from the "less prepared" groups benefit *more* from engagement, particularly in terms of effects on grades, persistence, and preparation. Discussion about content and construct validity of survey instrumentation is vital to the advance of data intended to help researchers understand how to best help students persist and succeed. Mounting evidence suggests that students with more fragile entrance profiles seem to gain significantly from their participation in campus-wide decision making, and from making more direct contact with faculty leading to the possible conclusion that campus administrators who deny access to effective shared governance mechanisms reduce opportunities for students to gain traction academically and persevere through rough periods.

Summary Points

- The fewer of us who comprise "the whole," the less likely we will be to advocate effectively to maintain a stable full-time faculty base available to deliver quality education or the necessary support to students in order to retain them and help them complete their studies.

- Multiple research findings indicate that full-time faculty engaged with students is the foundational component to increased student retention, persistence, and completion. The more the managerial model of corporate efficiency is valued over the tradition of relying on faculty discussion, expertise, and mutual engagement, the less shared governance will have value to those with the purse. Ultimately, this means that the role of faculty in the overall design of their teaching and service functions will receive less support and will be valued less by the public at large. The result on the quality of educational delivery is also at stake.

- Administrators play a central role in ensuring the quality of higher education, not by making academic decisions themselves, but by supporting transparent shared governance across campus constituents in all practice. Quality in shared governance leads to increased educational quality.

- Campuses with a commitment to high academic quality are more likely to have expected, rewarded, and acknowledged best practices in the design and use of shared governance mechanisms.

- When a smaller proportion of faculty engages, and a larger proportion avoids engaging, quality academic delivery is at risk. What suffers is the foundational mission of the university.

- A lack of effective shared governance is affected by the role played by administrative leadership: presidents of boards, chancellors, and campus presidents. If they fail to encourage, accept, and value the critical role of an expert faculty in the major decisions of the campus (or university system), the resulting outcomes are typically counterproductive to efficient and quality delivery of the academic mission. Such attitudes and value systems transfer downward to provosts, deans, department chairs, and finally to faculty who are encouraged and rewarded for embracing a silo model.

- Faculty can and do play a significant role in supporting or ignoring the functions of shared governance. To the extent that engaging faculty is a central issue for the robustness of a curriculum and the resources required to deliver it, individual faculty members have responsibilities to the whole beyond their individual or disciplinary interests.

- The more full-time faculty there are meeting classroom and other academic activities, the better will be the outcomes for student retention, persistence, and completion. At the same time, the more faculty there are, the more there are to rotate into the tasks of shared governance,

- The goal of shared governance is to unleash the expertise of those who are delivering the mission of the institution—its faculty. Ignoring their deliberated wisdom costs the institution in loyalty to it. There is also the danger of an increasing distrust between managers and the skilled work force assigned to designing the pathways to academic fulfillment.

- Lack of engagement of a significant number of faculties in shared governance erodes the quality of decision making, and challenges the potential for broad support of initiatives. It condenses the distribution of the hard work onto a few, who can quickly become overworked and demoralized. A lack of support across the campus or system erodes the quality of the academy itself.

- At-risk students are more likely to succeed when they engage in campus life. Faculty engagement in and out of the classroom is valuable to all students, but it has the greatest impact on, and is most effective for, at-risk and less prepared students.

- Students and faculty profiles for successful engagement are similar; administrators who support shared governance *in word and deed*, and who encourage transparency, debate, and deliberation, provide a campus atmosphere for faculty to actualize their expertise in designing and delivering strong academic programs via effective shared governance. Best-practice campuses tend to have best-practice outcomes with their students who demonstrate higher levels of student retention, persistence, and completion.

- The value of governance is measured in action, not talk, in just rewards and acknowledgment of service.

Readers may find it helpful to use the questions listed below to assess the climate on your campus for shared governance and transparent processes. It might be best to review the questions with members of several faculty bodies to gain insight into current governance needs and strengths. After answering all the questions either Yes or No, add up the total. Note: The higher the total score, the more value is accorded to faculty authority and expertise via representative shared governance. Questions that result in a 0 response indicate areas for which consideration of change might seem reasonable. (Please note that questions with negative correlations of faculty authority result in a change in the value of Yes and No responses.)

Authority of the Faculty, Respect for Shared Governance as a Decision-making Process

- Does your administration consult with the elected faculty leadership for the selection of constituent elected representation on all committees it initiates before naming any faculty to a task force or a committee? Yes = 1, No = 0

- Does administrative leadership consult with governance to determine the structures, processes, and goals for such committees and work? Yes = 1, No = 0

- Is it common for the administration to ignore governance leadership or to request lists of potential faculty members that it then "'culls'"? Yes = 0, No = 1

- Is faculty governance representation independent of administrative choice and favor? Yes = 1, No = 0

- Do your administrators "assume" that inclusion of the Chair of the Faculty on many or all committees means that "the governance mechanism of the Faculty" writ large is now represented? Yes = 0, No = 1

- Are requests for inclusion of a broader range or increased number of faculty selected via representative faculty governance ignored or considered diffident? Yes = 0, No = 1

Student Engagement

- Is inclusion of representative student membership considered important by administrative leadership? Yes = 1, No = 0

- Is inclusion of representative student membership considered important among the elected faculty leadership? Yes = 1, No = 0

- Do students have opportunities for faculty/staff mentoring in shared governance processes? Yes = 1, No = 0

Transparency and Budget Review

- Are elected members of the faculty involved in a meaningful review of the campus budget with input from all operational units? Yes = 1, No = 0

- Are all data from all sectors of the budget—all income and expenditures, not merely allocations—available for transparent review? Yes = 1, No = 0

- Do academic departments have input into their allocations, income, and expenditures? Yes = 1, No = 0

Academic Decision Making

- Is the initiation of academic programs, institutes, majors, minors, college requirements, and academic practices a result of faculty governance design, review, and approval, or is such initiation "imposed" by administrators and then "rubber-stamped" by governance? Yes = 1, No = 0

- Are shared governance generated, mutually negotiated goals, processes, timetables, and appropriate resources the rule for academic decision making? Yes = 1, No = 0

- Are such decisions and mandates a result of meaningful consultation among and between constituents via shared governance processes? Yes = 1, No = 0

- Do decisions align with governance by-laws? Yes = 1, No = 0

Communication

- Is there meaningful public and thorough communication and consultation within and among constituents? Yes = 1, No = 0

- Do all constituent governance units have access to communication with their full membership and with each other? Yes = 1, No = 0

Administrative Selection

- Are faculty via faculty governance included in appropriate numbers and constitution in all administrative hiring decisions from the chancellor to the hiring of a dean and determination of department and institute chairs? Yes = 1, No = 0

Review of Goals, Outcomes, and Performance

- Are year-to-year performance benchmarks identified and evaluated by an inclusive process for quality outcomes of all operating units/individuals? Yes = 1, No = 0

- Are benchmarks and evaluation processes arrived at via consultation and shared governance processes? Yes = 1, No = 0

- Are critiques of processes built in to decision making, welcomed, and encouraged rather than avoided, denigrated, or ignored? Yes = 1, No = 0

- Are suggestions for change of process and outcome incorporated into future decision making? Yes = 1, No = 0

- Is there ongoing transparent and comprehensive evaluation of administration and professional staff and units equivalent to the comprehensive review and assessment required of faculty pursuing continuing appointment, tenure, and promotion? Yes = 1, No = 0

- Are the processes and goals of such review of administrative and professional performance inclusive of shared governance representatives? Yes = 1, No = 0

Value of Service via Shared Governance

- Are rewards for faculty and student engagement clear, valuable to constituents, determined via consultation, and applied fairly? Yes = 1, No = 0

Conclusion

Representative engagement is the "public common" of the faculty in both governance and union representation. Low levels of engagement in the structures designed to harness faculty expertise and authority in decision making places faculty authority and expertise at risk because it means that there is no format for channeling the collective wisdom of the whole in the fundamental function of the professoriate. Without a collective way of asserting its authority and the considered input and efforts of many engaged faculty, each of us has limited opportunity to protect the value and quality of the public university.

If *we*, the Faculty, want to ensure more access to the best use, and considered value, of our training, talents, and experiences, then *we* will be required to become more active in speaking up. We must advocate for, and organize to protect, the profession by promoting the importance of the intellectual and social capital we represent and are charged with producing. We are the ones who need to consistently and persistently advocate for shared governance in decision making, administrative support, and the positive valuation of what best-practice shared governance provides to the vibrancy and health of the American university.

Board members and administrators who understand and advocate for the effective, transparent actualization of shared governance will be supporting an important route to the highest quality of public education (Bahls, 2013; Bok, 2013).

While each of us comes into the Academy with individual investments in specific disciplines and highly individualized specialties, our professional obligation to maintain the institution that supports our work places our professional interests beyond our individual accomplishments. We become members in a broader public sphere in the domain of public goods. In the public university, that domain is central to the university's mission and, therefore, to ours. In this regard, Gerber's (2001) commentary remains relevant:

> In too many of our colleges and universities today, governing boards and presidents are claiming that more "flexible" forms of management must replace the practice of shared governance so that institutions may respond more readily to the latest educational fads and the preferences of their student-consumers. Such an approach fails to take into account that there are some elements of the curriculum that have enduring value and must be preserved, regardless of the level of student "demand" at any given time.
>
> Faculty control over curricular matters, a central element of what the AAUP means by shared governance, will not completely insulate our colleges and universities from many of the broad social pressures that challenge high academic standards and question the value of learning for its own sake. But, faculty are far more likely to be defenders of academic integrity than are administrators or governing boards that rely on a managerial philosophy that considers only a very narrowly conceived "bottom line." If faculty does not retain primary responsibility for academic matters within a system of shared governance, liberal education, with its emphasis on the development of critical thinking and humane values, may eventually become an arcane concept. (p. 23)

According to Kaul and colleagues (1999):

> Global public goods are goods that have a significant element of non-rivalry and/or non-excludability *and* made broadly available across populations on a global scale. They . . . are broadly available within countries, and are inter-generational; that is, they meet needs in the present generation without jeopardizing future generations. (pp. 2–3)

For those of us who work in a public university system, little else defines a public good better than the public university. Our institutions thrive when their missions generate, transmit, and communicate knowledge and when that knowledge supports a broad meaning of public utility and value. In this way we advance our understanding of how to solve our collective challenges and meet our collective needs while providing quality, affordable, and accessible education to many.

Acknowledgments

The authors are grateful for the participation and perspective of the SUNY Old Westbury student government leaders, Paraskevas Savva and Camilla Swasey, during the 1st Annual SUNY Voices Conference. We also express our thanks to our faculty colleague, Kathleen Greenberg, and to Deborah M. Rhem-Jackson, former Assistant Vice President for Academic Affairs/ College Readiness Programs at SUNY Old Westbury, for their insights and helpful contributions during the 1st Annual SUNY Voices conference and in the subsequent communications that led to the preparation of the manuscripts for which the two chapters the co-authors of this chapter presented and further developed for publication.

References

American Association of University Professors. (1966). *Joint statement on governance of the American Association of University Professors, the American Council on Education, and the Association of Governing Boards of Universities and Colleges.* Washington, D.C.

Bahls, S. (2014). *Shared governance in times of change: A practical guide for universities and colleges.* Washington, D.C.: Association of Governing Boards Press.

Bensimon, E.M. (2009). "Foreword." In S.R. Harper & S.J. Quaye (Eds.), *Student engagement in higher education* (pp. xxi–xxvi). New York: Routledge.

Bensimon, E.M. (2007). The underestimated significance of practitioner knowledge in the scholarship of student success. *Review of Higher Education, 30,* 441–469.

Bok, D. (2013). *Higher education in America.* Princeton, NJ: Princeton University Press.

Cabrera, A.F., Nora, A., Terenzini, P.T., Pascarella, E.T., & Hagedorn, L.S. (1999). Campus racial climate and the adjustment of students to college: A comparison between white students and African American students. *Journal of Higher Education, 70*(2), 134–202.

Carini, R.M., Kuh, G.D., & Klein, S.P. (2006). Student engagement and student learning: Testing the linkages. *Research in Higher Education, 47*(1), 1–24.

Carlson, S. (2014). Administrator hiring drove 28% boom in higher-ed work force, report says. *Chronicle of Higher Education.* Retrieved from http://chronicle.com/article/Administrator-Hiring-Drove-28-/144519

Carson, B. (Spring/Summer, 2014). Administrative bloat in the age of cutbacks. *The Bulletin*, University Faculty Senate, State University of New York, 17–18.

Colby, A., Ehrlich, T., Beaumont, E., & Stephens, J. (2003). *Educating citizens: Preparing America's undergraduates for lives of moral and civic responsibility.* San Francisco: Jossey-Bass.

Cruce, T., Wolniak, G.C., Seifert, T.A., & Pascarella, E.T. (2006). Impacts of good practices on cognitive development, learning orientations, and graduate degree plans during the first year of college. *Journal of College Student Development, 47*, 365–383.

Desroschers, D., & Kirshstein, R. (2014). Labor intensive or labor expensive: Changing staffing and compensation patterns in higher education. *Issue Brief.* Washington, D.C.: American Institutes for Research, 1–33.

Gerber, L.G. (2001). Inextricably linked: Shared governance and academic freedom." *Academe, 87*(3), 22–24.

Ginsberg, B. (2011). *The fall of the faculty: The rise of the all administrative university and why it matters.* New York: Oxford University Press.

Harper, S.R., & Quaye, S.J., eds. (2009). *Student engagement in higher education.* New York: Routledge,

Kaul, I., Grunberg, I., & Stern, M. (Eds.). (1999). *Global public goods: Managing globalization.* New York: Oxford University Press.

Kezar, A. (2007). Creating and sustaining a campus ethos encouraging student engagement. *About Campus, (11)*6, 13–18.

Kezar, A. (2005). Promoting student success: The importance of shared leadership and collaboration. *Occasional Paper #4.* Bloomington, IN: National Survey of Student Engagement.

Kezar, A., & Maxey, D. (2014). An examination of the changing faculty: Ensuring institutional quality and achieving desired student learning outcomes. *CHEA Occasional Paper,* Council for Higher Education Accreditation, Washington, D.C.

Kuh, G.D. (2009). What student affairs professionals need to know about student engagement. *Journal of College Student Development, 50*(6), 683–706.

Kuh, G.D. (2007). How to help students achieve. *Chronicle of Higher Education, 53*(41), 1, 12.

Kuh, G.D. (2005). *Promoting student success: What campus leaders can do.* National Survey of Student Engagement, Bloomington, Indiana.

Kuh, G.D. (2003). What we're learning about student engagement from NSSE: Benchmarks for effective educational practices. *Change, 35*(2), 24–32.

Kuh, G.D., Palmer, M., & Kish, K. (2003). The value of educationally purposeful out-of-class experiences. In T.L. Skipper & R. Argo (Eds.), *Involvement in Campus Activities and the Retention of First Year College Students* (pp. 19–34). *The First-Year Monograph Series #36.* Columbia, SC: University of South Carolina National Resource Center for the First Year Experience and Students in Transition.

Magolda, P. (2005). Promoting student success: What student leaders can do. *Occasional paper #8.* Bloomington, IN: National Survey of Student Engagement.

Morrill, R.I. (2013). Problems and promise: On higher education in American. *Harvard Magazine, 116*(2), 26, 28–30.

Trowler, V., & Trowler, P. (2010). *Student engagement literature review.* York, England: Higher Education Academy.

Umbach, P.D., & Wawrzynski, M.R. (2005). Faculty do matter: The role of college faculty in student learning and engagement. *Research in Higher Education, 46*(2), 153–184.

3

Hands across the Table

Integrating Students into
Shared Governance

Oluwadamisi Atanda, Síocháin Hughes,
Daniel Ryan, and Emily Sohmer Tai

Collaboration among students and others, such as faculty, staff, or administration, in governance settings can be difficult. A group of former faculty and student governance leaders examine proven strategies that promote cooperative exchange among students and faculty governance leaders.

- *Daniel Ryan provides historical context, discussing the legacy contemporary shared governance structures in the American academy owe to the traditions of the medieval European university.*

- *Síocháin Hughes, who chaired the CUNY UFS Committee on Student Affairs from 2012 to 2014, explains how she built stronger ties with the City University Student Senate, a cross-campus student governance body that drew together student governance leaders from across the 21 campuses of the City University system.*

- *Emily Sohmer Tai, in collaboration with Oluwadamisi Atanda (former Queensborough Student Association President and recipient of the 2012 Award for best CUNY Student Governance Leader of the Year), describe the multi-year development of a successful integration of student leaders into a shared governance system on a single CUNY campus.*

Together, these authors argue that the elimination of the rift between students and other governance leaders can not only enrich the university, but make realizing the pedagogical objectives of undergraduate education much more likely. By laying a foundation for cooperative exchange between students and faculty in the classroom, the values and habits of civic engagement to which public higher education is dedicated are effectively reinforced.

Introduction

Emily Sohmer Tai

The City University of New York (CUNY), an institution that has grown from the "Free Academy" established in 1847 to a network of 24 units (7 community colleges; 11 senior colleges; the Macaulay Honors College, and 5 graduate and professional schools), accommodates a system of overlapping shared governance structures. Each CUNY institution maintains its own individual governance plan to facilitate dialogue between three core constituencies: faculty, administrators, and students (City University Governance Plans). Two overarching governance bodies—the City University Faculty Senate (established in 1968) and the City University Student Senate (established in 1972)—meanwhile draw representation from the bodies established by local governance plans to represent the consensus across faculty and student communities to the City University's Central Administration (City University Faculty Senate website, 2013; City University Student Senate website, 2012).

Administrative partnerships with faculty, as well as administrative partnerships with students, are well established across the landscape of shared governance at CUNY. Building effective partnerships between faculty and students has been a more challenging task, complicated by the disparities in the way faculty and students may view curriculum and the college experience. We nevertheless contend that such partnerships are essential, if shared governance is to work effectively, as a fully representative resource for problem solving and institutional improvement. As educators, we suggest that it is our responsibility to fully engage students in shared governance, as part of the preparation a college education affords its recipients for participation in civil society. Such participation is, moreover, deeply embedded in the history and traditions of the western European university.

I.
Shared Governance and Faculty-Student Partnerships: A History

Daniel Ryan

The role of students in higher education has waxed and waned since the establishment of the academy. In fact, in 12th-century Italy, the term *universitas* referred to the students—those individuals who banded together and collectively paid entrepreneurial teachers for their instruction (Brundage, 2008; Rashdall, 1936). Coming from all over Europe, students sought certain protections from the state and received them from Emperor Frederick II in the form of a *Privilegium Scholasticum* (also referred to as *Authentica habita*). This provided them with some of the same protections accorded the clergy, from whence their instructions were drawn (De Ridder-Symoens, 1992). Sometime after a papal bull issued by Pope Gregory IX of 1233, according what Rashdall has termed "university privileges" to faculty at the University of Cambridge, faculty banded together at institutions across Europe to protect themselves from students, and the concept of *collegium* was formed (Leader, 1988; Rashdall, 1936). This move gave the *collegium* the right to choose its members, but little else. Configured by the traditions of the Bologna *nations*—the student associations that had founded the first university in Bologna—the *universitas* still dictated curriculum, hours of instruction, and student life (Cobban, 1971, 1980). This arrangement continued for several centuries. Students whose demands were not met simply voted with their feet, migrating to a different city that contained an institution more in line with their requirements. Institutions modeled after the Bologna mode were opened in Paris, France (1150), Oxford, England (1167), Modena (1175), and Heidelberg (1386).

The most visceral demonstration of the power of the students was demonstrated in Oxford, England, in 1355. Two students had visited the Swindlestock Tavern and had a disagreement with the tavern owner about the quality of their drinks. Words were exchanged, and the students threw their drinks in the tavern owner's face. As the students rallied around their peers, the locals rallied around the tavern owner, igniting a violent confrontation known as the Saint Scholastica's Day Riot. The Riot, also known as the Saint Scholastica Day's Massacre, lasted 2 days and left 63 students and 30 local residents dead (Miller, 1993).

Toward the end of the medieval period, faculty slowly assumed more power as they petitioned local municipalities to provide income for salaries, successfully arguing that higher education was a public good. By the early modern period, this rise of paternalism had shifted the power in universities to the faculty and local princes. By the 18th century, in Protestant as well as Catholic Europe, where institutions had been in existence primarily to train clergy and the wealthiest of citizens, the rise of philanthropy gradually eroded the power of the church. This, too, solidified the power of the professoriate, as they took on more and more of the responsibility for decision making that had heretofore been handled by the clergy. In the "New World" where New College (Harvard); William and Mary; Collegiate School (Yale); the College of New Jersey (Princeton); and King's College (Columbia) were founded, Americans embraced the concept of faculty control over aspects of student life, but relied on the Scottish Reformation model that put authority over the institution in the hands of laymen, similar to what was happening at Edinburgh and at Trinity College in Dublin (McGrath, 1970).

By the end of the 18th century, power over the governance of the University tended to shift in deference to various funding sources. Professional activities in American universities were limited almost exclusively to teaching. By the middle of the 19th century and with the passage of the Morrill Land Grant Acts, and, later, the elaboration of the "Wisconsin Idea," a new emphasis was placed on service to the community in which the institution was located. The Morrill Acts of 1862 provided land grants to each state for the establishment of agricultural schools and resulted in new schools being established throughout the Union, and later throughout the former Confederate states (7 U.S. Code 301 & 304). By the end of the 19th century, the focus shifted again, as institutions such as the University of Chicago looked to the example of the German University in according priority to academic research, with some power shifting to those individuals within the *collegium* who could bring new revenues to the institution (Rudolph, 1990).

Since the latter half of the 20th century, various factors—the war in Vietnam; the shift in perception from viewing education as a public to a private good; the growth of the "administrative class;" declining state support; the rising cost of tuition; the growth of dependence on adjuncts and online education; and changing demographics within the student body itself—have worked, increasingly, to shift power away from faculty (Bowen & Schuster, 1986; Slaughter & Leslie, 1997).

In part, this shift has corresponded to the increased power of students. For example, students successfully banded together and demanded change—at Berkeley (the Berkeley "Free Speech" movement); at Gallaudet

University (Deaf President Now!); and at Cooper Union (free tuition) (Anderson, 2013; Free Cooper Union, 2012; Gonzales, 2014). Students have raised their voices to be heard both on and off campus.

While students have forced their way into conversations on various topics (within a wide range, including athletics, changes in curriculum, and sexual assault policies), there has yet to be a significant shift toward student involvement in formal governing boards. A recent (2010) study by the Association of Governing Boards of Universities and Colleges found that, at Independent Colleges, only 20% had a student as a member of the governing board, and at only 8.5% of the institutions did the student have a voting role. That compares to faculty, who are represented on 27.8 % of boards, with 14.9% having a faculty member with voting privileges, and staff having a role on 33.6 of all boards, with 19.5 having a staff member with a voting role.

No discussion of shared governance can be fully meaningful without a legitimate role for students. It is worth pointing out that, absent that meaningful role, students often find other significant, but sometimes more disruptive, methods to make their voices heard. Engaging students in governance in a purposeful way elevates the structure to true shared governance. Such engagement welcomes students into the *collegium*, and honors the best traditions of the medieval university. These traditions originated, after all, with students who, seeking knowledge from proficient teachers, created associations for the purpose of supporting their instruction.

II.
Building Faculty-Student Partnerships in Shared Governance I: The CUNY UFS and the CUNY USS

Síocháin Hughes

While student representation might remain elusive on many of the campuses of America's private colleges, the tumultuous years of campus protest during the 1960s resulted in the establishment of governance structures that welcomed student voices at the City University of New York (Gibbons, Petty, & Van Nort, 2014; Hall, 2008). The University Student Senate of the City University of New York was founded in 1972, operating with a mission that contained key points related to students. The mission guaranteed that the City University of New York would (1) protect the rights of the student body, (2) further the cause of public higher education, and (3) promote the general welfare of its student constituents and the university, by preserving, as per the Student Senate's Constitution, "accessibility; affordability, and excellence within the City University of New York." The University Student Senate draws its delegates from all the constituent campuses of the City University of New York, and is charged with ensuring that all required student representatives are provided to all elected government leaders throughout the City and State of New York, as well as in the federal government. In the winter of 2015, for example, members of the University Student Senate testified in support of President Obama's proposal to offer students the opportunity to attend community college tuition free (City University Student Senate, February 23, 2015). Moreover, members of the University Student Senate Executive Committee sit, with vote, on committees of the City University Board of Trustees. The full University Student Senate meets as a body one Sunday per month during the academic year (City University Student Senate Constitution, 2013).

The establishment of the University Student Senate in 1972 was preceded by the establishment of the City University Faculty Senate only 4 years earlier (Tai, 2013). It, too, draws delegates from across the campuses of the City University of New York to support faculty; meets monthly (one Tuesday per month, during the Academic year); and, through its chair and Executive Committee, represents faculty views on committees of the CUNY Board of Trustees. Each of the committees of the CUNY Board of Trustees—the Committee on Academic Policy, Programs, and Research; the Committee on Faculty, Staff, and Administration; the Committee on Fiscal Affairs; the Committee on Facilities Planning and Management; the Committee on Fiscal Affairs; and the Committee on Student Affairs— accordingly accommodates one voting representative of the faculty and one voting student representative. Committee meetings are also attended by Faculty and Student alternates, and the University Student Senate and Faculty Senate Chairs, as ex-officio members of each committee (City University of New York, Board of Trustees, Bylaws).

Representatives of the faculty draw their information about faculty perspectives from a network of UFS committees that draw on the expertise of the UFS membership to review and recommend matters of Academic Policy. There Is a UFS Committee on Academic Freedom; a Committee on Libraries and Information Technology; a Committee on the Status of the Faculty; and a Committee on Student Affairs. This last committee is charged to "advocate for and guide students in their endeavor to acquire a rich and meaningful education that helps students succeed in their lives" (City University Faculty Senate Charter, 1968).

From 2012 to 2014, the University Faculty Senate Committee on Student Affairs was chaired by Síocháin Hughes, Adjunct Professor of Studio Art at Hunter College, and Graphic Designer & Academic Coordinator of Hunter's Academic Center for Excellence in Research and Teaching (ACERT). During Professor Hughes's tenure as chair, the Committee operated under the following mandate to extend the above charge as follows:

> In this endeavor . . . we will: Build on our role as faculty to establish bridges of supportive, collaborative communication between students, faculty and administration. We will promote collegial student representation on faculty committees as appropriate and collegial faculty representation on student committees as appropriate. And we will found a positive presence with the University Student Senate and with student government on our campuses by attending meetings, and making significant strides towards personal outreach. . . . We will initiate a multi-faceted report on the status of student affairs at CUNY, with the intention of presenting the work at a UFS Plenary in spring, or by developing it into a proposal for a UFS conference under the working title, "Best practices for supporting student/faculty communities." The report may explore details including, but not limited to: what works; what works best for CUNY and what works best on your campus; challenges and concerns for faculty, students and administrators; forms of governance; governance and administration; working together at the university as a whole and on individual campuses. The report and potentially, the conference will extend and energize our efforts towards strengthening Student Affairs across CUNY.

While a few years might feel like a long time to students, as faculty and administration are well aware, the totality of student presence on campus is quite limited. Students are on campus as they are developing their careers. Faculty and administration, are, by contrast, well established in their own careers and more certain of their future directions. This differential puts students at a considerable disadvantage should they seek to influence policy. Yet students bring a unique and valuable perspective to policy debates. The student perspective can become particularly valuable when administrators and faculty consider such challenges as efforts to improve graduation rates, student engagement, and student success—elements that are often scrutinized by legislators and watched closely by college administrators but do not always translate to success in the classroom. Because they are a temporary presence with ideas that are more likely to be supported by anecdotes rather than numerical data, student voices are often viewed as naïve and ephemeral. However, when these voices can be used to achieve a political advantage, it might not always be in the best interests of public education in general, or in the best interests of students in particular.

In *The Fall of the Faculty*, Benjamin Ginsburg argues that the explosive growth in administration has led to the decline of faculty power in terms of institutional influence, and that this development has run concurrently with the growing corporate financing of the university. According to Ginsburg, this has led to a wide-spread consumerist approach to education, de-emphasizing intellectual rigor and traditional importance of the liberal arts in favor of preparing students for industry. His observations underscore what many faculty members have observed with frustration, and what political players have, in their turn, blamed on faculty (Ginsburg, 2011). As faculty, we may retreat from this painful scenario into the rewards of research and teaching, but there is more that we can (and owe our students to) do.

Faculty members are significant to students, not only as mentors and educators who energize and enliven academic and professional engagement, but as people from previous generations who provide caring guidance to the newest generation of professionals. Our significance is felt not only by the individual students we teach, but more broadly, through the archetypal relationship we have as professor and student. While faculty influence over the university and educational matters might be at risk, faculty members need to realize, and take ownership for, the power of our position as educators. At the same time, we must recognize the value of students, who represent important voices that need to be heard. Students and faculty have a natural affinity, and can achieve mutual goals in the academic environment. If high-quality education is to survive the era of transition that Ginsburg and others have decried, marked by diminishing public funding for higher education, burgeoning administrative ranks, and increasing dependence on private and corporate donors, it is time to build bridges of collegial alliance between students and faculty so they can effectively advocate on each other's behalf and stand strong against the deterioration of the value of education. To do so, we need a new model of leadership for faculty-student relationships, one that calls for mutual respect and multi-generational wisdom and leadership. This was the basis of my work in building collaborative communication between the UFS and the USS.

The problem is our own *focus*. By diverting attention from what's important, indirect and political aggression impedes progress, stymies results, and creates a wedge between faculty and students. When we as faculty allow ourselves to "focus on the ants on the picnic table while the bears are eating the children," we lose the future generation of students. It is important that we not allow ourselves to be manipulated by crisis.

When I came into my position as chair of the Standing Committee on Student Affairs, exactly such a condition was present. Faculty members were preoccupied with the current controversy over the introduction of a Board of Trustees resolution on Creating an Effective Transfer System that resulted in the introduction of a new core curriculum framework across the City University (City University of New York Board of Trustees, 2011). The curriculum, which came to be known as "Pathways," was defended by the Administration on the grounds that it would facilitate transfer across the 2- and 4-year units of the City University and save students and the University money by sparing students the need to take courses beyond the number of credits required to complete their degrees. A large number (although not all) of City University Faculty opposed the measure, on the grounds that the requirements of the new Pathways Curriculum, and the mandatory three-credit course design it imposed, diminished the curriculum's academic rigor. Students, by contrast, were largely in favor of the new curriculum, which was supported by the City University Student Senate, although a few student governance leaders also voiced concerns about educational quality (Busch, 2013; City University, Board of Trustees, 2011; City University Faculty Senate, 2011–2014; *Daily News*, 2012; *Inside Higher Ed*, 2013; Skinner, 2012; Vitale, 2014).

It took a great deal of effort to refocus the conversation onto Student Affairs while this controversy was at its height. Out of the Pathways crisis, however, the directive to build communication between the UFS and the USS was initiated—a very positive outcome from an initially discouraging situation.

The key to building bridges of collaborative communication is to maintain focus on what is at stake and what is to be gained. This should take priority over and above any temporary squabble, irritation, or distress. Essentially, we must stop crying over our setbacks, like so much spilt milk, and forge new and positive strategies to continually improve the educational situation. In my work on the Committee on Student Affairs, my mission was to cultivate mutual attitudes of self-awareness and openness to divergent viewpoints that could deepen and sustain meaningful lines of communication. And my vision has been, as one might in a family, to encourage people to see beyond individual differences and find the love of each other—to "build the love."

In meeting with students in governance positions, I became aware that though the students didn't know me, they held me in high regard as a professor. I experienced the relationship between student and faculty as a timeless archetype, like parent and child. Through this, I drew the conclusion that this is the relationship that faculty has been cultivating all along. This is the relationship that undergirds our most effective teaching, as mentors and as pedagogues. Mutual high regard is always the most productive foundation for team effort, and cultivating this is far more substantive than any temporary measure put in place simply to gain student support.

We must continue this effort to meaningfully connect with students outside the classroom. Concurrently, we must encourage students to take ownership of their roles in governance—indeed, in all forms of leadership. In turn, we must also respect them as equals in leadership and partners in governance. This is the foundation for cooperative exchange, through which the timeless values and habits of civic engagement can be established.

III.
Building Faculty-Student Partnerships in Shared Governance II: The Student Perspective

Oluwadamisi Atanda with Emily Sohmer Tai

My foray into shared governance at Queensborough Community College wasn't exactly unexpected. In high school, right before I transitioned to Queensborough, I served as president of the student council, responsible for acting as liaison between the student body and school administration. But my interest in shared governance had deeper roots than that presidency. The high school I attended was in Lagos, Nigeria. Nigeria is a developing country, with a poor governance track record. The rights of ordinary citizens were often trampled on by the elite. Government accountability and transparency were rare. It wasn't uncommon to read about arbitrary government arrests and suppression of protests. These conditions contributed to my interest in activism. Governments and institutions alike are more productive when collaboration occurs across the board, between those who govern and the governed.

At Queensborough Community College, I encountered a governance structure that had great potential; it was robust and healthy, but not without flaws. My predecessors had worked constructively with members of the faculty who took seriously the role of student involvement in the college decision-making process. But faculty-student partnership at Queensborough was often limited, for two major reasons: First, students are distracted by other obligations. Immersed in various academic, professional, and social commitments, students are often left with little time to participate in governance activities, which can be time consuming. Sometimes, students also lack awareness (or understanding) of the campus shared governance opportunities available to them. A second difficulty is that some faculty members are indifferent to student participation in governance.

I was extremely fortunate that my governance team consisted of students determined to make their voices heard. We also had opportunities to work closely with Queensborough President, Diane Call, and Academic Senate Chair, Professor Emily Tai, both of whom were ushering a new tide of increased faculty-student partnership. Still, even with a great team and receptive faculty, we were not immune to challenges. One challenge I faced at the onset was a lack of information and explanation concerning the extent to which student involvement was needed. Apart from the "big meetings"—such as the monthly gathering of our college's Academic Senate, where student leaders held eight votes or meetings of the College Advisory Planning Committee, which were chaired by Queensborough's president—many students, including me, felt that student presence wasn't essential (Queensborough Academic Senate Bylaws; Queensborough Community College Governance Plan).

And yet, I would argue that such collaboration *is* essential. Faculty-student partnership begins with the mutual recognition that each party contributes a unique perspective to the table. I witnessed this first-hand, during a meeting of the Academic Senate's Committee on Assessment and Institutional Effectiveness. I listened as faculty members and administrators bickered about including additional questions in the semester-end student-faculty evaluations. These evaluations are intended to elicit feedback about the quality of lectures and usefulness of course materials. At some point during the meeting, I spoke up, providing a student's perspective: Most students I knew couldn't care less about the evaluations. Every person in the room seemed to go numb. I explained that professors usually hovered over us as we completed the evaluation, and knowing full well who was going to assign our final grade for the course, we were sure to draw nothing but hearts and stars all over the evaluations. The discussion immediately changed, and the new challenge before the committee was no longer including more questions in the evaluations but how to ensure confidentiality and objectivity. At that moment, I realized that the presence and input of students in the decision-making process is not only vital—it can be transformative.

During the introduction of the controversial "Pathways" curriculum, an issue that divided administrators and teaching staff, a unique opportunity emerged for student involvement. The students' stance, many argued, had the potential to tip the scale in one direction or the other, because of the arguments both faculty and administrators made that their opposing positions were each taken in the best interests of students. Both administrators and teaching faculty actively endeavored to find opportunities to meet with student governance leaders to explain their respective positions. These were particularly difficult, and I daresay exciting, times for the campus and larger university community. The relevance of student representation in college discussions was amplified. For us, as student representatives, this process revealed the potential for students to influence policy, as well as the challenges that lay within shared governance.

Part of the process required us to participate in long, intermittently tedious, meetings to review lengthy texts. We were also asked to present our insights about the texts at small, high-stakes meetings. We had to stretch outside the impact of our own experience to consider policies that would go into effect beyond our tenures as student government officers— we had to look at everything in terms of the larger scheme of things.

Throughout this debate, I was forced to wear several hats. It was challenging to effectively communicate all of the substance and complexity of the policy to the student body. Sometimes my position seemed different from that of the majority of the student body. One of the biggest learning experiences for me was to make sure that I voiced the needs of other students, no matter what my personal sentiments were. In the end, I had to balance their views with my own well-informed judgments, shaped by my attendance at critical hearings and discussions about the policy. I also needed to ensure, in this situation and others, that I was tactful in expressing disagreement, given the dynamics of decision making on a college campus. One day I might be openly disagreeing with the administration about their smoking ban; the following day I might have to request administrative support for the expenses of refurbishing the student union building. Needless to say, diplomacy was a skill not to be neglected.

While I was a student leader at Queensborough, I found the shared governance culture to be very lively. Faculty leaders were persistent in their efforts to include students in important discussions, such as during the revision of the college's governance plan. This governance plan, a critical document, specifies the structure of the governance system through which college policy will be developed and implemented. I was pleasantly surprised at the degree to which students were consulted in the revisions of the document. Professor Tarasko, who chaired the Faculty Executive Committee, and I were in regular communication. Because students were engaged throughout the revision process, we were better able to appreciate the procedures used within the college, as well as the commitment of faculty members. I am eternally grateful for the patience and respect with which my team and I were treated throughout these interactions; we were engaged not merely as extraneous and uniform ex-officio participants, but as equal colleagues. I strongly believe that this relationship permeated the college campus and improved faculty-student relations overall.

This was quite unlike my experience at another unit of the City University of New York: City College, where I served as an officer with the Government and Law Society, an organization under the Undergraduate Student Government. At City College, disagreements between student representatives and the administration were frequent. Regular communication between the two parties did not occur. Often, for whatever reason, the administration would share details about a project only after it was underway. I recall the controversy that surrounded the administration's takeover of the Guillermo Morales/Assata Shakur Student and Community Center (Kaminer, 2013). Reports were that student government officers, like the rest of the City College community, were informed about the decision to reassign the space only after it was reassigned. This caused widespread uproar across campus, and students, including their elected representatives, were outraged by the takeover. In my estimation, the backlash could have been greatly minimized had student representatives been consulted and informed throughout the transition.

Overall, my experience at Queensborough Community College was without doubt enriching, and my participation within the shared governance apparatus made it more so. Faculty-student partnership is central to the success of the college because it fosters a culture of collaboration. It provided my colleagues and me with the opportunity to advocate for our peers concerning issues we considered important. We honed critical networking and negotiation skills. We were able to learn about the inner workings of higher education and the formation of policies. But, perhaps most importantly, we learned how to work with others, learning to find compromise even deep in the thicket of a debate.

Conclusion

Emily Sohmer Tai

Shared governance is *praxis*: the affirmation of an academic tradition. Affirmations of principle alone do not make shared governance work; it is constructed, over time, in daily interactions. The evidence for a successful shared governance partnership is never manifest in any single policy. It is, rather, discerned across the wide variety of matters that fall within the purview of college governance. In looking back to the traditions of the medieval university that Dr. Ryan has discussed, we can learn that it is up to us to build a system of shared governance that marries the student-centered Bologna model to the faculty-centered model that prevailed at Paris, or at the medieval university of Cambridge, in order to ultimately create a system in which students and faculty participate in a common dialogue to shape university policy. Faculty members, as Professor Hughes and Mr. Atanda have argued, can learn much from students as they work together in a governance system. Interactions with students outside the classroom can, moreover, enrich interactions with students in the classroom, as faculty members gain insights into student priorities and perspectives. But faculty members should also appreciate the power of the governance experience to enhance student learning as a dimension of civic engagement.

In the academic environment of the 21st-century American higher education campus, where student engagement has been shown to contribute to student success, and experiential learning activities have been recognized as valuable instruments for promoting such engagement, we would like to close by proposing that campuses truly commit to shared governance by integrating participation in shared governance into their curricula, as service learning experiences there would be clear links between shared governance and more traditional curricula (e.g., in the humanities and social sciences). Integrating shared governance into the curriculum might simultaneously reinforce students' grasp of theoretical topics encountered in the course in the liberal arts and science study, as well as deepening student understanding of the ways in which these disciplines have practical applications (Center for Community College Student Engagement; Strage, 2000). The integration of shared governance into college curricula might, meanwhile, help students to better appreciate their power, as civil actors, to effect positive change through governance processes, and, perhaps, deepen their commitment to civic participation post-graduation. Indeed, we would even venture to suggest that faculty who de-emphasize the participation of students in college governance squander a critical experiential learning opportunity for students. Faculty governance leaders can, and should, teach by example. If we truly believe that shared governance is what makes a good university great, we owe it to our students to include them in the process—and, by so doing, show them how it works.

Acknowledgments

In addition to acknowledging one another, Dr. Sharon Cramer, and the Editorial team of this volume, the authors would like to acknowledge Dr. Terrence Martell, Chair of the City University Faculty Senate and CUNY Trustee, 2012–2016; Muhammad Arshad, University Student Senate Chair and CUNY Trustee 2013–2014; Joseph Awadjie, University Student Senate Chair and CUNY Trustee, 2014–2016; William Phipps, Executive Director, City University Faculty Senate; Fernando Araujo, Executive Director, CUNY University Student Senate; Dr. Diane Bova Call, President of Queensborough Community College, CUNY; and Professor Alexandra Tarasko, Professor of Nursing and Chair of Queensborough Faculty Executive Committee, 2012–2015.

References

Anderson, N. (2013). Gallaudet marks 'Deaf President Now.' *The Washington Post*. Retrieved from http://www.washingtonpost.com/local/education/gallaudet-marks-deaf-president-now/2013/02/07/17666740-6fdc-11e2-8b8d-e0b59a-1b8e2a_story.html

Association of Governing Board of Universities and Colleges. (2010). *Policies, practices, and composition of governing boards of independent colleges and universities*. Washington, D.C.: Association of Governing Board of Universities and Colleges. Retrieved from http://agb.org/reports/2010/2010-policies-practices-and-composition-governing-boards-independent-colleges-and-unive

Bowen, H.R., & Schuster, J.H. (1986). *American professors: A national resource imperiled.* Oxford: Oxford University Press.

Brundage, J.A. (2008). *The medieval origins of the legal profession: Canonists, civilians, and courts.* Chicago: The University of Chicago Press.

Busch, M. (2013). What CUNY Pathways means for undergraduates. *The Nation.* Retrieved from http://www.thenation.com/article/what-cuny-pathways-means-undergraduates/

City University Faculty Senate. (1968). Charter of the University Faculty Senate. Retrieved from http://www.cunyufs.org/CHARTER.pdf

City University Faculty Senate. (2011–2014). Pathways responses. Retrieved from https://sites.google.com/site/universityfacultysenatecuny/senate-action/resolutions-on-pathways

City University of New York. Board of Trustees. Bylaws. Retrieved from http://policy.cuny.edu/bylaws/#Navigation_Location

City University of New York. Board of Trustees. (2011). Resolution on creating an effective transfer system. Retrieved from http://www.cuny.edu/academics/initiatives/pathways/about/archive/archive/text-draft/Reso.pdf

City University of New York. Central Administration Website. Governance plans. Retrieved from http://www2.cuny.edu/about/administration/offices/legal-affairs/governance-plans/

City University Student Senate. (2013). Constitution. Retrieved from https://drive.google.com/file/d/0By5Yp9XLcAgQelhtWHJTRnBNOUE/edit

City University Student Senate. Mission statement. (1972). Retrieved from http://www.usscuny.org/about-us.html

City University Student Senate. (2015). USS testifies in support of President Obama's proposal for free community college tuition. Retrieved from http://www.usscuny.org/uss-testify-in-support-of-president-obama-proposal-for-free-communtiy-college.html

Cobban, A.B. (1971). Medieval student power. *Past and Present, 53,* 29–66.

Cobban, A.B. (1980). Student power in the Middle Ages. *History Today,* 30 (2). Retrieved from http://www.historytoday.com/alan-b-cobban/student-power-middle-ages/

Cornell University Law School. Legal Information Institute. *7 U.S. Code § 301—Land grant aid of colleges.* Retrieved from https://www.law.cornell.edu/uscode/text/7/301

Cornell University Law School. Legal Information Institute. *7 U.S. Code § 304—Investment of proceeds of sale of land or scrip.* Retrieved from https://www.law.cornell.edu/uscode/text/7/304

De Ridder-Symoens. H., ed. (1992). *A history of the universities in Europe* (Vols. 1–2). Cambridge: Cambridge University Press.

Editorial. (2012). Pipe down, profs. *Daily News.* Retrieved from http://www.nydailynews.com/opinion/pipe-profs-article-1.1220729

Free Cooper Union. (2012). Retrieved from http://cusos.org

Gibbons, W.C., Petty, A., & Van Nort, S.C. (2014). Revolutionary times revisited: Students' interpretation of the City College of New York student protests and takeover of 1969. *The History Teacher, 47* (4), 511–528.

Ginsberg, B. (2011). *The fall of the faculty: The rise of the all-administrative university and why it matters.* Oxford: Oxford University Press.

Gonzales, R. (2014, October 5). Berkeley's fight for free speech fired up student protest movement. *NPR.* Retrieved from http://www.npr.org/2014/10/05/353849567/when-political-speech-was-banned-at-berkeley

Hall, S. (2008). Protest movements in the 1970s: The long 1960s. *Journal of Contemporary History, 43* (4), 655–672.

Hoeveler, J.D. Jr. (1976). The University and the Social Gospel: The intellectual origins of the Wisconsin Idea. *The Wisconsin Magazine of History,* 282–298.

Kaminer, Ariel. (2013). Protests as City College closes a student center. *New York Times.* Retrieved from http://www.nytimes.com/2013/10/22/nyregion/protests-as-city-college-closes-a-student-center.html?_r=0

Leader, D.R. (1988). *A history of the University of Cambridge: Volume 1: The University to 1546.* Cambridge: Cambridge University Press.

McGrath, E.J. (1970). *Should students share the power: A study of their role in college and university governance.* Philadelphia: Temple University Press.

Miller, C. (1993). The Saint Scholastica Day Riot: Oxford after the black death. Retrieved from http://fch.fiu.edu/FCH-1993/Miller_1993.htm

Queensborough Community College. Academic Senate. Bylaws. Retrieved from http://www.qcc.cuny.edu/governance/academicSenate/asBylaws.html

Queensborough Community College. Governance plan. Retrieved from http://www.qcc.cuny.edu/governance/plansPoliciesProcedures/governancePlan.html

Quick Takes. (2013). CUNY faculty vote no confidencein transfer program. *Inside Higher Ed.* Retrieved from https://www.insidehighered.com/quicktakes/2013/06/03/cuny-faculty-vote-no-confidence-transfer-program

Rashdall, H. (1936). *The universities of Europe in the Middle Ages* (Vols. 1–3). London: Oxford University Press. Retrieved from https://archive.org/stream/universitiesofeu01unse/universitiesofeu01unse_djvu.txt

Rudolph, F. (1990). *The American college and university: A history.* Atlanta: University of Georgia Press.

Skinner. C. (2012, December 10). CUNY Profs call for halt to curriculum re-do. *The New York World.* Retrieved from http://www.thenewyorkworld.com/2012/12/10/pathways-resolution/

Slaughter, S., & Leslie, L.L. (1997). *Academic capitalism: Politics, policies, and the entrepreneurial university.* Baltimore, MD: Johns Hopkins University Press.

Strage, A.A. (2000). Service learning: Enhancing student learning outcomes in a college-level lecture course. *Michigan Journal of Community Service Learning 7,* 75–81.

Tai, E.S. (2013). Forty-five years of tradition: Looking back on City University's Faculty Senate. *UFS Blog.* Retrieved from https://sites.google.com/site/

universityfacultysenatecuny/UFS-blog/45yearsoftraditionlookingbackoncunysu
niversityfacultysenate

University of Texas, Austin. Center for Community College Student Engagement.
Retrieved from http://www.ccsse.org/center/

Vitale, A.S. (2014). The fight against Pathways at CUNY. *Academe.* Retrieved
from http://www.aaup.org/article/fight-against-pathways-cuny#.VdjyJcpzPmI

Part II

Broad-Based Shared Governance Explorations and Solutions

4

Sharing Shared Governance

The Benefits of Systemness

Sharon F. Cramer and Rochelle Mozlin

Large statewide higher education systems face challenges when attempting shared governance. This paper examines shared governance within the State University of New York (SUNY). Definitions of shared governance are provided and examined, followed by an identification and analysis of "holes." The authors conclude by proposing a paradigm illustrating how attention to both structural and interpersonal features of shared governance can lead to benefits for individuals, campuses, as well as the system.

Introduction

How do decisions get made? Within each institution of higher education, as within every family, there are predictable stages in the decision-making process: identifying need, exploring options, weighing priorities against resources, considering implications for different decisions, and ultimately making choices. While there are common processes for every decision, regardless of its type (e.g., approaching how to effectively evaluate general education offerings is relatively similar to deciding to move to a new house in a community with better schools), each decision is also idiosyncratic.

The challenges of decision making, as well as communicating, organizing, and disagreeing within a shared governance model within an individual institution are many. Within large statewide systems of higher education, these challenges are exponentially increased. The State University of New York (SUNY) is such a system. Established in 1948, SUNY now includes 64 campuses and serves over 460,000 students. SUNY is the largest state comprehensive public higher education system in the country.

In 1953, the University Faculty Senate (UFS) was established through the *Policies of SUNY's Board of Trustees*; it was designed to be the "official agency through which the University Faculty engages in the governance of the University." The *Policies* (2014 edition, p. 18) further establish that the Senate shall be concerned with effective educational policies and other professional matters within the University.

In this chapter, we examine how the members and leaders of University Faculty Senate within SUNY, in conjunction with Chancellor Nancy Zimpher, use a system-wide approach. This allows for general as well as individualized responses to governance-related challenges such as decision making within and across member colleges and universities via the term "systemness." *Systemness* is defined by Wikipedia as "the state, quality, or condition of a complex system, that is, of a set of interconnected elements that behave as, or appear to be, a whole, exhibiting behavior distinct from the behavior of the parts. The term is new and has been applied to large social phenomena and organizations (health care and higher education) by advocates of higher degrees of system-like, coherent behavior for delivering value to stakeholders." Wikipedia explicitly mentions Zimpher in this definition as follows: "The higher educational use of the term was instituted by The State University of New York's (SUNY) Chancellor Nancy L. Zimpher in the State of the University Address on January 9, 2012. Zimpher noted systemness as "the coordination of multiple components that, when working together, create a network of activity that is more powerful than any action of individual parts on their own" (Zimpher, 2012a).

This chapter also defines and highlights several resources developed by the Governance Committee of the University Faculty Senate (e.g., *The Governance Handbook, The Campus Governance Leader's Guide*). Examples will be presented that illustrate how systemness provides a forum for thoughtful consideration of concerns that may initially appear heterogeneous but often have much in common. In reflecting on actions that sometimes emerge from adversity, strength has been found. Challenges faced on individual campuses (as well as throughout the System) led to sharing of the experiences, perspectives, and voices, resulting in SUNY's dynamic processes of shared governance. This chapter illustrates how shared governance within SUNY has facilitated independent, campus-specific responses to governance challenges as well as enhanced performance of the more routine "activities of daily shared governance."

What is Shared Governance?

Origins of Shared Governance

Most academics agree that the modern roots of "shared governance" can be found in the 1966 *Joint Statement on Government of Colleges and Universities* by three groups—the American Association of University Professors (AAUP), the American Council on Education (ACE), and the Association of Governing Boards of Universities and Colleges (AGB). The statement is the starting point for most discussions of shared governance, in part because it continues to provide a foundation for broadly defining the main campus constituents who would be part of the shared governance partnership: "governing board members, administrators, faculty members, students, and other persons" (AAUP statement, p. 1, found in Appendix 1, *University Faculty Senate Governance Handbook* (2013 edition, p. 47).

The statement is likely so frequently referenced because it clearly vests the responsibility of curriculum with faculty, in the following way: "A key element of the 1966 statement is that it identifies faculty as having 'primary responsibility' for such fundamental areas as curriculum, subject matter and methods of instruction, research, faculty status, and those aspects of student life which relate to the educational process" (*UFS Governance Handbook*, 2013 edition, p. 9).

Defining Shared Governance

Defining "shared governance" is difficult. Leo Tolstoy's opening sentence of *Anna Karenina* (1877), describing family life, is relevant here: "Happy families are all alike; every unhappy family is unhappy in its own way." Successful governance organizations are accurately described by many, if not all, of the characteristics below, whereas the unsuccessful ones usually have idiosyncratic structural or interpersonal challenges (or both). Three example definitions are provided below, each of which highlights a different aspect of shared governance.

SUNY Shared Governance Transformation Team Definition (2011)

> Shared governance in higher education refers to the structures and processes through which faculty, professional staff, administration, governing boards and, sometimes, students and staff, participate

in the development of policies, and in decision making that affect the institution.

This definition highlights both the diversity of the stakeholders and the variety of methods by which policies and decisions can be developed within institutions of higher education. Implied in the wide constituency base is the need for a process of negotiation that can take concerns of all members into consideration. By differentiating "structures" from "process," the definition underscores the need to have functional structures in place (e.g., representation within campus governance structures for many voices, procedures for election, dialogue, etc.), as well as room for the more subtle means through which ideas shared in less formal conversations can be incorporated into the decision-making process.

Principles of Shared Governance (AAUP Joint Statement on Shared Governance, 1966)

Important areas of action involve at one time or another the initiating capacity and decision-making participation of all members of the institutional component. Difference in the weight of each voice, from one point to the next, should be determined by the reference to the responsibility of each component for the particular matter at hand.

These principles capture a different aspect of the shared governance process, wherein the topic under consideration to some extent drives the membership of those involved in discussions, and in decisions. These principles argue against a "standard" method for shared governance, and instead hone in on *what* is being examined. The responsibility for identifying and deciding is shared by all, promoting the model within which every member of the campus takes responsibility for governance design and members work together toward outcomes. Ideally, finger pointing and blame are replaced by stepping forward to identify both problems and solutions.

American Federation of Teachers (AFT) Comment on Shared Governance (2002)

We believe that all college and university employees—top tenured faculty, junior faculty, temporary and part-time/adjunct faculty, graduate teaching and research assistants, professional staff with and without faculty rank, the classified and support staff that keep the educational enterprise going—should have a guaranteed voice in decision-making and a role in shaping policy in the areas of their expertise. (AFT, p. 3)

The American Federation of Teachers publication promotes the participation of "all" college and university employees. Omitted are administrators and students. This description links the dialogue to particular areas of expertise, thus ensuring that policy is not something that "just happens," but rather should include those who are directly involved.

How Does Shared Governance Function within SUNY?

Representation on the SUNY University Faculty Senate (UFS) consists of elected Senators from the 36 state-operated campuses and 2 senators appointed by the chancellor from system administration. The number of Senators representing each campus is determined by a weighted formula. There is a structure of standing committees within the UFS, the members and Chairs of which are appointed by the UFS Executive Committee. Three Plenary Sessions of the University Faculty Senate (each lasting 2 days) are held each academic year, in the fall, winter, and spring. Rotation among the campuses as sites for these meetings, with each campus hosting a meeting approximately every 10th, year, provides UFS members an opportunity to visit other campuses. Campus Governance Leaders (CGLs) from individual campuses are invited to attend the Plenary Sessions.

At the Plenaries, Senators and CGLs are given the opportunity to meet in sectors to discuss common concerns and issues. During a question and answer session with the chancellor (referred to as the Sharing of Concerns), each sector representative has the opportunity to present the chancellor with several questions that emerge from the sector meetings. Other Plenary activities include reports and updates from committees, key administrators from System Administration, and invited guests.

The dialogue between the sector representations and the chancellor connects directly to guidance provided by D. Bruce Johnstone. When Dr. Johnstone served as Chancellor of the State University of New York, he developed "Seven Precepts for Campus Presidents" (1991). He encouraged presidents to use these ideas in their dealings with the governance units on their campus. The first aspires toward the type of interaction that promotes "shared governance": "Respect your elected faculty senate and seek to involve and strengthen it. View it positively, as a partner and indispensable helper, rather than as a natural adversary or as a body whose enhanced strength or effectiveness needs to diminish yours" (Appendix 5 of the *UFS Governance Handbook 2013*, p. 63). This recommendation, from a chancellor, that presidents find ways to partner with elected senators, provides a guideline that has been central to the University Faculty Senate's dialogue with each chancellor over the decades. Although topics vary from year to year, promoting ongoing, meaningful interchanges with each University Faculty Senate has been a consistent commitment of SUNY chancellors. A major challenge for Senators in their relationship with chancellors is to avoid the urge toward either placating or being confrontational; instead, Senators must find ways to authentically and deliberately examine both problems and solutions. The two individuals primarily responsible for this are the chancellor and the president of the University Faculty Senate, but both are well aware that they are leaders representing the concerns and varied viewpoints of their constituents throughout the SUNY system.

Birnbaum (2004), in his critique of shared governance, advances a far more cynical view. He warns that one of the main difficulties facing shared governance is the need to honor and bring together separate entities, each of which has separate priorities:

> The three main parties to academic governance focus their attention on different things: trustees are concerned with responsiveness, administration with efficiency, and faculty with academic values. Each group has been socialized in different ways, is exposed to different aspects of the environment, has competence and expertise in different areas, and sees the institution from a unique perspective. Effective governance requires that the viewpoint of each group be considered in making decisions. (p. 17)

Birnbaum concludes that it is unrealistic for such diverse groups to work effectively together. The challenge of "shared governance," and its integration of the agendas and resources of multiple campuses into a shared vision of policy, relates to the complexity of multiple campuses effectively working together as a system. Chancellor Zimpher initially shared the term "systemness" in her January 2012 Address:

> The State University of New York has so many assets, but there is not one greater than our "systemness." Beyond the individual

strengths that each of our 64 campuses possess, there is a powerful and unmatched capacity to reach our most ambitious goals
together and to realize our highest achievements. In 2012 and
beyond, SUNY will tap into that power of "systemness" to create a more affordable, productive, and accessible university, while
doing its part to generate economic development, create jobs,
and prepare the workforce of tomorrow for New York State.
(Zimpher, 2012b)

Zimpher's notion of "systemness" (referenced in a 2012 publication of the
Rockefeller Institute of Governance, Zimpher, 2012c) and its application
to shared governance and the University Faculty Senate challenge Birnbaum's pessimistic conclusion. By incorporating campus-based governance
structures (via the Campus Governance Leaders, or CGLs, as well as the
University Faculty Senators), campus faculty and unique campus concerns
are represented. Through the involvement of the chancellor (and other key
SUNY administrators) at the Plenary meetings of the University Faculty Senate, an administrative perspective is incorporated. Additionally, the president
of the campus hosting the plenary is always represented, either in person or
by a senior campus administrator. At many plenaries, the president not only
gives an initial welcome to the Senate but also attends parts of the meeting.
    Concerns are expressed by different sectors, and a direct response
from the chancellor to the sector representatives enables all to hear and
consider how the discussion of issues raised have relevance to their campuses. Campus administrators and campus governance members gain
insight into the perspectives of both the chancellor and the sectors as
their University Senators report back to the campus—providing not only
current information about what is being shared from SUNY System at
the plenaries but also describing how faculty and staff on other campuses
are using shared information.
    The University Faculty Senate supports shared governance in a variety
of ways, including through its Governance Committee. This committee,
one of the Senate's standing committees, serves as a resource for the UFS,
its Senators, and CGLs via gatherings at meetings of the University Faculty
Senate and use of an active listserv.
    Despite campus differences, "systemness" can be descriptive of, and a
resource for, campus governance leaders and members. Langland (2011)
poses a question for consideration:

How can shared governance be made compatible with processes
    that require a radical redefinition and reorganization of an

institution? . . . How can faculty imagination, pragmatism, and governance be enlisted to discern and preserve what is fundamental to higher education and to redesign our public institutions around those core values? (p. 556)

Although she does not provide answers to these questions, she urges that "faculty governance . . . cease to be reactive and become anticipatory, leading institutional transformation rather than lamenting it" (pp. 556–557). These descriptions go to the heart of the "systemness" approach toward shared governance that has been central to the work of the SUNY University Faculty Senate. Of necessity, the problems and challenges related to shared governance become clearer with further scrutiny. The following section identifies a number of "holes" that shared governance must address in order to be successful.

Holes in the Shared Governance Model at SUNY and in General

Analysis of the challenges faced in the successful implementation of shared governance quickly uncovers two main categories of difficulties: structural and interpersonal. The *structural* weaknesses are more easily seen. They often consist of the absence of fundamental resources (e.g., some SUNY Senates have out-of-date bylaws or are required to spend so much time discussing and approving routine matters that more substantive topics cannot be addressed) or failure to have a system in place for hearing from all members of the governing body or the campus. The *interpersonal* weaknesses are often hidden, but can undermine effective structure through erosion. The following identification of three holes illustrates how much of a gap can exist between the idea of shared governance and the reality.

Structural

Faculty, staff, administrators, and others have different—sometimes contradictory—perspectives or priorities. The structure of higher education relies on specific roles of its members. Each member—faculty, staff, administrators, and students—not only has a specific job to do, but has primary responsibilities that generally outrank shared governance in terms of importance. In many cases, this can mean that governance varies in terms of where it resides in the priority list for each individual, as well as in the context of needs of the individual.

Bahls (2014) identifies the need for shared governance to serve as a basis for transcending individual responsibilities and perspectives.

> When shared governance is understood and practiced as a system for identifying and aligning priorities, institutions will be able to move through moments of friction more smoothly. Shared governance can—and should—provide boards, faculty and administrators with a way of working collaboratively toward a common vision . . . [to] design and support a system for moving together in the same direction. (p. 17)

Ideally, each person will learn to appreciate both institutional needs and the responsibilities of others, enabling all to fully participate in governance activities in a timely way. However, in some cases, friction between personal and institutional perspectives and priorities occurs. Resnick Pierce (2014) identifies "differences over the Nature and Pace of Change" (p. 13), which can lead to many differences of opinion as being at the core of shared governance difficulties.

At the campus level, absence of fundamental structural features can sometimes be impediments to a governance organization. Pragmatic problems, such as elections-related communications problems, can result in low voter turnout. Governance leaders may not have recruited enough qualified candidates to run for office, leading to failed elections. Other forms of communication difficulties (e.g., inadequate or misleading communication about a governance-based decision) lead to frustration or confusion on campus. Governance difficulties can occur because input sought on the academic or strategic plan may not be received or used, and the resulting confusion can have dangerous, divisive implications. At the system level, such difficulties are compounded exponentially. For example, lack of information about a proposed revision of a system-wide funding formula can lead to a wide range of intense, negative emotions that could be eliminated (or at least mitigated) with a timely flow of relevant, detailed explanations.

Interpersonal: Lack of Trust between Faculty, Administration, and Governing Boards

At the First Annual SUNY Voices Shared Governance conference in April 2014, the embedded theme of "trust" appeared in multiple sessions. During the opening remarks, H. Carl McCall, Chairman of the SUNY Board of

Trustees, identified "trust" as essential for shared governance—without it, progress cannot be made. SUNY Chancellor Nancy Zimpher went even further, when she said, "collaboration moves at the speed of trust." The Merriam-Webster online dictionary defines *trust* in the following way: "belief that someone or something is reliable, good, honest, effective, etc." Can this belief withstand the tests of the inevitable challenges that will occur in the complex environment of a campus within a system as large as SUNY?

Hardy (1991) examined the process of decision making within university governance and concluded that power is a cornerstone of the governance process. She observed that "collegiality and politics [are] two sides of the same coin" (p. 411). She recommends that we carefully scrutinize the decision-making process so as not to get misled by the illusion of collegiality, encouraging us to "look more carefully at the role of leadership in building consensus and commitment—at the collegial use of power" (Hardy, 1991, p. 418). Bahls (2014), on the other hand, puts trust in a key position: "There is no strict formula for making shared governance work. In fact, shared governance begins with a quality that faculty is critical to shared governance because those elements can sustain the faculty and board when mutual discussions become difficult. Trust helps nurture an environment in which it is safe for all constituencies to push and challenge each other respectfully" (p. 77).

Much of the basis for trust emerges over time, and presumes a basic idea—to give the other person(s) the benefit of the doubt, leading to the "mutual respect" Bahls references above. The shared governance model rests on a sturdy foundation of respectful interpersonal relationships. Relationship building forms the basis of trust, which goes a long way toward creating a supportive climate for effective shared governance. Speck (2011) identifies absence of trust as a key problem: "If either rigor or respect is omitted from shared governance, the result is not mutuality but unhealthy relationships that bespeak of fracture and the failure of productive compromise" (p. 227). Others (e.g., Pope, Kezar) have identified trust as the bedrock of shared governance that is often missing.

Structural and Interpersonal: Changing Membership and Leadership at All Levels Can Erode Trust and Perpetuate the Status Quo

Turnover among governance members and leaders as well as new campus administrators leads to lack of shared history and restarts for many governance units at the start of each year. For example, there is an annual need to repeat governance orientation activities and clarification of governance procedures. These logistics are only the most obvious part of a need for at least annual restarts. Balken (2011) provides a vivid example: "With the exception of the university president, who stepped down in 2010 after serving for fifteen years, as well as a few members of his cabinet, we have experienced rather dizzying administrative turnover in the last fifteen years. The university has had eight provosts since 1995 . . ." (p. 564). Not only is continuity a problem, but difficulty can occur in establishing the credibility of new individuals who seek to serve and lead.

Kezar's (2004) analysis of factors contributing to effective governance noted the transformation associated with increased involvement and commitment of key people. "Governance became an activity that participants could see meaningfully shaping their environment and creating an effective context for learning as well as a thriving institution" (p. 42). Absence of such key people, who often take on necessary leadership roles, can create challenges. A common problem is absence of succession planning: Members of governance organizations suddenly startle when they realize that only a few new people are engaged in the ongoing sequence of governance responsibilities.

More routine, and yet still troubling, can be the inevitable divide between "longstanding" members of the governance group, who can view comments and actions in a historical context, and "rookies." On the positive side, the rookies' input may offer fresh perspective; on the negative side, their early contributions may be off topic in subtle or overt ways. Also, rookies can feel excluded, sensing a divide between insiders and outsiders. As they become more familiar with the governance process, some may perceive themselves to be unwelcome, as they see the experienced members and leaders maintaining the exclusivity of an insiders' club that is closed off to them. Sensitive governance leaders make efforts to close this divide—including informal mentoring or opportunities for open forums on controversial topics with long histories—but such a disparity among members can undermine the cohesion of the governance unit and the representation its members provide to the campus as a whole. This is an issue that may occur only intermittently, but it remains important and should not be ignored.

An effective governance body requires interested and capable governance members. A campus may be limited in terms of the pool of potential governance members—and leaders. Kezar (2004) examined different impediments to effective governance, as well as what led to success in governance. Like Pope, she identified trust as an important component, but she also pointed to the need for leadership, which engenders trust. Her conclusion was that "leadership, trust and relationships supersede structures and processes in effective decision making. A governance system can operate with imperfect structures and processes, but if leadership is missing, and relationships and trust damaged, the governance system will likely fail for lack of direction, motivation, meaning, integrity, a sense of common purpose, ways to integrate multiple perspectives, open communication, people willing to listen, and legitimacy" (pp. 44–45). Trust influences all aspects of effective governance. If a leader does not have the confidence of members, then hesitation and doubt undermine action. In many cases, governance organizations seek ways to reinvent themselves, to find the "perfect process." Instead, Kezar urges a return to fundamental matters of trust. In a later publication (Kezar, Carducci, & Contreras-McGavin, 2006), she and her colleagues focus on leadership as a topic that requires reconceptualization as a "multidimensional phenomenon," with "no single way" to be a leader (p. 176). With no single right answer, for governance members or leaders, the challenge exists for all to consider how to best find, and use, resources for their campuses.

Structural and Interpersonal: Idiosyncratic Campus Needs and Structures Make It Difficult to Benefit from Others' Solutions

To many on the front lines of governance, it is not immediately obvious how resources developed for one campus can be adapted for and used by others. Each campus appears to be unique. When considering a system as big as SUNY, the idea of this heterogeneous group forming and using a common language and resource base can seem, at times, impossible. At times, members of governance will be unable to generalize benefits of others' solutions to meet their own needs.

Doubts exist. Lachs (2011) published his reflections on his experiences as chair of the Vanderbilt University Faculty Senate in *The Chronicle of Higher Education*. He concluded, "shared governance is a myth." His summary is one to which all individuals who have served in a governance role can relate:

> Faculty members have no special competence running organizations: many of them lack the practical sense required for making savvy and timely decisions concerning the complexities of institutional life. Moreover, they have little or no interest in the details of

administration. They may want tenure, promotion, higher salaries, and convenient parking, but only so that they may attend to their research and teaching. In this view, faculty members are neither capable of nor interested in managing the university . . . if that is right, as many a president will affirm in a moment of candor, why create the make-work charade of faculty committees, faculty membership on search committees for administrators, and ineffectual faculty senates? Why not admit the reality that the sharp line between management and labor has found a home in the university, and that faculty members are nothing more than employees? That may not be a happy state of affairs, but it would be wholesome to admit it, ridding professors of at least some of their self-importance and thereby enabling them to form a more accurate picture of their station.

The pessimistic perspective described in this widely read article is not unique to Lachs. Many, with their own disquieting experiences with governance, can relate to the discouraging sense of being marginalized when involved in governance. Being part of a large system, many individuals complain that their uniqueness becomes submerged when broad-based initiatives are prioritized over the needs of specific campuses. Although some writers (e.g., Balkun, 2009, 2011) are more optimistic about shared governance, it is difficult to imagine how one of the largest multi-campus systems could create a way for a group of people to develop trust, encourage leadership, and lead toward an effective way of promoting systemness in the governance process.

All is never perfect, and no matter what is done to address challenges, some holes will continue to exist. As an example, members of the SUNY system experienced a recent difference of perspective with regard to "shared services." The Chancellor and members of two pairs of campuses differed in their outlook with regard to "shared presidencies." Vacancies at proximal campuses made the potential cost savings of a presidency on two campuses appealing to administration, while for campus faculty members, such a prospect was highly troubling. In spite of dialogues, the administration's prerogative prevailed. Some might view this as evidence that "shared governance" is a mere Trojan horse, with the appearance of collaboration leading to an outcome that violates those principles. However, several years later, the Chancellor (at a University Faculty Senate Plenary) declared "the experiment with shared presidencies [is] officially dead." The candor of the conversations within the senate, on the part of senators and the Chancellor, illustrated the underlying trust that had been established. This opened the door to future conversations about controversial issues and illustrated that effective shared governance is an ever-evolving issue.

In many other cases, when stepping back and viewing the entire "shared governance" enterprise through the lens of multiple campus collaboration, new and valuable perspectives are obtained. Transformed perspectives, gained from dialogue with others, offer the opportunity to see even the holes in a new light. SUNY has created just that vantage point, through the "systemness" aspects of the University Faculty Senate. In the above case, the result was a proactive faculty engaged in governance processes at both the campus and university levels.

Filling in the Holes: Systemness Solutions

The paradigm provided in this chapter is the integration of "systemness" into the shared governance model. Plenaries exemplify the paradigm: At three annual meetings of this elected governance group (representing a broad spectrum of campuses), it has been possible to deepen members' knowledge about governance topics in a relatively short time. An example of this paradigm at work can be seen in thoughtful analysis of important topics (within committees or by the Senate as a whole), leading to resolutions. These are sponsored and approved at the University Faculty Senate level and then go back to each participating campus for endorsement. The loop is closed when the president of the SUNY University Faculty Senate presents these resolutions to the chancellor or to the SUNY Board of Trustees.

Chancellor Zimpher's commitment to systemness and shared governance was evident in the article on shared governance she wrote for the October 2012 special issue of the publication of the University Faculty Senate. Her article "Shared Governance Drives our Greatest Accomplishments" included the following observation regarding the many significant challenges faced by institutions of higher education: "[I]t will take the full force of an effective university system to rise to these occasions; a system in which all involved are committed to the overall vision and willing to work together to see that it is achieved. Shared governance is a critically important first step toward this end" (p. 4).

Systemness provides a method for shortening the learning curve regarding shared governance. The interweaving of solutions developed at the campus or the committee level with challenges faced on other campuses has promoted dialogues in many settings. Although not intentionally, the four factors in the model that Kurland (2014) identified as yielding a "shared understanding of, and commitment to, the mandate [of shared governance]" (p. 74) can be seen in the description of the structural solutions below: *clarity of roles and responsibilities, transparency, communication,* and *agreement on expectations and responsibilities* (pp. 74–75). In her research study of a governance committee over 2 years, she observed that if the committee is directly involved in "visioning or validation work," both the committee and its members are more likely to successfully be characterized by each of the four factors. The more opportunities afforded members of the University Faculty Senate committee members to learn about and contribute to broader SUNY-wide concerns, the more likely the members might be to experience connectedness to overall SUNY goals. The results can continue to integrate specific needs with broader resources.

Structural Solutions for Shared Governance

Bolman and Deal (2008) identify four frames for use in reframing examination of organizational functioning. The first, the structural, ensures that the essential structural elements of the organization are complete and up to date. As shown below, there are intentional structures within the UFS to facilitate effective inclusion of new members and productivity of the group as a whole.

UFS Brings People Together at Plenaries

Meeting three times annually in formal Plenaries, members share information, develop shared perspectives, and hear how other campuses are approaching shared challenges. There are opportunities to hear from the entire membership, as well as to engage in small-group discussions with counterparts (e.g., sector members). After hearing up-to-date information about SUNY issues and resources from System leaders, Senators are given time to discuss priorities and options that pertain to both their own campuses and others throughout the system. Kurland (2014) observed that "three aspects of communication emerged that impacted shared governance: too much information, too little information, and the strategic use of communication to facilitate consensus" (p. 75). An example of how movement from "too much" to "strategic use of" information can be seen within the group of those who lead their campus's governance unit, known as "Campus Governance Leaders."

For the past 11 years, all Campus Governance Leaders (CGLs) have been invited to the UFS Plenaries. Travel costs are underwritten by the UFS. A goal for inviting this group is to give them sufficient time during the academic year to meet each other and become conversant with relevant SUNY-wide topics. Although at the start of the year, this might be experienced as "too much information," the meetings are structured so that eventually the leaders are able to make strategic use of the information they hear.

- The CGLs elect a Convener annually who is then invited to attend meetings (as a nonvoting guest) of both the Governance Committee and the Executive Committee of the UFS.

- The CGLs are given the same opportunities as Senators to meet to discuss "issues of concern" and report them to the entire senate body in the presence of the chancellor. Often these issues are being considered (or have been considered) on other campuses, and a particular issue, brought forth by one of the CGLs, is not unique to a single campus.

- Between meetings, CGLs interact and share ideas via an active listserv. This is available to all CGLs, many of whom are not able to attend the plenaries consistently. These avenues of interaction have fostered shared governance through the entire SUNY System:

  o The CGLs are given the opportunity to share "best practices" in promoting faculty engagement in shared governance and improving the effectiveness of campus governance.

  o The work of the Governance Committee is more closely aligned with the needs and concerns of the CGLs.

  o Discussions during UFS plenaries are more robust with the insights and inputs of the CGLs.

  o The collective intelligence and governance experience of the CGL group and/or the UFS and/or the System can be mined to facilitate solutions to challenges to faculty governance, big and small.

In addition to the CGLs, participants at the Plenaries include the SUNY Chancellor, the President of the SUNY Student Assembly, and the President of the Faculty Council of Community Colleges (FCCC). The latter two are invited to each Plenary, not only to give a report, but also to hear the information and concerns shared at each meeting. The give and take within the Plenaries is followed up by reports at each campus, as well as at the Student Assembly and FCCC, as the UFS President is invited to attend each of their meetings and share a report, thus increasing the information-sharing between organizations. These reports are consistent with two of the characteristics Kezar (2005) identified as promoting effective collaboration: "Sense of priority from people in senior positions" and [participation from members of] "External groups" (p. 55).

Over the course of each academic year, the members of the University Faculty Senate, and the CGLs, become clearer about "agreement on expectations and values." As each year begins, members new to the body have to do what Kurland (2014) describes as "developing a shared understanding (p. 75)," which includes procedures as well as content. New leadership—of the Senate as a whole or of committees, requires an adjustment. When a cohesiveness of the body is achieved, the work of the Senate is better able to proceed. The addition of an annual orientation institute for new CGLs and student governance leaders has enabled the SUNY University Faculty Senate to begin the acculturation process very early on. Questions can be raised, and faces and names put together at the outset of the leaders' terms, thereby potentially shortening the learning curve process by humanizing it.

Under the leadership of Chancellor Zimpher, a new prominence for shared governance was created, via "SUNY Voices." Shared governance was identified as one of the chancellor's initiatives, following her identification of SUNY priorities. As defined on the SUNY website, "The SUNY Voices initiative is a branding mechanism for giving visibility to SUNY's unique focus on shared governance throughout the system, but it also provides support for strengthening shared governance at the system level, at the campus level, and between and among the campuses and SUNY System Administration." It has enabled those throughout the system to participate in system-wide events, involving UFS, FCCC, and members of the Student Assembly.

The Governance Committee Serves
Both UFS and SUNY

Most directly involved in the topic of shared governance is the UFS Governance Committee. The charge of the Governance Committee addresses multiple levels of governance: "The Committee shall concern itself with University-wide governance and shall provide guidance on matters of campus governance. The Committee shall interact with local governance leaders of the University" (*SUNY University Faculty Senate Bylaws and Procedures, 2013*, p. 12). Kezar (2005) identifies the need for "integrating structures . . . [that] are key to sustaining collaboration and to linking work that is usually done in isolation" (p. 54). In her extended examination of collaboration within higher education (Kezar & Lester, 2009), she further elaborates on how these integrating structures function on an individual campus:

> Integrating structures ensure that there are not any barriers in communication, budgeting or technology. People on campuses have noted how nay-sayers (those who do not believe in collaboration) are looking for problems in order to provide evidence that collaboration will not work. Integrating structures is one of the ways to make sure you do not hit the bumps along the road to collaboration (or at least hit fewer). When information sharing is clear, when people problem solve together, and when technology works, nay-sayers have fewer problems to highlight. (pp. 123–124)

For the UFS, the Governance Committee serves as a very important integrating structure, providing clarification and opportunities for individuals throughout the SUNY system to examine pertinent challenges together. An action plan for the Governance Committee is prepared each year, and activities designed to support governance at all levels are included. The Governance Committee is also available to consider questions and formulate answers as the need arises. Through the years, many resources have been developed that continue to provide guidance and important information to UFS Senators, Campus Governance Leaders (CGLs), and faculty across the System. The *Governance Handbook*, a resource for governance in UFS and on campuses, is reviewed and updated every 4 years. The *Governance Handbook* is recommended as "the place to start" when questions arise concerning shared governance at any level in SUNY.

The *Governance Handbook* is available 24/7 on the UFS website: http://system.suny.edu/media/suny/content-assets/documents/faculty-senate/ GovHandbook-Final-2013.pdf/. The Governance Committee is developing a Shared Governance Resources webpage to facilitate access to all documents relevant to shared governance at all levels within the System (links to campus bylaws, resolutions from the UFS pertaining to shared governance, policies of the Board of Trustees of the University, etc.).

Other documents the Governance Committee has developed are also available online:

- Campus Governance Leader (CGL) Orientation and Welcome Guide
- New Senator Orientation Guide
- Common Parliamentarian Procedures
- Campus Governance Best Practices Report (2007)

These resources help bridge the gap between rookies and longstanding members of governance structures. The need to reinvent the wheel is significantly reduced, and trust can be enhanced.

In 2013, the UFS Governance Committee, in conjunction with its counterparts in the FCCC and Student Assembly (SA), started to offer an orientation meeting for campus governance leaders. This idea emerged from the development of the *Orientation Guide* publication and the realization that an opportunity for conversation and presentations would be valuable in advance of the start of the term of office for new leaders, but could also be helpful to those who had served already. During its first year (2013), invitees included leaders from both the UFS and the FCCC. Beginning in its second year, the invitees expanded to include leaders from SAs throughout SUNY (UFS and FCCC campuses) as well as a few representatives from the City University of New York (CUNY).

Funds for these orientation meetings and for the 2014 and 2015 Shared Governance conferences came from the SUNY Voices budget—another benefit of a system-wide commitment to governance.

UFS Provides Resources to Meet Routine Responsibilities As Well As Expanded Responsibilities at Times of Crisis

Routine. In the cycle of campus activities, each campus faces tasks that may not have been done in recent memory, tasks such as conducting a search for (or evaluating) a senior campus administrator. The individual involved in leading the activity most recently may have departed, or minimal records may have been kept. The *Governance Handbook* provides resources for campus use in these sorts of situations. In addition, members of the University Faculty Senate Governance Committee are available to discuss these and other governance-related topics.

A recent revision of campus bylaws at one SUNY institution, for example, was facilitated by use of the UFS website containing links to many SUNY bylaws. In addition, the UFS parliamentarian provided feedback regarding the changes under consideration. These informal dialogues generally take place throughout the year, and the Chair of the Governance Committee is available to assist on many governance-related topics.

Times of crisis. Sometimes the need for assistance is much more challenging. The UFS has two tools available for campuses confronting a conflict between faculty governance and the college administration: campus consultation and visitation.

Campus consultation. A consultation is a somewhat informal process that leverages faculty governance expertise within the university to assist a campus experiencing significant governance issues. It should be viewed as a process that can be used proactively to prevent a major breakdown between faculty and campus administration. A consultation is recommended when a serious conflict arises in which internal efforts at resolution have been repeatedly unsuccessful. Consultation takes place when an impasse has been reached, but there is no likely imminent crisis, such as a vote of no confidence.

Visitation. In the event of a serious, prolonged conflict on campus between faculty governance and administration, and when there is serious consideration of a vote of no confidence, it is strongly recommended that the campus president and the campus faculty governance leader(s) jointly request the help of the University Faculty Senate in resolving the dispute via a visitation. They should make this request in the form of a letter of invitation to the President of the University Faculty Senate asking the Senate President to render assistance by appointing a Visitation Committee to come to the campus.

For Visitation Committee membership, the Senate President will seek people with broad governance experience. Such people are distinguished by reputations for reasonableness and integrity, and for their capacity to avoid being either advocates or adversaries in their dealings with administrators and faculty. The Visitation Committee's membership will always include a person from SUNY System Administration acting as a member of the committee for the Senate and not in an official capacity as a SUNY System administrator. Such a person will often have had prior service on the Senate and/or served as a SUNY System liaison to the University Faculty Senate.

The Visitation Committee will serve in the capacity of making an inquiry, in cooperation with the campus governance leader and the campus president, and submitting a report. The report may include suggestions and recommendations for actions by both the local governance body and administration. The Chair of the Visitation Committee will send the Final Report of the Visitation Committee to the President of the University Faculty Senate, who will submit the Final Report to the president of the campus and to the campus governance leader and the chancellor. The Chair of the Visitation Committee or the President of the University Faculty Senate may be asked about, and may choose to comment on, the visitation process by the University Faculty Senate, the campus community, or the public. Members of the Visitation Committee should recognize that the substance of the deliberations, the content of the report, and its recommendations are sensitive issues; they should exercise care in maintaining confidentiality.

Systemness offers the individual campuses of SUNY an opportunity to capitalize on what has been learned through experience. It is inevitable that there will be a steep learning curve on matters that involve challenges. To this end, SUNY's systemness allows for benefits of learning. It would be impossible for a campus to provide the objectivity, in times of crisis, that can be offered by the UFS. Experience, and distance from the participants' passion of the topics, can lead to proper analysis of the situation and recommended solutions.

Interpersonal Solutions to Shared Governance

Participation in UFS and Systemness Provides On-the-Job Leadership Training

Different levels of engagement (committee membership, elected University Faculty Senator(s) from each campus, UFS officers, Executive Committee positions) provide for progressively more advanced leadership opportunities as well as role models for effective leadership. At the same time, term limits established by UFS for committee membership, senators, and officers provide opportunities for more experienced faculty members to reverse their trajectory and bring their leadership and knowledge back to their campuses and other organizations within the SUNY system.

An excellent example of the leadership training process can be seen in the Campus Governance Leaders (CGLs). On some campuses, the same individual will remain the CGL for many years, whereas on others there are term limits (from 1 to 3 or more years). Thus, some are very experienced, and others are brand new to their roles. They have much to share with each other.

Participation in UFS and Systemness Enhances Collaboration

Birnbaum (2004) articulated the importance of faculty involvement in educational policy more generally, including setting institutional objectives, planning, budgeting, and selecting administrators. However, finding ways for faculty and administrators (as well as other stakeholders) to work together can require a re-adjustment of perspective. Academic inquiry, fundamental to faculty, may be anathema to administration. The ability to understand the perspective and priorities of others (and perhaps agreeing to disagree) is basic to effective collaboration.

Gallos (2009) recommends a collaborative approach toward governance in order to maximize the effectiveness of shared governance:

> A collaborative perspective on senate work is far from Pollyannish. It is steeped in research and experience . . . , and it seeks to reclaim the intended collaborative foundations of academic shared governance. It asks faculty senates to balance—not replace—their reactivity with proactivity, wed their strong advocacy to strong inquiry, and take the lead in moving closer to the real joint decision making that campuses espouse—and so desperately need. University senates become forums for shared understanding, not battlefields for campus control; places where faculty and administration regularly come together to suggest, listen, and learn—and where both look forward to the exchange." (pp. 137–138)

The SUNY University Faculty Senate has successfully created the kind of forum Gallos describes. Because it draws members from throughout SUNY into the governance process, systemness provides great leverage, which becomes evident during the informal (sector) meetings that occur during the University Faculty Senate Plenaries. Members of a sector will discuss a common problem all are facing (e.g., dealing with a budget shortfall, coping with upcoming changes in general education requirements), and the conversation includes moments of amazement. On some campuses, administrators and governance leaders share little time or information, whereas on others there is genuine dialogue that helps to frame alternative solutions. The differences help all to question the status quo on their own campuses and to consider structural options that might not have otherwise been identified. It is within the Senate that the benefits of in-depth analysis, which faculty members bring to their work, can be transferred to the governance process and prevent re-inventing the wheel and perhaps more creative solutions to vexing issues.

Participation in UFS and Systemness Establishes Trust

Structurally effective shared governance relies on an outcome of collaboration and, ultimately, trust. How can trust be achieved when, in many ways, different members of a campus are speaking their own languages? This is not only rooted in the academic disciplines of each member but in the values they have attributed to the topics brought up by others. How effectively individuals learn to translate the concerns of others determines the likelihood that better understanding and improved levels of trust will occur—minimal translation leads to reduced understanding and lowered trust, and vice versa. Debates and discussions within the University Faculty Senate serve as a laboratory for enhancing understanding of multiple issues from the varied perspectives of the campuses and the sectors. Pope (2004) recognizes that participants must learn to trust each other as well as the process:

> As institutions differ according to mission, size, governance structure, and other characteristics, it is necessary to analyze various types of institutions to determine the ways in which faculty trust and participation in governance differ within these varying settings. Faculty at these various institutions may have contrasting perceptions of what trust is, and how it operates within the governance process. By understanding these differences, a more complete taxonomy of faculty trust in higher education governance can be achieved. (p. 83)

Pope concludes with this recommendation: "Drawing upon the definitions of trust—including its four dimensions of competence, openness, benevolence, and reliability—. . . faculty and administrators in higher education may use this construct to improve the effectiveness of shared institutional governance" (p. 83). Within the University Faculty Senate, the development of trust is seen across multiple years, with the election of sector representatives, Vice President, Secretary, and president of the University Faculty Senate. The four components of trust are essential in the presidential election, as the president not only represents the senate throughout the state in multiple forums but also represents faculty throughout the system with a nonvoting seat on the Board of Trustees. Thus, in many ways, trust and access are embedded in the interpersonal solutions crucial to shared governance.

Conclusion

SUNY maintains many models of governance. Structurally, all must be consistent with the Board of Trustees' *Policies,* but that allows for many models. What each unit strives for is effectiveness, promoting attentive awareness of key institutional concerns, followed by consideration of the viewpoint of many stakeholders. The opportunities to learn about alternatives used on other campuses via the systemness resources available through the University Faculty Senate allows for expanded options.

Trakman (2008) provides the following advice, relevant to governance members throughout SUNY:

> "Good" university governance . . . does not simply happen. It is usually the product of painstaking effort to arrive at suitable governance structures, protocols and processes. "Good" governance is also about timing and judgement: it requires boards of governors to recognize when a governance model is not working, why and how to repair it. Ultimately, governance models are created by people to govern people. They are only as good as they who devise and apply them, as well as those who live by them. (p. 77)

At the end of each academic year, the UFS honors one of its own with the Chugh Award for Outstanding Service. This recognition is named after a widely respected, humble past leader of the organization. Chugh's own insights after serving on a campus committee illustrate the recognition bestowed on the award's recipient:

My work . . . helped me see firsthand the role an individual faculty member could play in the work of the institution. It made me aware that each member of the campus community irrespective of his/her official title and seniority had a stake in the institution and could influence it through such participation. Good ideas coming from anyone whether faculty, administration, and staff to enhance the operation of the institution were welcomed. (Chugh, 2012)

Giving the award highlights the contributions made by individuals who have committed to the type of excellence in governance Trakman describes. Sharon Cramer, the 2011 recipient of the Chugh award, when receiving the award, summarized governance leadership in the following way:

"What do we look for in those who will serve, and eventually become our governance leaders?

- *Understanding that "invisible work" is an inevitable aspect of what we do.* Countless hours are invested in governance, and rarely are they known or acknowledged. We have all realized that we work "behind the scenes" most of the time.

- *Patience* and *care* are required for good governance. Hard as it can be to slow down and listen, such a commitment to seeing a process all the way through is essential.

- As shown throughout all the work of our University Faculty Senate, *passion for governance* is something we share. We express our passions differently, but still, our passion is there (Cramer, 2011).

A key value of systemness is the opportunity afforded members to aspire to new levels of excellence, personally, within their governance units, as well as for their campuses. It is in this way that systemness has its most powerful impact.

Note

This paper was the basis for a poster presented at the "Harnessing Systemness, Delivering Performance" Critical Issues in Higher Education Conference, November 2012, New York, New York, as well as at the SUNY Voices Shared Governance Conference in Albany, New York, in April 2014. Both authors are senior faculty members at two separate institutions, represented within SUNY's University Faculty Senate. Each has made longstanding commitments to system-wide faculty governance, including serving as Chair of SUNY's University Faculty Senate

Governance Committee. Each received the Chugh Award for Service to SUNY's University Faculty Senate. Both have served in numerous roles as governance leaders on their campuses and within the system.

References

American Federation of Teachers (AFT) Resolution. (2002). Retrieved at http://www.aft.org/resolution/shared-governance-colleges-and-universities

American Federation of Teachers Higher Education. (n.d.). Foreword: Shared governance in colleges and universities: A statement by the Higher Education Program and Policy Council (pp. 3–10). Washington, D.C.

Bahls, S.C. (2014). *Shared governance in times of change: A practical guide for universities and colleges.* Washington, D.C.: Association of Governing Boards of Universities and Colleges Press.

Balkun, M.M. (2011). Making shared governance work: Strategies and challenges. *Pedagogy, 11*(3), 562–569.

Birnbaum, R. (2004). The end of shared governance: Looking ahead or looking back. In W.G. Tierney & V.M. Lechuga (Eds.), *Restructuring Shared Governance in Higher Education, New Directions in Higher Education #127* (pp. 5–22).

Bolman, L., & Deal, T. 2008. *Reframing organizations: Artistry, choice and leadership.* 4th ed. San Francisco, CA: Jossey-Bass.

Chugh, R. (2012). *Service to the University.* Unpublished manuscript, referenced with permission of the author.

Cramer, S.F. (2011). Chugh award acceptance speech at Spring 2011 UFS Plenary, published in the Fall 2011 UFS *Bulletin.*

DeNardis, L.J. (2001). FOCUS: Shared governance. *Presidency, 4*(3), 38–39.

Gallos, J.V. (2009). Reframing shared governance: Rediscovering the soul of campus collaboration. *Journal of Management Inquiry, 18.* doi: 10.1177/1056492608326326

Gideon, G. (2012). "The challenge of 'shared governance': Recent debates over University policies have called Yale's decision-making procedures into question. Retrieved from http://www.yaledaily.com/news/2012/apr/12/close-challenge-shared-governance

Hardy, C. (1991). Putting power into university governance. In J. C. Smart (Ed.), *Higher Education: Handbook of Theory and Research, Vol. VI* (pp. 393–426).

Kezar, A. (2004). What is more important to effective governance: Relationships, trust, and leadership or structures and formal processes? In W.G. Tierney & V.M. Lechuga (Eds.), *Restructuring Shared Governance in Higher Education, New Directions in Higher Education #127* (pp. 35–46).

Kezar, A. (2005). Moving from I to We: Reorganizing for collaboration in higher education. *Change, 37*(6), 50–57.

Kezar, A.J., Carducci, R., & Contreras-McGavin, M. (2006). Rethinking the "L" word in higher education: The revolution of research on leadership. In K. Ward & L. E. Wolf-Wendel (Eds.), *ASHE Higher Education Report, 31*(6).

Kezar, A.J. & Lester, J. (2009). *Organizing higher education for collaboration: A guide for campus leaders.* San Francisco, CA: Jossey-Bass.

Kurland, N.B. (2014). Shared governance and the sustainable college. *International Journal of Sustainability in Higher Education, 15*(1), 63–83.

Lachs, J. (2011). Shared governance is a myth. *The Chronicle of Higher Education, 57*(23). Retrieved from http://proxy.buffalostate.edu:2214/ps/i.do?id=GALE%7CA248594681&v=2.1&u=buffalostate&it=r&p=AONE&sw=w&asid=d915502511c7ad2c9d00b6d25a01bee1

Langland, E. (2011). Shared governance in an age of change. *Pedagogy, 11*(3), 554–557.

Pope, M.L. (2004). A conceptual framework of faculty trust and participation in governance. In W.G. Tierney & V. M. Lechuga (Eds.), *Restructuring Shared Governance in Higher Education, New Directions in Higher Education #127* (pp. 75–84).

Resnick Pierce, S. (2014). *Governance reconsidered: How boards, presidents, administrators, and faculty can help their colleges thrive.* San Francisco, CA: Jossey-Bass.

Speck, B.W. (2011). The myth of shared governance in higher education. *International Journal of Organizational Theory and Behavior, 14*(2), 200–235.

State University of New York. (2014). *Policies of the Board of Trustees.* Retrieved from https://www.suny.edu/student/university_suny_history.cfm

State University of New York. (2013). *SUNY University faculty senate bylaws and procedures.* Albany, NY. Retrieved from http://system.suny.edu/media/suny/content-assets/documents/faculty-senate/Final-Revisions-Bylaws-Procedures-2013.pdf

Taylor, M. (2013). Shared governance in the modern university. *Higher Education Quarterly, 67*(1), 80–94.

Trakman, L. (2008). Modelling university governance. *Higher Education Quarterly, 62(1/2),* 63–83. Retrieved from http://en.wikipedia.org/wiki/Systemness

University Faculty Senate Governance Handbook (2013). Albany, NY: State University of New York. Retrieved at http://system.suny.edu/media/suny/content-assets/documents/faculty-senate/GovHandbook-Final-2013.pdf

Zimpher, N.L. (2012a). *2012 State of the University Address.* The State University of New York.

Zimpher, N.L. (2012b). *Systemness to drive success in 2012.* The State University of New York.

Zimpher, N.L. (2012c). "Systemness" keeps college affordable, productive, accessible. *The Nelson A. Rockefeller Institute for Government.* State University of New York at Albany.

Zimpher, N.L. (2012d). Shared governance drives our greatest accomplishments. Special Issue on Shared Governance. *Faculty Senate Bulletin.* A publication of the State University of New York, p. 4.

5

Governance Structures

Perspective on Administrative
Task Forces in Shared Governance

Duncan Quarless and Minna S. Barrett

When institutional needs arise that cannot be addressed via existing structures (because they are considered inadequate for a particular set of circumstances), new governance structures must be developed. This chapter explores the use of task forces as one such structure in governance. This examination of the use (and potential misuse) of the "task force" as a standard "tool" for effective governance in higher education arises from questions concerning its "fit" within the contextual framework of governance that is truly "shared."

This chapter focuses on three overarching principles that serve to evaluate the use of task forces as a tool for shared governance:

1. *Establishing the need for the task force (in terms of the scope of the charge, the professional faculty expertise required to address the charge, and the constituencies affected by the potential recommendations that result). This includes assessing the related consultative relevance and collaborative impacts associated with its use.*

2. *Examining the charge of the task force within the context of the larger framework of shared governance. This relates to the question of whether or not it serves a complementary function to the existing governance structures.*

3. *Working with as much transparency in the intent and operation of the task force as permitted by the process. This relates to the good faith effort for the openness and sharing of information that constitutes democratic governance.*

The Task Force Tool for Shared Governance: A Nonstarter?

Task Forces: A Structural Context

Introduction

In the preface of the *Statement on Government of Colleges and Universities*[1] reported by the American Association of University Professors (AAUP), three concepts that underscore governance were articulated: a central idea, a fundamental purpose, and a targeted primary audience.

1. The central idea is one of "appropriately shared responsibility and *cooperative action among the components of the academic institution." The implicit presupposition here is that a proper division of labor imputes suitable responsibilities to the contributing operational units of shared governance. The concurrent expectation of the operational units is one of cooperative, dutiful effort.*

2. The fundamental purpose is "to foster constructive joint thought and action, both within the institutional structure and in protection of its integrity against improper intrusions." The statement was offered to provide some conceptual framework for academic governance.

3. The primary audience is reflected implicitly within the preface, and more explicitly by the authoring bodies, as observed in the content and section headings of the statement itself, which address the governing board, the president, and the faculty.

The academic institution, of course, exists to be responsive to the needs of students. The statement therefore notes the need to properly assess student need and to promote student voice within governance. Moreover, operationally, the institution is more than simply the governing board, president, and faculty; instead, the statement is directed to the principal authoritative voices of the academic institution, speaking for the paradigm of shared governance as compared to a more typical corporate model.

Shared governance born out of this historical context thereby became a working construct to operationalize "mutual understanding," "joint effort," and "inescapable interdependence" among trustees, administration, and faculty. This paradigm was introduced to establish the general educational policy and internal operations of the institution (defining areas of authority and responsibility), and to distinguish them from the quite different external relations of the institution. This was the framing ideology for shared governance that brings deferential purity to academic institutions of higher education in establishing the general education policy of the institution.

The educational program is thereby subject to a combination of unique and normalized operational standards (e.g., the institutional charter, mission, education law). Moreover, the central idea and fundamental purpose ascribed to the ideology presumably protects the institution from external influences unduly bent on erratic or unilateral decision-making processes that would act contrary to the general education policy of the institution. Thus, for example, the decision to change a liberal arts and science institution to a vocational trade school, based perhaps on local political forces, would not be the sole purview of the trustees.

A number of trends have created more gradual pressures that are antithetical to shared governance in academic institutions of higher education. These developments influence how higher education is funded, how access is determined, and who governs the institution. These patterns include such contributing factors as:

- the synergy between reduced state funding to public education and the move toward privatization, as guided by related commercial and political demands;

- the nature of enrollment, the changing student pool, and related changes in enrollment selectivity and number of enrollees, as driven by the associated budgetary allocations and public expectations;

- and, the culminating current realities in the marketplace for PhDs, impacting academia as a comparatively less accessible job market for tenure-track employment over the past couple of decades particularly among 4-year colleges and universities (Zusman, 2005).

These more subtle and gradual pressures are redefining, for example, the nature of the professional status and employment opportunities of PhDs in academia, where non–tenure track and part-time employment percentages among the faculty are steadily rising. In turn, the principles and values by which academic institutions are governed are also affected. The concomitant gradient effect is one that is moving shared governance in a direction that resembles the more standard business models of corporate industry.

Venable (1998) has described six interconnected features of authentic shared governance, which (by extension) are advanced here to serve as the litmus test for true consultative purpose in the administrative use of task forces. These are (1) a climate of trust, (2) information sharing, (3) meaningful participation, (4) collective decision making, (5) protecting divergent views, and (6) redefining roles.

These six features are perhaps best thought of as gauges of institutional climate and its contextual culture regarding how task forces are used. These characteristics are subject to the dynamic tension described herein in the consideration of task forces in either integrating or serving as parallel shared governance structures.

Authority and Responsibility

Consultation in the most general terms is the process by which the representative constituent bodies within the institution are given consideration in the decision-making outcomes of the institution.[2] It is generally applied to the governance relationship between the faculty and their respective administrations. Notably, consultative process ideally works within the previously defined context of the *Statement on Government of Colleges and Universities*. Consultation, therefore, is not to be meddlesome filibustering, or scheming factions covertly influencing impending decisions, but rather proper and substantive enrichment of the decision-making process.

For example, the Faculty Bylaws of SUNY Old Westbury[3] in Article I: Definitions defines "Consult" as follows: "In all places in the Policies where 'consult' or 'consultation' is used the term shall be interpreted to include a formal recommendation or vote or other action of record (as, for example, minutes of reports indicating discussion and action by appropriate committees) by the Faculty, its appropriate elected committees, or both, sufficiently explicit to show the extent and effectiveness of such consultation. It is understood that 'consultation' does not necessarily imply decision-making authority." In defining the authority of the faculty, these same bylaws later assert faculty authority to "include matters of educational interest and research and of academic policy . . . responsible, individually and collectively, for, 1. maintaining academic standards;

2. recommending the granting of degrees; 3. developing the College's educational, research, and service programs, and 4. conducting these programs."

Additionally, in the general discharge of these areas of direct and primary responsibility and authority, there is an expectation of faculty involvement in related institutional matters that affect the educational program, where faculty have "an appropriate role as participants in institutional decision making . . . through formal and systematic consultation through established governance structures and processes."

Consultation, as a desirable feature and a centerpiece for decision making in shared governance, is noted for its impact in everything from strategic enrollment management (Goff, 2008) to assessing institutional effectiveness (Hrabowski, 2011). In order to specifically tackle the question of the "relevant" use of task forces in shared governance, the first of three principal questions must be addressed: Does the task force serve a true consultative purpose?

With respect to higher education (particularly in the public sector), this question is best broached recognizing the tension that exists between the administrative authority vested in the trustees and the campus president, and the professional authority of the faculty. This tension creates the areas of overlap of two potentially divergent systems: the system that represents the legal authority of the trustees and the administration to handle all of the legal obligations and commitments of the institution (including its overall fiduciary responsibilities); and the system that represents the professional authority of the faculty to establish the educational programs of the institution (Birnbaum, 2004). The subsequent practical structural and operational controls of these two systems have also been described as emphasizing vertical and lateral coordination respectively (Bolman & Deal, 2013, pp. 43–66).

These constitute a natural tension inherent in the structural units of governance between the hierarchal orientation of the administrative structure (typically functioning in a vertical coordination), and the horizontal orientation of the faculty-based structure (typically functioning in a lateral coordination). Although somewhat generalized, the professional authority by which the faculty operates in an academic type institution values lateral coordination within "the academy," where collegiality, collaboration and consensus forge trust and respect. This lateral coordination recognizes vested responsibility and authority in the officers within the academy as collaborative equals to the general ranking populace of the faculty in the decision-making processes.

Faculty governance units typically exemplify this type of coordination where the faculty senate chair sits at the tip (base) of an inverted pyramid: the collective faculty having ultimate authority, their senate vested with limited authority when the full faculty is not convened, followed by the senate executive committee and lastly the senate chair. The legal authority by which the trustees and the campus president (campus administration) operate values vertical coordination, where the campus president sits (at the tip) atop a more typical hierarchal pyramid of responsibility and authority (Gerber, 1997). That system vests the president with ultimate operational authority (including in many cases the systematic decision-making timeframe), accountable to the trustees in order to satisfy the need for regulatory control (i.e., checks and balances of administrative governance) of the official and legal matters of institutional governance.

At their extremes, the organizational control whose emphasis is exclusively focused on the legal authority of the trustees and the administration expectedly discounts the necessity for faculty participation in the decision-making process; while the organizational control whose emphasis is exclusively focused on the professional authority of the faculty likely directs itself to internal operations that are not readily responsive to all of the demands that bring stability to the institution (Trakman, 2008).

The former is likely the case, for example, where the trustees and the administration, acting in the interest of their shareholders in publicly traded or large private corporate entities, assume predominance over such things as curriculum (Farrell, 2003; Millora, 2010; Wilson, 2010).

The latter is likely the case, for example, where the faculty assumes improper authority over the fiduciary management of the institution (Scharffs, 2005; Weeks, 2002). In the case of the latter illustration, the institution may be made vulnerable to unintended legal obligations in cases where improper fiduciary authority is assumed (Weeks, 2002).

Faculty fiduciary responsibility more suitably relates to the role of the faculty within the learning environment of the educational program (the integrity and proper use of faculty authority in their relationships with students—advising, instruction/curricular costs, proper acknowledgment of student contributions in the case of discovery, patents, etc.) (Scharffs, 2005; Weeks, 2002).

The governing elements of authority and responsibility are characterized within the interplay of these two extreme systems (the legal one and the professional one). Authority and responsibility are thereby best identified within a well-defined institutional purpose, which is the foundation for the structural governance elements that result, and the synergistic qualities that define the working relationships between governance constituencies (Birnbaum, 2004).

Birnbaum posits:

> Although the great diversity of colleges and universities is widely recognized, this appreciation has not been properly extended to an understanding of diversity in their governance. The culture, structure, programs, personnel and technology of different institutions all influence participant expectations of how decisions are to be made and influence is to be allocated. For that reason, conceptual discussions of the importance of "shared governance" are often fruitless unless the characteristics of the institutions being discussed are specified. (p. 7)

This viewpoint contends that the conceptual context for a meaningful application of shared governance is one that is couched in the institution's purpose. This purpose is somewhat generalized along a continuum between two polar institutional archetypes: academic and market.

> The extreme *academic* archetype has its emphasis in the social implications of the education program as "deeply rooted in a culture that prizes academic freedom, critical discourse, creativity, and liberal learning." This type of institution for example invariably upholds the professional status of faculty as autonomous scholars in the formulation of the education program.
>
> In contrast, the extreme *market* archetype has its emphasis in the marketplace implications of the education program as a means to a much more narrowly defined vocational student (consumer) outcome. In institutions of this type, "Faculty are transmitters of training material, not autonomous scholars." (Birnbaum, 2004, p. 8)

Consequently, the virtues of shared governance and "consultation," as previously described, by convention are correlated to institutions with strong tendencies toward the "academic" pole, since "market" institutions have "no compelling reason for implementing processes and structures of shared governance"(Birnbaum, 2004, p. 8).

Institutional purpose, however, is seldom purely characterized at either of these polar opposites. Ostensibly, there are some climatic indicators (structural and relational) that help to gauge where an institution may fall along the continuum. For example, an institution with strong "academic" tendencies will extol academic freedom (as a relational dynamic) in the development of its education program. By comparison, an institution with strong "market" tendencies will extol the vocational aspects (mainly through a strong structurally defined dynamic) of the education program largely to the exclusion of anything else. The "academic" places its vision on the development of the "social capital" of the institution that results from such things as intellectual curiosity, civic engagement, and scholarship (social implications), while the "market" places its vision on the development of the "corporate capital" that results from exclusive focus on students as consumers of the institution's product in their individual training for the marketplace (corporate implications).

Moreover, Enders (2005) and Birnbaum (2004) concur that institutions continuously face pressures that bring about their departure from what Enders describes as the "professional state" (one that favors "academic" culture) by efforts to change public higher education through models of reform. These models of reform arise from the governance tension in the public sector through the interplay between two abstract dichotomies: "the state versus the market and the profession versus the organization" (p. 36). That is to say, the state in its oversight of the public university is not exempt from the pressures of the market, and the self-regulation of the profession is subject to the pressures placed on it by the institution (organization), and vice versa. In speaking of this condition in Western Europe, Enders notes, "But all models share to a certain extent a withdrawal of trust in the procedural arrangements that traditionally governed the professional state and a withdrawal of trust from the university as a matter of government policy" (p. 37). In the United States the impact is being observed on federal student aid policy, accountability standards, and the rise of for-profit institutions in higher education (Millora, 2010). And, unsurprisingly, the perceived success of for-profit institutions has also been presented largely through the lens of the market view.

Accordingly, since public nonprofit institutions do not normally operate at either extreme, but incorporate elements of both, defining the institutional purpose along the continuum between these polar extremes is crucial for establishing how consultation is viewed within governance. For example, both the "academic" and the "market" views emphasize their service to students, but there are differences: The academic has a focus on the student as a learner to be developed as part of the "social capital" of the institution, whereas the market has a profit-driven focus on the student mainly as a consumer of a product (Birnbaum, 2004; Enders, 2005; Gumport, 2001; Millora, 2010).

In the face of very austere economic circumstances, and the global technological advancements, institutional responsibility is likely to be tasked with areas of shifting priorities within shared governance, with the institution's cultural paradigms increasingly nuanced (Bergquist, 1992; Lawrence, 2013; Tierney, 2004). Bergquist (1992) captures the nature of the academic cultures of U.S. higher education in terms of its history, evolution, and diversity of U.S. higher education.

The original four academic cultural types—collegial, managerial, developmental, and negotiating—provide some additional typological description to institutional cultures rising from the climates that produced them. These cultures also cover the categorical setting (ranging from junior college through the university center).

The *collegial* and *managerial* types largely give rise to the other two. All of these cultural models maintain the professional status of faculty. The differences between the four types that are perhaps most prominent pertain to the focal means by which faculty influence the institution and govern themselves. The nature of these cultures must be thought of in some ways as being fluid, providing dynamics from which potentially "new" academic cultures arise. True to form, two additional archetypes have recently been added to the original four cultures reflecting the global social and technological external pressures on academic institutions (Bergquist, 2008).

These social and economic pressures are affecting other internal areas as well, possibly diminishing (if not encroaching on) faculty purview over the educational program. For example, one could examine how perceptions of the role of faculty governance (with respect to collegiate athletics) are affected by the diverse influences to expand supports for collegiate athletics, in times of competing financial priorities affecting the educational program (Lawrence, 2013).

This type of pressure brings with it some subtle variations to the academic culture (e.g., political behaviors within the culture as a means to maintain the influence of faculty in the fiduciary decision making in student affairs areas). The inclination in institutions with strong collegial decision making, where authority is also decentralized, may be to use such structures as joint task forces as a means to bridge existing structural units. Alternate governance structures, with more relaxed organizational frameworks (e.g., task forces) are likely to find greater utility in governance, particularly in times of great social and economic stress in the institution.

Additionally, the changing social and economic pressures undoubtedly will affect the nature and scope of consultation within the institution.

The question of what constitutes consultation, and more specifically how it is employed in using task forces, will arguably always be linked to a desired change to solve a "perceived" problem that the existing governance structures are considered structurally (and perhaps relationally) inadequate to properly assess and address within some prescribed timeframe.

It follows that the recommendations that proceed from such undertaking will likely address the need to reform the institution in some way. The question of consultative purpose is connected to institutional purpose in this regard, particularly where administrative task forces are concerned, since the administration has the unique place of deliberating legal authority to act (i.e., authority associated with managing legal affairs that particularly affect its external relations). The faculty perspective then is one either to view the task force work as "apropos," "quid pro quo," or perhaps "fait accompli."

This sequence aligns itself along the continuum between the two polar extremes, where "apropos" is likely the perspective on how the task force work is incorporated in the decision-making process for an institution strongly oriented to the academic pole; "quid pro quo" is the likely perspective for an institution somewhere in between the two poles; and "fait accompli" is the likely perspective for an institution near the market pole. It is important to note here that perspective need not be equated with the accurate reality of the situation, but it nonetheless influences the relational sphere of institutional governance.

Thus, when institutional purpose is clearly defined, the nature of governance (i.e., structural and relational dynamics) interdependently follows. An institution with strong academic purpose and values will most likely be closely aligned to shared governance, just as one with strong market purpose and values will most likely be closely aligned with a more top-down rational management, particularly during austere times and strong public discontent. When governance and institutional purpose are both properly defined, they can function in a coordinated way and thereby achieve and improve institutional effectiveness (Enders, 2005, pp. 39–41; Leach, 2008, pp. 18–20).

The nature of the fundamental role of the faculty is inseparably linked to the institutional purpose. And in academic institutions of higher education, shared governance that seeks to reduce the faculty role is likely to diminish institutional effectiveness as it weakens the "social capital" of the institution (Heaney, 2010; Kezar, 2004; Minor, 2003). Building the social capital of the institution by advocating for increased participation in governance has many noted benefits.

For example, strategies increasing participation have a greater potential for a vested shared interest and a spirit of cooperation, which results from the sense of influence in the decision-making making process (Birnbaum, 2004, p. 17; Duderstadt, 2004). Moreover, the means to build this social capital can include both standard and nonstandard "forums," such as established mixed senates (which include the participation of constituencies other than just the faculty) and temporary joint-task forces (which similarly represent and operate under multiple authorities—faculty, professional staff, and students) (Birnbaum, 2004; Kezar, 2004; Lapworth, 2004).

These types of governance structures, bent on building social capital, are more likely the prominent dynamic of an academic institution. Unsurprisingly, such is not contrary to effective governance in that it leads to additional benefits of the social capital: broadening the consultative influence, developing leadership among constituencies, and strengthening the trust and cooperation of constituent groups (Birnbaum, 2004; Kezar, 2004; Lapworth, 2004; Leach, 2008, pp. 14–17).

The case for building social capital should not be trivialized in terms of its potential effects on leadership. While leadership and authority are not one and the same, they have something in common by virtue of their actual impacts. Bolman and Deal (2013) note that "People choose to obey authority so long as they believe it is legitimate. Authority and leadership are both built on voluntary compliance" (p. 344). Notably, the overt demonstrative exercise of authority should not be equated with leadership. Similarly, the general discharging of one's duties as a manager also does not equate to leadership.

According to the quantitative-analytic theory of leadership, good leaders are effective in handling tasks and people (pp. 338–343). The complementary research on leadership involves more qualitative research that is case study based in real-world practice (qualitative-holistic studies), which adds more subtle and relational focus (i.e., it adds a more nuanced human element) (pp. 343–344). Bolman and Deal, in reframing the viewpoint on leadership, conclude that "Wise leaders understand their own strengths, work to expand them, and build diverse teams that can offer an organizational leadership in all four modes: structural, political, human resource, and symbolic" (p. 369).

A unifying principle here is that leadership is contextual, involving both elements of organizational structure and relationships among institutional constituents. It follows in our current context of shared governance that institutions that extol "academic" virtues would be presumably predisposed to value leadership over the mere exercise of authority.

Concomitantly, this trait of the academic institution that emphasizes social capital also relates to its purposeful overall impact, which ultimately includes students, as Birnbaum (2004, p. 10) notes of the pressure to drive "academic" institutions to the extreme of "market" institutions: "And changing character and identity risks losing the core expertise, commitment to mission, and long-term perspective that gives the university its unique character (as well as what contemporary marketers would refer to as its 'competitive advantage')."

In consideration of all of the aforementioned desirable attributes of the "university," Birnbaum concludes: "The principles of shared governance enunciated in the 1967 Joint Statement continue to serve these institutions, and the larger society, well. . . . The basic question to ask is not whether we want to make governance more efficient, but whether we want to preserve truly academic institutions" (Birnbaum 2004, p. 26).

Consequently, responsibility and authority must be linked where there is validity in the decision making (Kezar, 2004; Leach, 2008, pp. 12–21; Minor, 2003). Validity should be thought of mainly in the relational terms of what happens after the decision making.

In this context, it is the subsequent nature of compliance as an outcome of the decision making that is in view. This should not be viewed in absolute terms of compliance or noncompliance by all of the affected constituents. This validity should be thought of as some measure of the "voluntary compliance" (and perhaps the associated productivity of effort) that follows as a product of the decision making and, subsequently, what is understood to be the ultimate accountability for the decision.

In relation to the question we have explored here—"Does the task force serve a true consultative purpose?"—we must again consider the type of institution. If an administrative task force is used in an academic type institution, such that responsibility and authority are linked in a managerially directed structure (e.g., vertical coordination with severely limited participation by nonadministrative constituencies) both within the task force work (structure, charge, consultative work) and the process to implement a decision-making outcome, the administrative decisions that result are likely to be perceived as "invalid."

Specifically, there is greater potential for the consultative process under such conditions to be deemed inadequate, the decisions flawed, and the overall decision-making process invalid. An unintended perception here (e.g., among the faculty) may be inevitable—even if not verbally communicated explicitly—that those who are truly authorized to act on a final decision are the ultimate decision makers. With that responsibility, so too are they ultimately accountable.

Hence, consultation seeks legitimate voice and consideration in the decision-making process. Heaney (2010, p. 75) writes: "People who are accountable for decisions must have the authority to make them. However, those with authority to make decisions can make them in an environment that solicits the involvement of all stakeholders. Participants understood that power and authority remain factors in shared governance."

The complexity in the details is in defining roles in the decision-making process. These roles depend on authority that is not solely vested in the final decision maker(s), but rather in the "power" of those who participate in the decision-making process (Heaney 2010, p. 76). Of note: This reference to power also includes the empowerment of students in decision-making processes. The means for addressing this complexity involve structural and relational elements.

Presumably, the work of a task force must include an expertise that is brought to the work (either resident within the task force or by external consultation) and a consideration of the contextual impacts in terms of the desired outcomes of the task force recommendations (e.g., infrastructure, resources, affected constituencies).

With respect to consultation, this can be tricky, but the consideration, within the reasonably prescribed timeframe, should include:

- constructing a task force that will facilitate some optimal consultation across structural governance unit constituencies both for the purpose of acquiring relevant institutional information and parameterizing potential recommendations; an example might be to look for structural units that represent broad-based constituencies (e.g., mixed senates if such exists within the institution) for recommendations on constituent members to the task force, who will in turn facilitate the essential and proprietary communications related to the task force's work, and

- situating the task force work within the relational elements of the institution.

An example may be to consider existing policies within the institution (e.g., faculty bylaws) and exercise practical communications with institutional constituencies that uphold both "the letter" and "the spirit of the law" (i.e., some openness in the communications about progress, prescribed timeframes, and procedural aspects for the decision making).

Consultation, working within this context of authority and responsibility, is also subject to the working tension between the two systems (the legal, managerial oriented system of the administration and the professional collegial system of the faculty). This tension affects how consultation is defined, the scope of its application, and its capacity to meet timely demands. The scope of faculty involvement in institutional decision making has been reported in the literature in the areas of budget, strategic planning (including enrollment), administrative hires, negotiating external relations, and assessing institutional effectiveness (Hrabowski, 2011; Mallon 2004; Minor, 2003).

A number of critics have spoken of the various concerns associated with governance in academic institutions ("the university"). These have become the frequently noted criticisms of shared governance in its diverse forms. For example, a frequently cited criticism is that the university is comparatively sluggish in the face of changing times, as compared to the private sector. This occurrence of so-called "untimely delay in the decision-making processes" is often attributed to the democratic process involving consultation (Duderstadt 2004).

Duderstadt describes the academic institution (a more collegial model), as the "voluntary culture of the university" involving the "process of consultation, communication and collaborations," as contrasted with the (corporate) business and industry process of "command-control-communication." This voluntary culture of "consensus leadership" is one that must also change such that decision making neither requires having to seek the consensus of all concerned constituencies prior to action (pronounced as a luxury no longer afforded academic institutions in the type of external climate of a rapidly changing world) nor breeding the reactive responses of special political interests that look toward the status quo and are at odds with strategic leadership.

Duderstadt's position can be described as follows:

> Universities need to better define those areas where the special competence of the faculty requires their consent (e.g., academic programs and policies); those areas where faculty advice will be sought and considered, but not considered authoritative (e.g., funding priorities), and those areas where faculty need not be consulted (parking?). (p. 85)

These gradations arguably help to better define the nature of the influence in the decision-making process. This does not necessarily diminish, for example, faculty influence, but rather more effectively uses faculty influence within decision making. Duderstadt also noted the faculty engagement and participation (what Birnbaum would ascribe to the "social capital") invested (having its focus) in departmental matters where there is greater appreciation of their power and influence (i.e., strong links between their authority and their responsibility).

This focus of participation and effort of the talented faculty at the department level, he contrastingly laments in observing a paucity of the engagement of such talent for matters of university governance where the view of such participation is perceived to be merely advisory. In consideration of consultative purpose, this contrast in interest and participation is a notable disadvantage to the institution. In recognition of the need to strengthen faculty governance to benefit the university level governance, Duderstadt speaks of the need to vest faculty bodies with executive rather than advisory authority (p. 84).

The context for consultation in shared governance is premised in structural and relational considerations. The structural and relational characteristics of the institution are often matched to its archetypal profile as somewhat generally defined along the continuum between two categorical opposites (the academic and the market). The admixture of these archetypes, which are polar opposites, naturally correlates with the institutions overarching purpose.

This purpose defines:

- the role that constituent groups play in the decision-making processes of the institution (e.g., faculty status and participation in the formulation of the educational program and related decisions that affect its implementation);

- the institution's values, which are housed in structural units and relational dynamics. Institutions with strong academic character and purpose are predisposed to structural work units that favor more collegial governance, and relational activity (e.g., communications) that supports the same, and the related values of governing ideals such as academic freedom and liberal education. The values are characterized as supporting the development of the "social capital" of the institution (e.g., intellectual curiosity, civic engagement, and scholarship).

A proper consideration of what constitutes consultation (and whether or not temporary governance structures, such as administrative task forces, can be effectively used for critical decision making) are similarly impacted by the structural and relational dynamic. The practical impacts of these structural and relational considerations, with respect to constituent groups, define the nature of their participatory engagement in governance as situated in the relationships between authority and responsibility, influence, power, and accountability in decision making.

As noted earlier, these practical impacts include, for example, whether or not the nature of the consultation promotes the engagement and expertise of talented faculty to be advantageously employed, as a means to improve the decision-making and problem-solving effectiveness of the institution.

Task Force: Structural Integrity in Governance

The task force is included in a growing list of governance "tools" that have been used in higher education over time. These tools undoubtedly serve in many cases as governance structures, with such examples including strategic planning committees (Bryson, 2011), future search (Weisbord, 2000) and Joint Big Decision Committees (JBDC)(Corak, 1992; Schuster, 1994). The anatomy and function of a task force, however useful, represent what may be considered a parallel governance structure to whatever exists within the institution at the time of the task force initiation (Hartley, 2003; Mallon, 2004). Mallon includes the more recent prominence of "centers" within the university structural units of governance, expressing concern that alternate governance structures have great potential for complicating institutional governance. Mallon postulates that under the conditions of these alternate governance structures, "institutional [higher education] governance can be best understood not as an overarching concept but as an aggregation of disjointed structures, processes, and employment patterns." By extension of this argument, the task force structure potentially adds to what is referred to as a "complex maze of governance, where participants' responsibilities and authority are increasingly confusing and uncertain" (Mallon, 2004, pp. 62–63).

While Mallon applies the concept of *disjoined governance* specifically to the consequential power and influence associated with the emergence of "centers" and "institutes" as governance structures at university centers, several universally applicable points are made.

- First, the potential to extend the participation to include multiple governance entities is not (in and of itself) likely to enhance the effectiveness of shared governance at the institutional level. Rather, it is an impediment, increasing its complexity and unwieldiness.

- Second, the related autonomous plurality of interest and influence of multiple governance structures is not likely to contribute to shared governance at the institutional level. Rather, such structures potentially move what are generally considered complementary operational unit structures to the mainstream of governance. This is problematic, as these structures function to the detriment of departmental integrity, influence, and budgetary allocations.

- Third, these alternate governance structures often operate in a fashion that is contrary to collegial governance. For example, they often, have "directors" appointed to indefinite terms, operating as authoritarian voices. These individuals operating within their hierarchal, vertically coordinated structures and their authoritarian relational disposition, may limit consultative participation in the decision making within the very structure that they represent. The implication here is that the inclusion of centers or institutes (or by extension any other "parallel" governance structure) into the mainstream of institutional governance may attenuate consultative expertise and participation to the potential detriment of the institution.

- Fourth, to the extent that an alternate governance structure has the flexibility to act according to its "autonomous" interests (often directed to commercial relationships external to the institution), the nature of its decision making and influence may not serve the collective interests of the institution.

- Finally, these alternate governance structures may be unduly influenced by market values, which impact the professional processes of the academy (e.g., "faculty" hires, tenure decisions, other staffing decisions), thereby negatively affecting the institution's academic resolve (Mallon, 2004).

In sharp contrast, Hartley (2003) identifies the positive potential of task forces. Hartley focuses attention on the use of the task force governance "structure" as a tool in the principal change strategy of academic institutions. Hartley's case study of one private college that used task forces as a key strategy for a comprehensive change effort identifies several noteworthy benefits of the use of task forces, with the caveat that they are incorporated under the umbrella of the collective institutional agenda. When task forces are used in this complementary way, they serve as an innovative bridging tool with the potential to forge strong change coalitions. They are unburdened by the standard operation of the existing governance structures and provide a more relaxed focus on the specific "change" element (task).

The focused attention brought to the "task" is a narrowing of the breadth of operation that is normally characteristic of working committees or even subcommittees. It is worth noting that committees are often additionally burdened by the day-to-day operational concerns of the governance structures to which they belong. The task force charge offers a narrowing of operational scope, as well as flexibility. Both the organizational structure and operational form of the task force are likely synergistic characteristics associated with its finite lifespan.

The specificity of "task" feature of the task force also provides flexibility in the coordinative management of the task force itself. While more standard governance structures form their memberships through such things as elections, searches, or other prescribed procedures, task forces are not of necessity restricted in these ways. Moreover, existing structures are also generally constrained by organizational structures with more clearly defined member roles that apply to the broader operational scope of the committee, senate, cabinet, etcetera. All of these constrain the activity of the existing governance structure with a fidelity that is typically limited to its immediate constituents.

The tractability of the task force form potentially predisposes its members to a more creative and collaborative operation. Bolman and Deal (2013) offer some perspective on the use of task forces as they bring the focused human capital and expertise for problem solving. Task forces also function within a broader structural social frame, designed to accomplish the intended work. The leader of the task force, addressing a very specific, time-limited charge, can facilitate creative and innovative thinking among members to pragmatically address pressing problems.

The cautionary note, however, involves its proper application as a tool and not the sole essence of the overall operational structure. Bolman and Deal (2013) identify, for example, that the task force, by its very nature, while providing the much-needed lateral communication to address new problems or questions within the institution, also potentially diverts attention from "ongoing operating issues" (p. 58). The task force, therefore, exists as a bridging governance element that by its design brings creative energy, talented expertise, and innovation to accomplish a narrowly defined task. It must therefore have a terminal lifespan that is linked to its charge (task). Task forces do not replace existing structures. They provide timely responses for newly developing problems or needs within the institution.

In contrast, when properly incorporated, the task force becomes a viable part of the overall structural frame. "The structural frame looks beyond individuals to examine the social architecture of work. Though sometimes equated with red tape, mindless memos, and rigid bureaucrats, the approach is much broader and more subtle. It encompasses the free-wheeling, loosely structured entrepreneurial task force as well as the more tightly controlled railway company or postal department. If structure is overlooked, an organization often misdirects energy and resources" (Bolman & Deal, 2013, p. 66).

When the task force operates solely in conformance with a well-defined charge, the tendency for a more collegial operation provides the impetus for a lateral coordination (Bolman & Deal 2013; Hartley 2003) under a common goal. The bridging phenomenon inherent within the nature of task forces themselves orient them in a more collegial way that transcends unilateral focus on any particular governing unit. This lateral coordination operant within task forces is applied to the activities (acquiring and sharing information, identifying the intersecting and collective concerns associated with the task, etc.) that bridge constituent governance units. With respect to the task force members, the relaxed environment of the task force provides the liberty to bring constituent expertise to the consultative process in a unique way. The coordination solidifies the individual and collective responsibility of the task force members to properly respond to the charge.

A task force's team-based structures place greater emphasis on a looser horizontal form that supports other lateral forms (e.g., network configurations) rather than more rigid hierarchical structures. Hartley found that this condition led to improved participatory communication (including opportunity for collegial debate) across what would be considered several dispersive constituency groups. This finding is also consistent with Bolman and Deal's categorizing task forces as a lateral technique and form, offering the potential to bridge some of the complexity of an otherwise disjointed governance especially in situations that "require collaboration of diverse specialties or functions" (Bolman & Deal, 2013, p. 55). There is the added value of such with respect to behavioral change, such as enthusiastic cooperation, among constituencies (Bolman & Deal 2013; Hartley 2003).

Task force members, while accountable to their respective constituencies, are less inclined to be defensive of their respective institutional role and freer to focus both on the quality of the process (work) and support of the outcomes (reporting/implementation). Hartley (2003) noted that this dynamic strengthened both the professional (work) and personal relationships across constituencies. The process, which included discussion and debate, ultimately led to consensus support for the initiative ("The Summit Plan"), which changed the nature of the education program to add new instructional features deemed appropriately complementary to the institutional mission.

The most crucial benefits of the use of task forces were the development of social and political capital, providing the necessary momentous support for the change agenda. This is attributable to at least two factors:

(1) the broad and participatory consulting of the task forces and their members across the larger contributing constituencies, and

(2) a process that was not unduly stagnated or derailed by potential naysayers that was likely to characterize the more typical shared governance structures and deliberations (in that particular case study).

Overall, this process was not the timeliest but was reasonably progressive. The observation here was that in the existing governance structures, certain voices were exerting considerable influences that were possibly skewing the consultative effort in the decision-making processes. The use of task forces was deemed prudent and equitable, in that the naysayers had their substantive opportunity to be heard throughout, as well as in the final stages of the debate within the democratic process that ultimately led to the adoption of the plan in that case study. It was noted in Hartley's (2003) study that the use of task forces broadened participation, thereby attenuating potentially disparate influence by dissenting minority on both the process and the outcomes.

Task force use, however, is not a cure-all. As Hartley points out in the "Summit College" study, consensus building (even when it employs task forces) has some minimal consultative time requirement. These findings are instructive, but perhaps are not specifically applicable in the absence of other contextual institutional characteristics, which often do more to define relationships than mere structures (e.g., relationship based values).

The literature provides support for task forces as prospective (practical) tools to help provide an improved timeliness of consultation within, and across, potentially diverse constituencies. Task forces also embody all of the aforementioned benefits ascribed to cultivating social capital. Use of task forces should be considered in terms of their influence in decision-making processes, where roles are clearly defined. This influence is characterized by the authority and responsibility vested in the task force. Task forces that bridge existing governance structures are poised to address operational gaps in the fixed structure. Thus, consultation with respect to the use of task forces is one that asks whether or not their use truly affirms shared governance.

The integrity of the structural frame (i.e., proper recognition of governance/operational units) of the institution for shared governance, as previously established, is a critical consideration when introducing parallel governance structures such as task forces. The decision to use a task force is therefore not simply an academic one. The structural context is important but represents what can be referred to as one side of a two-sided coin. The other consideration is one that provides relational context for how parallel governance structures are used to accomplish institutional purpose.

Administrative Task Forces: Can They Serve Anything Other than an Administrative Purpose?

Task Forces: A Relational Context

Many stresses may be challenging the tenets of shared governance and contributing to a loss of faculty status in higher education (Birnbaum, 2004; Bornstein, 2012; Enders, 2005). A host of evolving demands on institutions include the growing economic strains, rapidly changing instructional technologies that are redefining classroom contact time and other aspects of pedagogical practice, changing student demographics and the associated political climate for all of the aforementioned demands (King, 2013). The political pressure to abandon shared governance points toward corporate models that centralize authority and decision making in the administration, and consequently other key elements of the institutional operation such as strategic planning and the nature of institutional assessment as well (Waugh, 1998).

The question of consultative purpose in the use of task forces, as previously described, is one that is centered on both the ultimate authority of the authorizing agent and the consultative responsibility of all the task force members, and the authorizing agents. Accordingly, among them, collaboration becomes key. If it is a core institutional value, all the better. More is required among task force members than simple cooperation, since authentic collaboration is likely to support a conscious effort to arrive at mutual understanding in the joint effort needed to achieve the desired outcomes associated with the task force charge.

Understandably, a task force operating under the auspices of shared governance represents and links the authority to act with an inescapable interdependence to act responsively—even in the face of what may be disparate internal and external pressures. Moreover, the manner in which authority and responsibility are operationally defined in accomplishing the task should be considered not only in the light of the immediate charge but also in terms of how it serves in developing the transformative collaborative leadership of the institution (Gardiner, 2006). The latter is of special importance because it is a crucial and potentially contentious aspect of the perceived "capital" and the allocated influence and authority for the decision making within the institution (Gardiner 2006; Waugh 1998).

Task Force Authenticity for Shared Governance

Institutional Climate

The gauge of the institutional climate associated with the governance is also characterized by institutional purpose, as discussed earlier in this discourse, but also by how well matched the operational governance of the institution is to that purpose. Comprehensive change strategies (or for that matter any strategic plan) must account for the institutional climate. Birnbaum (2004) uses the descriptors of "hard" and "soft" to summarily classify this climate. His presupposition is one that uses "academic" type institutions as the point of reference, which leads to the conclusion that that type of institution will respond more effectively (i.e., with voluntary compliance by constituencies) to "soft" governance.

It should be noted here that in a large public higher education system of diverse institutional missions integrated under the umbrella of the system itself, such as the State University of New York (SUNY), the presumption of a pure "academic" typology might not be sufficiently adequate to account for some of the nuances associated with the individual climates of respective SUNY campuses (e.g., the academic culture of the institutions faculty and students), particularly with respect to how parallel governance structures are received.

The presumption for campuses that would be characterized as more closely fitting the academic typologies is that they are more likely to receive parallel governance structures in a seamless way if they are integrated as a feature of an overall "soft" governance—one that places greater emphasis on relational considerations and laterally coordinated ("soft") governance structures. The seamless match in such cases eases the focus on the bureaucratic formalities of rules and processes. In contrast, "hard" governance is better matched to the "market" typology, which typically operates and values more rigid hierarchal "hard" structures and relational considerations tending more toward the vertical coordination that characterize "hard" governance.

The institutional climate in both cases is more conspicuously identified by the nature of its readily manifest governance structures, but more latently by its relational characteristics across constituencies (i.e., culture).

As noted earlier, task force use within an academic culture aligns itself to structures that are less hierarchal, where the authorizing agent imputes a greater power to the task force. The search for sound practice in shared governance spans the variation in structures, operational methods and models associated with the deliberative faculty bodies and their integration within institutional governance (Heaney, 2010; Minor, 2004). The various structures include governance units defined by institutional constitutions (Heaney 2010), hybrid academic units such as institutes and centers (Mallon 2004), and diverse faculty senate models (Minor 2003).

While task forces that "organically" develop out of the shared interests mediated through existing governance structures may be preferable in addressing collaborative decision making (Boyd, 2013), the literature strongly supports the premise that the most valued qualities of shared governance do not appear to be predicated on any particular governance structure, but rather bring credence to the structural elements of governance (Boyd, 2013; Hartley, 2003; Kaplan, 2004; Kezar, 2004; Kurland, 2014; Mallon, 2004; Minor, 2004; Schoorman, 2010). These qualities are those that define relationship more than structure or policy. Notably, however, these desirable qualities in building relationship need the support of the structural and related operational elements (Kezar, 2004). Kezar notes the significant synergy between the two (structural and relational) in institutional decision making, for example:

> It is important to note that structures and processes tend to influence relationships, leadership arrangements, and trust. . . . For instance, if faculty and administrators develop a process to ensure consultation and the advice produced by that consultation is used, trust is developed.
>   . . . Similarly, but perhaps less formally, relationships and leadership can have an effect on structures and processes. In this way structures and processes begin to look different in practice than they do on paper. . . . For example, a committee might begin with a specific charge, timeline, and set of procedures, yet through conversations the charge might be modified, new people might be added to the committee, and meeting procedures might be altered. In other words, structures and processes are not static. (p. 37)

The concluding argument is that institutional resource (investment) that is directed to the relational characteristics of the institution (e.g., leadership development and relational development across constituencies) will improve the governance, as "These actions (fostering leadership development and building relationships) will also contribute positively to the intangibles of human interaction, such as trust. Investment in training for leaders is perhaps the best way to create better relationships and trust since leaders are pivotal in the development of both of these areas" (p. 45).

A Culture for Understanding and Building Trust

The climate of trust, as Gardiner describes it (citing Tierney 2004), is integrity in the relationships between governing boards, campus presidents (and by extension their administrators), and the faculty. This integrity is noted as a "consistency between words and deeds" (Gardiner 2006, p. 212), which puts greater onus on those who have decision-making authority.

The climate for trust has its basis more strongly couched in a relational context rather than a structural one. Birnbaum (2004) describes this as the "soft" governance that builds trust by giving greater weight to the social interactions that include cognitive processes that lead to more collaborative decision making, and the perceived legitimacy that leads to voluntary compliance (procedural justice) (Heaney, 2010).

In Del Favero's (2003) view this is the social nature of governance that has the capacity to bring the conflicting cultures of the administration and faculty into a conceptual framework that emphasizes social exchange, social capital, and network forms of organizational structure. In this same relational context, Tierney (2004) describes the potential for building trust, where differing points of view can be bridged out of a campus community culture that values some presumption of the goodwill that promotes the common good.

This notion of campus cultures as having a greater link to decision-making outcomes than actual structures is also consistent with findings out of a comprehensive study conducted by Kaplan, where authority as vested in existing components of the governance structure did not produce the hypothetically presumed group interests of those exercising that authority (Kaplan 2004, pp. 31–33). Kaplan therefore suggests that further study be devoted not to the structures but rather the processes by which these structures are engaged, as institutions also respond to the dispositions (e.g., resource-related allocations and political pressures) of the external environments in which they exist. Kezar (2004) adds that Kaplan's findings are consistent with organizational theories of governance that demonstrate that behaviors are loosely tied at best to bureaucratic structures. Kezar further posits:

> Relationships and trust are hard to separate; good relationships lead to trust, and trust develops good relationships. There are two relationships in particular in which trust is critical to effective governance: the relationship between faculty and administrators (often epitomized by the relationship between senate chair and president), and the relationship between the president and his or her board. If trust does not exist in these relationships, effective governance is unlikely. (p. 44)

The conclusion of note here is perhaps best simply stated. The institutional climate as having a more prominent focus on governance structures is better served by a relational (institutional culture) focus that addresses the more substantive intangible underpinnings of governance: building trust and developing effective capacities for governance by focusing on the human capital vested in working relationships between campus constituencies and the development of the related leadership potential of the institution.

Transparency: Openness and Information Sharing

As previously noted, authority does not automatically equate to effective leadership, nor does it always strengthen the validity for action or its outcomes. From the perspective of shared governance, voluntary compliance is a desired behavioral change among campus constituencies, as it is linked to decision-making processes.

Earlier it was noted that this type of compliance does not merely depend on the authority that is exercised in a decision-making action. The exercise of authority may simply be seen as duties discharged out of a position within a hierarchal structure (i.e., a structural context of limited relational/cultural value).

In an "academic" institution, the relational dynamic of leadership has the potential for far greater impact in this regard. An effective and productive outcome depends on perceptions of the "legitimacy" of campus "authorities" and their respective institutional governance structures (including, ultimately, the president). This is subsequently reflected in the effective implementation of a decision within the institution. In essence, the greatest value associated with exercising authority in the decision-making processes for shared governance is expectedly the result of strong relational influences not structural ones. This was previously illustrated in considering how trust is developed.

Transparency is another relational value of academic institutions which resonates within a culture of trust. Transparency and openness are relationship-based qualities for shared governance, particularly in terms of perceptions of legitimacy (Birnbaum, 2004; Bolman & Deal, 2013). This transparency is also predicated on the disposition for information sharing.

Gardiner identifies information sharing in the context that also redefines roles and develops leadership. He correlates the nature of the leadership to the nature of shared governance within an organizational structure. This representation (of transactional, transformational, and transcendent leadership) looks at the shared governance continuum that moves leadership from merely transactional to transcendent.

- *Transactional* leadership favors a hierarchal top-down structure as the model.

- *Transcendent* leadership is the model that implements information sharing and achieves true collective decision making among
"associates" (Gardiner, 2006).

Kezar (2004) similarly emphasizes the practical implications associated with the emphasis on leadership as a means for improving the overall
effectiveness of governance (pp. 41–42), concluding: "A new perspective
is gaining support: campuses can build effective governance through an
investment in leadership development and through mechanisms that nurture faculty, staff, and administrative relationships (for example, sponsor-
ing campus wide events)" (p. 45). These "mechanisms" are likely to favor
transparency in the relationships. The initial leadership focus is placed
on those representing positions with vested authority in decision-making
processes from among the participating campus constituencies.

While formal communication structures disseminate information, the
disposition for sharing information is relational transparency. Heaney
(2010) notes

> Although formal constitutions define structures, these documents
> cannot guarantee civility, trustworthiness, or transparency. With
> a commitment to these qualities of relationship and the effort to
> maintain them, the university can achieve its potential as an adult
> education institution, which engages students, faculty, and staff
> in creating the future democratically. (p. 78)

The manner in which existing structures are transparent—mediate information sharing, participatory exchange, and frame debate—is indicative of
the extent of managerial orientations in the governance. The managerial
influence of "market" culture for example often favors centralizing authority and concomitantly limits information sharing—a corporate decision-
making methodology (Waugh, 1998).

Transparency and openness form the cornerstone for forging effective working relationships in the decision making of inclusive university
democracy, and as such are connected to procedural and structural implements. Hartley (2003) notes the importance of transparency as a positive
factor in the perceptions of the legitimate use of governance structures
(e.g., task forces) that work also to constructively engage even naysayers.

Kurland (2014) notes the importance of the relational transparency
associated with advancing the sustainability change agenda of the college
involved in that study through a consultative process that included the
use of an "informal governance structure." This effect of transparency

is also noted within faculty governance as an element of social justice. Schoorman (2010) integrates the relational transparency and openness for information sharing and forging consensus as a crucial decision-making engagement to promote faculty service through governance by using the object illustration of the curricular impacts associated with the introduction of diversity to the social justice pedagogy of that public college.

This dynamic application of relational transparency promoted and improved diversity in the faculty service (i.e., perspectives and people) through engagement in the institutional governance via the Faculty Assembly of a multi-campus public college. As Schoorman describes, "Within this context of decision-making, diversity is conceptualized as the sources and directionality of organizational communication. . . . Thus, the democratization of faculty governance entailed openness to all perspectives, an obligation to listen to and build consensus from this diversity, transparency in the decision-making process, and leadership accountability through listening and action."

The repetitive emphasis on transparency and openness in its diverse applications across a diverse range of institutions serves as a cue for the nature of the governance that is highly valued. This emphasis speaks to the "soft" nature of the governance in all of these cases, where the descriptions and the focus do not to any large extent address the structural context.

Relational Synergies: Decision Making, Divergence, and Perceived Role

Previously, the discussion of authority was framed in relationship to the power that ascribes responsibility to the decision making. In revisiting the significance of authority, substantive working relationships also bring accountability to this equation. These administrative campus responsibilities, in the best of circumstances, value faculty input as part of the social capital (e.g., professional expertise, leadership) of the institution. When all is working at its best, faculty have real influence in both the actual decision making (e.g., executive authority, evidence of faculty input in the implementation), and in the fair play that respects the process (trust, integrity, transparency) that led to the decisions (Birnbaum, 2004; Duderstadt, 2004; Kezar, 2004).

Advisably, administrators should parameterize their use of administrative task forces (and any other parallel governance structures), and thereby provide some measures for assessing its effective integration and purpose for shared governance. As task forces serve to address specific problems that have significant campus-wide and long-term impacts, one potential parameter is inherent in the complementary nature of the task force as a governance structure working to promote a participatory effort that includes senior faculty and affords the institution a collective insight that spans the talented problem solving constituencies of the campus.

This effect can be thought of as a measure of both the perceived consultative purpose and the extent and effectiveness of the consultation itself. Task forces are sure to be perceived as governance circumvention where the integrity of the structural and relational governance is violated. The structural contextual cues for an "academic" type institution are far less rigid but do have synergy with the relational contextual cues which are more highly valued in the organizational culture. The contributions of the organizational dynamic (culture) as well as the circumstances under which a task force becomes a "tool" determine its effective use.

Tierney (2003, pp. 11–14) identifies seven ways in which improper administrative action can create "organizational dissonance":

- convene a group, vest them with decision-making authority, and then not implement the decision;

- ask for input and then ignore it;

- wait for reaction, rather than proactively seek input;

- establish rules to mutually govern process and then break them;

- consistently seek input from an exclusive source (limit the scope of consultation and create perceived nondissenters);

- place faculty in leadership positions that require administrative skills and offer no professional development training or support; and

- limit resource and discourage comparative understanding by isolating the campus from useful external resources (e.g., communications/resources from professional associations, colleagues from other campuses, consortiums).

This path to ineffective decision making results from the cumulative effect of pernicious faculty engagement, severely diminished value given to diverse and divergent input, and the perceived discount of the faculty's role.

Similarly, faculty authority also bears relational accountability. Faculty members have professional authority over the educational program, which vests each faculty member with a responsibility to contribute to its success. The presumption is that all faculty members are responsible for the condition of the institution's educational program. This responsibility includes accountability for tweaking programs to be responsive to student learning. The accountability, while imputed to the institutional governance, rests on the faculty.

This fine-tuning has a great deal of interdepartmental dependence that must respond to needs at many levels (e.g., the institutional level, professional pedagogy, state education requirements). Faculty governance also has the onus to identify transcendent leadership adequate to address interdepartmental programming. In the face of such demands, faculty governance is not immune to the limitations of its own bureaucratic structure, which may not possess the lateral coordination that is necessary to readily address aspects of this institutional need (Gaff, 2007).

Conclusion

The ideological framing of shared governance has its operational context in those things that shape the structure and relationships in institutional governance. The organizational theories pertaining to such work (i.e., governance) are challenging the notion that the more manifest features of governance, that is, those pertaining to the structural frame (organizational governance units), are similarly the ones that determine its effectiveness. It is now more widely contended that structure is less important than the underlying culture it supports.

In providing some of the structural and relational context for consultation in this chapter, the emphasis on the intangibles that permeate shared governance (influence, trust, respect, transparency, leadership) support the position that relationship trumps structure. From the subject matter presented in this chapter, it is reasonable to conclude that the organizational frame is important for accomplishing the work, but relationships are likely a stronger determinant in the progress, productivity, and overall effectiveness of the collective work of the institution.

Additionally, connected with this attempt to understand the synergies between organizational structure and relational dynamic in shared governance, some perspective was given on the use of an alternative governance structure, the task force. Our examination of the task force ascertained its fitness as both a structural and relational tool for tackling some of the complexities in governance that arise as institutions face new operational challenges that existing governance units may be ill equipped to address.

The task force should represent the balance that shared governance brings to the institutional culture, as the substance and evidence of effective decision making through successful governance that captures all of the workings of academic institutional vivacity: strengthening the trust and cooperation of the faculty, validating the governance (leadership development and decision making) process, fostering the sound collective social dynamic of the institution, and honing the processes that support the institution's mission and outcomes.

There are two greater advisory notes from Hartley's (2003) study of Summit College:

(1) the use of task forces allowed for a more collaborative change strategy that facilitated broad participatory consensus, but also limited the president's authoritative control in the decision-making process;

(2) the very intention to bring creative and innovative energy to the change strategy that produced the "parallel" task forces (governance structures) was created by the president, which in some ways bypassed the existing governance structures.

The cautionary note pertaining to the latter (2) is that the use of a parallel governance structure under the president as the authorizing agent made that structure the creation of the president. The president's action established a new precedent in that case, which not only opened the campus president to unproductive criticisms but also gave way to additional deteriorating manipulations of the ongoing processes by the administrative successors to that president.

Thus, the literature suggests that the task force tool for shared governance has its most legitimate use assigned to circumstances where it complements existing structures, either arising with the support of the formal governance units or integrating as a bridging consultative structure. This legitimacy additionally is the product of a transparency that transcends, but also consequentially affects, procedural and structural elements of the decision-making process.

At its best, the task force is also associated with consultation across faculty, involving other stakeholder constituencies. While it is may be within the purview of any governance unit to employ a parallel governance structure such as a task force, the most judicious use of administrative task forces is likely to involve addressing areas where faculty consultation is considered more advisory than authoritative. By contrast, an astute use of joint task forces will likely find application in areas where faculty consultation is considered either authoritative or very desirable.

Acknowledgments

The authors are grateful for the participation and perspective of the SUNY Old Westbury student government leaders, Paraskevas Savva and Camilla Swasey, during the 1st Annual SUNY Voices Conference. We also express our thanks to our faculty colleague, Kathleen Greenberg, and Deborah M. Rhem-Jackson, former Assistant Vice President for Academic Affairs/ College Readiness Programs at SUNY Old Westbury, for their insights and helpful contributions during the 1st Annual SUNY Voices conference and in the subsequent communications that led to the preparation of the manuscripts for which the two chapters the co-authors of this chapter presented and further developed for publication.

Notes

1. The Statement (originally endorsed in 1967 and subsequently revised in 1990) in its entirety can be found at http://www.aaup.org/report/statement-government-colleges-and-universities accessed on The American Association of University Professors (AAUP), the American Council on Education (ACE), and the Association of Governing Boards of Universities and Colleges (AGB).
2. For other helpful readings on the subject matter, see Scott, J.W. (2002). The critical state of shared governance. *Academe*, *88*(4), 41, and Eckel, P.D. (2000). The role of shared governance in institutional hard decisions: Enabler or antagonist? *The Review of Higher Education*, *24*(1), 15–39.
3. These bylaws can be accessed at https://docs.google.com/viewer?a=v&pid=-sites&srcid=ZGVmYXVsdGRvbWFpbnxvbGR3ZXN0OYnVyeWZhY3VsdHlzZW5hdGV8Z3g6MmQ3ZjE5ZDMyNWYyM2JhNw. Excerpts are quoted from pages 2 and 4.

References

Bergquist, W.H. (1992). *The four cultures of the academy*. San Francisco, CA: Jossey-Bass Inc.

Bergquist, W.H., & Pawlak, K. (2008). *Engaging the six cultures of the academy: Revised and expanded edition of the four cultures of the academy*. John Wiley & Sons.

Birnbaum, R. (2004). The end of shared governance: Looking ahead or looking back. *New Directions for Higher Education, 2004* (127), 5–22.

Bolman, L.G., & Deal, T.E. (2015). Reframing organizations: Artistry, choice, and leadership (5th ed.) Somerset, NJ: John Wiley & Sons, Inc.

Bornstein, R. (2012). Transforming institutions through shared governance. *Trusteeship, 20*(5), 24–28. Association of Governing Boards of Universities and Colleges Publication.

Boyd, F., & Tiede, H. (2013). Collaborative decision making regarding salary policy: A case study. *Academe, 99*(2), 20–40, 3.

Bryson, J.M. (2011). *Strategic planning for public and nonprofit organizations: A guide to strengthening and sustaining organizational achievement* (Vol. 1). New York: John Wiley & Sons.

Corak, K. (1992). "Do big decision committees work?" *Planning for Higher Education, 21*, 20–24.

Del Favero, M. (2003). Faculty-administrator relationships as integral to high-performing governance systems new frameworks for study. *American Behavioral Scientist, 46*(7), 902–922.

Duderstadt, J.J. (2004). Governing the 21st century university: A view from the bridge. In W.G. Tierney (Ed.), *Competing conceptions of academic governance: Negotiating the perfect storm* (pp. 137–157). Baltimore, MD: Johns Hopkins University Press.

Enders, J. (2005) Higher education in times of discontent? About trust, authority, price and some other unholy trinities. In I. Bleiklie and M. Henkel (Eds.), *Governing Knowledge: A study of continuity and change in higher education—A festschrift in honor of Maurice Kogan* (Vol. 9, pp. 31–48). Netherlands: Springer.

Farrell, E.F. (2003). Phoenix's unusual way of crafting courses. *Chronicle of Higher Education, 49*(23), A10–A12.

Gaff, J.G. (2007). What if the faculty really do assume responsibility for the educational program? *Liberal Education, 93*(4), 6–13.

Gardiner, J.J. (2006). Transactional, transformational, and transcendent leadership: Metaphors mapping the evolution of the theory and practice of governance. *Leadership Review, 6*(2), 62–76.

Gerber, L.G. (1997). Reaffirming the value of shared governance. *Academe, 83*(5), 14–18.

Goff, J.W., & Lane, J.E. (2008). Building a SEM organization: The internal consult approach. *College and University, 83*(3), 20–27. Retrieved from http://search. proquest.com/docview/61954821?accountid=29096

Gumport, P.J. (2001). Built to serve: The enduring legacy of public higher education. In P.G. Altbach, P.J. Gumport, & D.B. Johnstone (Eds.), *In Defense of American Higher Education* (pp. 85–109). Baltimore, MD: The Johns Hopkins University Press.

Hartley, M. (2003). The promise and peril of parallel governance structures. *American Behavioral Scientist, 46*(7), 923–945.

Heaney, T. (2010). Democracy, shared governance, and the university. *New Directions for Adult and Continuing Education,* (128), 69–79.

Hrabowski, F.I., Suess, J., & Fritz, J. (2011). Assessment and analytics in institutional transformation. *EDUCAUSE Review, 46*(5), 14–16.

Kaplan, Gabriel E. (2004). Do governance structures matter? *New Directions for Higher Education,* (127), 23–34.

Kezar, A. (2004). What is more important to effective governance: Relationships, trust, and leadership, or structures and formal processes? *New Directions for Higher Education,* (127), 35–46.

King, G., & Sen, M. (2013). The troubled future of colleges and universities. *PS: Political Science & Politics, 46*(1), 83–89.

Kurland, N.B. (2014). Shared governance and the sustainable college. *International Journal of Sustainability in Higher Education, 15*(1), 63–83.

Lapworth, S. (2004). Arresting decline in shared governance: Towards a flexible model for academic participation. *Higher Education Quarterly, 58*(4), 299–314.

Lawrence, J., & Lawrence, M. (2013). Faculty perceptions of organizational politics. *The Review of Higher Education, 36*(2), 145–178.

Leach, W.D. (2008). Shared governance in higher education: Structural and cultural responses to a changing national climate. Available from SSRN 1520702: http://papers.ssrn.com/sol3/papers.cfm?abstract_id=1520702

Mallon, W. (2004). Disjointed governance in university centers and institutes. *New Directions for Higher Education,* (127), 61–74.

Millora, M.L. (2010). Market values in higher education: A review of the for-profit sector. *InterActions: UCLA Journal of Education and Information Studies, 6*(2), article 5. Retrieved from http://escholarship.org/uc/item/2q5856m8

Minor, J.T. (2003). Assessing the Senate: Critical issues considered. *American Behavioral Scientist, 46*(7), 960–977.

Minor, J.T. (2004). Understanding faculty senates: Moving from mystery to models. *The Review of Higher Education, 27*(3), 343–363.

Scharffs, B.G., & Welch, J.W. (2005). An analytic framework for understanding and evaluating the fiduciary duties of educators. *BYU Education & Law Journal.* Retrieved from http://digitalcommons.law.byu.edu/cgi/viewcontent. cgi?article=1204&context=elj

Schoorman, D., & Acker-Hocevar, M. (2010). Viewing faculty governance within a social justice framework: Struggles and possibilities for democratic decision-making in higher education. *Equity & Excellence in Education, 43*(3), 310–325.

Schuster, J.H., Smith, D.G., Sund, K.C., Kathleen, A., & Yamada, M.M. (1994). *Strategic governance: How to make big decisions better.* Bristol, UK: Intellect Books.

Tierney, W.G. (2003). Academic vantage points: Reflections on the university in the 21st century. *Center for Higher Education Policy Analysis, University of Southern California.*

Tierney, W. G. (2004). Improving academic governance: Utilizing a cultural framework to improve organizational performance. In W.G. Tierney (Ed.), *Competing Conceptions of Academic Governance.* Baltimore, MD: John Hopkins University Press.

Trakman, L. (2008). Modelling university governance. *Higher Education Quarterly, 62*(1–2), 63–83.

Venable, W., & Gardiner, J.J. (1988). *Synergistic governance, leadership teams, and the academic department head. Annual* Meeting of the Association for the Study of Higher Education. St. Louis, Missouri.

Waugh, W.L. (1998). Conflicting values and cultures: The managerial threat to university governance. *Review of Policy Research, 15*(4), 61–74.

Weisbord, M.R., & Weisbord, M. (2000). *Future search: An action guide to finding common ground in organizations and communities.* San Francisco: Berrett-Koehler.

Wilson, R. (2010). For-profit colleges change higher education's landscape. *The Chronicle of Higher Education, 56*(22), 1–19.

Weeks, K., & Haglund, R. (2002). Fiduciary duties of college and university faculty and administrators. *Journal of College and University Law, 29*(1), 153–187.

Zusman, A. (2005). Challenges facing higher education in the twenty-first century. In P.G. Altbach, R.O. Berdahl, & P.J. Gumport (Eds.), *American Higher Education in the Twenty-First Century: Social, Political and Economic Challenges* (2nd ed., pp. 115–160). Baltimore, MD: Johns Hopkins University Press.

6

SUNY Seamless Transfer Policy and Shared Governance

Elizabeth L. Bringsjord, Daniel J. Knox, David Lavallee, and Kenneth P. O'Brien*

On December 17, 2012, SUNY's Board of Trustees passed a resolution on Seamless Transfer, which was the latest in a long line of Board actions affirming and reaffirming SUNY's commitment to seamless transfer policy. The resolution represented a major shift—from a conceptual agreement on the importance of seamless transfer to the creation of the systemic infrastructure to implement this critical initiative. This chapter traces the evolution of SUNY's Seamless Transfer policy from development through current implementation, with a particular focus on the role of shared governance in the process.

Introduction

When the SUNY Board of Trustees passed a resolution on Seamless Transfer on December 17, 2012, it was but the latest in a long line of Board actions affirming and reaffirming SUNY's commitment to seamless transfer policy. In fact, the foundation of the SUNY system, as it had been devised

---

*The four co-authors have been active "participant observers" in the recent steps toward creating a seamless transfer system for SUNY. Each, at different stages, has been deeply engaged in the generation of and implementation of transfer policy at both the campus and system-wide levels. Our contribution is written from a shared point of view, our individual and collective experience, and from the distinct canons of our very different academic disciplines.

in the late 1940s, included the expectation that students could transfer from one institution to another. For example, the Temporary Commission on the Need for a State University's 1948 report called for a network of community colleges that, in addition to technical and vocational training, would provide the general education curricula that would enable students to transfer to baccalaureate programs.[1]

This vision, however, was not easily achieved; in fact, it proved highly elusive. In the more than 5 decades between the 1948 Report and the 2012 resolution, SUNY Boards had passed at least six resolutions reaffirming the basic policy of "seamless transfer" that had been was one of the foundational elements for New York's system of public higher education. Despite differences in wording, this series of resolutions provided both evidence of a consistent policy commitment and, given the need for frequent restatement, a failure of practice.

As noted in Marjorie Lavin's 1986 report, "Current Issues in Transfer and Articulation," part of the failure lay in the tradition of each campus (or department) faculty having curricular authority, which they jealously guarded.[2] Because of these idiosyncrasies, each of SUNY's state-operated campuses (those offering baccalaureate and graduate degrees) largely determined their own governance structure, co-existing only as a decentralized "confederation" of campuses. The governance of SUNY's 30 community colleges was even looser, as each campus administration reported to its own Board of Trustees, negotiated its own union contracts, and within general SUNY and New York State Education Department (NYSED) rules, wrote its own curricula.

Regarding transfer credits, SUNY's decentralized structure effectively meant that faculty in the state-operated campuses acted much like their colleagues at similar institutions across the country, reserving to themselves the right to pass judgment on the acceptability of credits earned in individual courses. The system provided few checks and balances against the arbitrary exercise of that power by faculty. On many campuses, for example, a department chairperson evaluated incoming transfer courses, and a change of chairperson might mean a change in how particular courses were evaluated. These variances in interpretation resulted in a lack of consistency in transfer credit evaluations between campuses and even within the same department over time.

Community college faculty also had great latitude to craft their own curricula, based on their own analysis of effective program design. As a result, the largest SUNY community colleges often offered courses covering topics that were traditionally included in the last 2 years of an academic major in a 4-year baccalaureate degree. In some cases, the identical textbook was used at both campuses for the courses in question—introductory level and upper level. Caught between the demands and prerogatives of competing faculty interests were the students, who frequently found themselves losing credit (not to mention money spent) for work they had completed successfully.

What follows is our collective view of how the SUNY system, between 1998 and 2014, brought policy and practice into closer alignment. And, unlike the experience elsewhere in the country with public systems of higher education, faculty authority was maintained over the curriculum.

SUNY-GER, December 1998

In December 1998, the Board of Trustees passed a resolution that established a system-wide set of General Education Requirements (SUNY-GER). From the start, SUNY-GER was strongly opposed by the faculty and professional staff governance bodies of the university and its campuses. It was criticized for both its content (which was viewed as consistent with more conservative forces battling the larger "culture wars"[3]) and the means of its creation: an imposition by the Board without the active engagement of faculty governance.

Faculty governance groups throughout the system considered the imposition of SUNY-GER to be a clear violation of the American Association of University Professor (AAUP)'s 1966 "Statement on Shared Governance," which had identified the curriculum as a major area of faculty authority. Fortunately, significant efforts by faculty governance and the SUNY Office of the Provost led to an approach that put faculty at the core of policy implementation. After an initial period of faculty resistance, the Provost Office organized system-wide advisory groups; its first incarnation (1998–2000) was the Provost's Task Force on General Education, which was succeeded by the Provost's Advisory Committee on General Education (PACGE). The PACGE played a critical role by engaging faculty from across the system to evaluate campus programs and courses.

In the next 2 years (2000–2002), the implementation of the SUNY-GER devolved to the campuses, which had submitted detailed implementation plans. These plans included great specificity and standardization of approach, with the expectation that identified courses would meet the designated learning objectives for each of the 12 categories.[4]

One of the ongoing problems with SUNY-GER was its differential sector implementation. SUNY's 64 campuses are grouped into four sectors by institution type: doctoral, comprehensive (master's) colleges, community colleges, and technology colleges. In terms of undergraduate academic programs, the principle difference between the sectors is that doctoral and comprehensive colleges offer bachelor's degree programs, while community colleges offer associate degree programs; technology colleges offer both bachelor's and associate degree programs. The SUNY-GER elements became a requirement for bachelor's degrees (30 credits in 10 specified content areas), while the system's community colleges agreed to require 21 credits in 7 of the 10 areas within associate degrees. In practice, however, associate programs often met the letter of the agreement by advisement rather than changes in degree requirements. This misalignment of curricula between sectors continued to create problems for students who transferred.

As part of SUNY-GER implementation, faculty committees worked with the SUNY Office of the Provost to develop a list of courses that would be transferrable among SUNY's campuses to fulfill general education requirements. And by providing both a *list* of courses from all sectors within SUNY, and an *on-going process* that modeled faculty-administration collaboration, the implementation allowed the university community to transcend the issues that first plagued the initiative and move transfer policy forward.[5] In the same period, Provost Peter Salins convened the General Education Assessment Review Group (GEAR) to develop the guidelines for assessing the campus programs in light of the new requirements.

Campus policies varied, but one way of looking at the result was that a system-wide faculty process had displaced the autonomous determination of transfer credit by individual faculty or departments for general education courses. In 2002, PACGE responsibility for course review was transferred to the Office of the Provost at System Administration. To maintain course information, SUNY created a centrally maintained database and campus registrars developed a General Education Transcript Addendum (GETA) to identify both the appropriate transfer credit and the requirements those credits satisfied. Although the database was challenging to create, and initially contained some errors, diligent review and correction resulted in it serving as an increasingly valuable resource for the system. More than any specific outcome, the collaborative *process* that evolved provided a model of shared governance that would later prove important to furthering seamless transfer.

In 2002, SUNY undertook another significant initiative to address the transfer of credits with the creation of the Teacher Education Transfer Template (TETT). Eleven baccalaureate campuses and 17 community colleges participated in matching their courses to the categories created for the template. Composed of staff from the Office of the Provost, campus administrators (David Lavallee, Provost at SUNY New Paltz, chaired the group), and faculty leadership, the TETT group identified a core curriculum and created new advisement tools, which significantly aided students who began their studies on one campus and finished their degrees on another.[6]

The Power of Students: the New York State Commission on Higher Education

When Governor Eliot Spitzer charged the newly appointed New York State Commission on Higher Education in 2007, with particular focus on the public systems (CUNY and SUNY), he included a student as a member of the Commission: Donald Boyce, the President of the SUNY Student Assembly.[7] When Mr. Boyce had transferred from a SUNY community college to a baccalaureate campus, the receiving campus made him repeat a course in which he had already earned an A. None too pleased, he made certain that the other members of the Commission were aware of the possible pitfalls of the SUNY transfer process. They listened; they heard his comments within the context of other anecdotal evidence of transfer problems. Then they acted. Following a highly critical discussion of transfer in the public systems, the Commission recommended that "the SUNY and CUNY Boards take steps to strengthen course and program articulation and transfer by 2011–12."[8]

Under new pressure from the Commission, and with the longstanding commitment to seamless transfer, the Board charged then-SUNY Provost Risa Palm to address the problem. In a distinct departure from the process employed a decade earlier with the SUNY-GER, the Office of the Provost immediately engaged faculty governance in organizing the Joint Committee on Transfer and Articulation, which was co-chaired by the governance leaders of the two system-wide faculty governance organizations: the Faculty Council of Community Colleges and the University Faculty Senate. This committee's membership included a majority of faculty who were selected by their respective governance bodies, several chief academic officers, campus administrators responsible for transfer policy, and provost office staff. After a careful examination of existing policies and practices, the Joint Committee recommended stronger transfer and articulation policies that for the first time would guarantee that courses normally taken in the first 2 years of a major would be accepted into the major requirements at other SUNY institutions. To ensure campus compliance, two sets of appeals processes were mandated, one initiated by a campus and the other initiated by a student. How many, and which, courses would be identified, however, was not yet resolved.

The Joint Committee's resolution was supported by the provost and both the Faculty Council of Community Colleges and the University Faculty Senate, which led to a formal endorsement by the SUNY Board of Trustees in November 2009. In addition to reaffirming the transfer principles set forth in an earlier Board resolution (#90-196), the 2009 resolution demonstrated an increased interest in expanding access to college by aligning P–12 schools with higher education.

The Zimpher–Lavallee Years, June 2009–July 2013

While a policy framework to support the transfer of credits earned in both general education and the foundational courses in a major, the curricula across SUNY campuses did not necessarily align. As described in the previous section, general education implementation differed by sector, and lower-division courses in the major often differed as well—even within the same disciplines. Consequently, students could often transfer credits successfully, only to discover that in some cases the credits did not easily fit into the sequence needed at their new institution. Therefore, significant work remained to align both general education requirements and the courses in the major, discipline by discipline, across the SUNY system.

At the beginning of her tenure in June 2009 the new Chancellor, Nancy Zimpher, received a clear mandate from the Board of Trustees to finally make student transfer "seamless" across all SUNY. In David Lavallee, who she recommended as Interim System Provost, she had found a partner who was both experienced with SUNY transfer issues and committed to the goal of seamless transfer. And Provost Lavallee had two faculty governance leaders elected in May 2009 who had previously worked with him on Joint Transfer Committee. The evolving working relationship among them was furthered by the appointment of Associate Provost and Vice Chancellor for Academic Programs and Planning Elizabeth Bringsjord to the Executive Committee of the University Faculty Senate. While they did not always agree on particular issues, they shared an understanding of the thornier issues of transfer across SUNY's numerous campuses and a willingness to address them.

To foster student mobility, the administration successfully presented a second Board of Trustees resolution in early 2010. This resolution established principles and goals for transfer of the courses typically taken in the first 2 years of a baccalaureate program, and it significantly enhanced flexibility in SUNY-GER by reducing the number of required academic areas from 10 to 7, while retaining the requirement of a total of 30 credits. At a minimum, all campus programs would have to meet the learning outcomes in mathematics and basic communication, as well as at least five of the other eight academic areas. This significant change in SUNY-GER recognized the limitations of the many smaller community colleges had in offering course(s) in all 10 content categories. At the same time, it allowed campuses the choice of either adopting the new flexible standard or continuing to require all 10 GE areas as they had for a decade.

Disciplinary Transfer Paths—1.0

Very early in his tenure, Provost Lavallee initiated a process aimed at developing disciplinary transfer paths, each of which would identify a number of core courses—typically four to six—that are most commonly taken in the first 2 years of an academic major. Once identified, these were to have ready transferability across all of SUNY's undergraduate programs. The critical question was, who would decide which courses would be identified for a major?

The process by which the courses were identified took approximately 12 months to complete, with the first phase of the project focusing on the most popular transfer majors (covering roughly 90% of transfer students). Campus chief academic officers, in consultation with department chairs or other lead faculty in each discipline, recommended faculty who were asked to serve on more than 30 "discipline-specific" committees. More than 400 faculty members, representing every SUNY sector and institution, were engaged in discipline-specific committee meetings designed to (1) identify specific foundational courses for their majors and (2) draft generic course descriptions for each of the courses. Most final course descriptors were similar in length to typical course catalog descriptions, but there was variation depending on the discipline. Overall, faculty found that lower-division coursework in many disciplines covered similar knowledge and skills across campuses.

Each committee included at least eight members of the teaching faculty, four each from 2- and 4-year campuses, beginning with the campuses that sent and/or received the greatest number of transfer students. Importantly, every SUNY campus had representation somewhere in the mix of discipline-specific committees. To design the contents of the Transfer Path, committees examined course and section data at 4-year campuses taken by students with 60 or fewer credits. This, rather than an examination of comparable course numbering, proved to the best strategy, since faculty discovered that some courses that carried a 300 number were actually populated by lower-division students. Course numbering in SUNY, as in almost all other state systems, is very inconsistent, which is why some other state systems have moved to a common course numbering system.

In some disciplines, such as communications, nursing, and social work, no typical patterns of coursework were apparent. In these cases, the disciplinary committee members engaged in discussions to identify courses in the major that would cover the knowledge and skills students need to complete in the first 2 years of full-time study in order successfully complete a bachelor's degree in an additional 2 years of full-time study. Disciplinary committees verified typical course lists by titles, and defined the content required for those courses by crafting generic course descriptions for each course. Together, the course lists and generic descriptions made up the content of each discipline's Transfer Path.

Each committee chair led the discussions and determined when the group had reached consensus on its recommendations. For majors that required significant discussion regarding course lists, the SUNY Provost designated an assistant or associate provost from his office to moderate discussions until the group reached a consensus on course lists, which would then allow a smaller group to work out the specific language of the course descriptions.

Once the Transfer Paths were established, each campus then mapped specific courses within their local programs to the generic Transfer Path courses, discipline by discipline. At the end of this process, 37 Transfer Paths had been completed in the most popular transfer disciplines, which accounted for over 95% of all transfer students within the SUNY system. When the proposed course lists and content descriptors were "finalized" by the faculty groups, campuses were notified through their Chief Academic Officers and given an additional 10 months to request changes. In fact, few campuses or programs responded during the extended comment period, and the requested revisions identified seven descriptors rather than courses that needed to change. The original discipline-specific committees discussed the suggestions; in nearly all cases, the suggestions were incorporated, and the descriptors were modified accordingly.

Finally, information about general education courses and requirements, as well as the database of Transfer Path courses, became available to both students and campus personnel through announcements to Chief Academic Officers, with copies to appropriate stakeholders. Notices were posted on the SUNY transfer website as newly available web-based transfer planning tools became available. Using the Transfer Path web platform, students and advisors could, for the first time, identify and plan coursework that would prepare students for successful study at multiple SUNY campuses.

The last point is critically important, since by 2010 transfer patterns had become more complicated than in previous decades. In practice, students increasingly moved "omni-directionally," which made every campus potentially both a sending and receiving institution. In New York, much like the rest of the country, more and more students were obtaining their bachelor's degrees from institutions other than that where they began their post-secondary studies. Transfer was no longer a matter of students moving from community colleges to bachelor's programs. Currently, such ("traditional") transfer accounts for slightly less than half of all SUNY transfers, while approximately one third transfer into community colleges, and the remainder transfer "laterally" from one 4-year campus to another. Within this new reality, aligning curricula across sectors is essential to support transfer student success.

The Board of Trustees Resolution of December 2012

In her January 2012 State of University address, Chancellor Zimpher laid out plans to drill down on core infrastructure issues, including "Seamless Transfer" (available online at https://www.suny.edu/about/leadership/chancellor-nancy-l-zimpher/speeches—presentations). The Chancellor gave an update on the progress to date on Seamless Transfer, once again emphasizing SUNY's commitment to helping students earn their degrees on time, whether they were choosing to continue their education or to start their careers. She highlighted the new mobility website and other transfer tools, and reiterated the 2010 Board of Trustees policy allowing transfer of 12 or more credits in the Transfer Pathway majors. She also praised the FCCC and UFS for their partnership in building the system for the complete transfer of AA and AS degrees to satisfy general education requirements at 4-year institutions. Calling it *"systemness* at work," the Chancellor hailed the progress as one critical part of SUNY's commitment to college completion.

The transfer issue was being re-conceptualized, both within SUNY and across the nation, not simply as the way in which students could begin at one institution (with more and more beginning their post-secondary work at community colleges), but also as an integral part of the "Access to Success" agenda. The administration worked with faculty governance at each step, though not always smoothly and certainly not always in agreement. In December 2012, the SUNY Board of Trustees passed its "Seamless Transfer Requirements" policy, a resolution that was designed to be the final word on seamless transfer across the SUNY system. This resolution represented a critical shift for the Board, from statements of principle about the importance of seamless transfer to the creation of the systemic infrastructure and technology needed to implement workable procedures and practice.

In fact, it did a good deal more. Citing SUNY's ongoing commitment to both academic excellence and seamless transfer, the resolution clarified curricular expectations in the following areas:

- "The first two years of full-time study of an undergraduate program leading to an A.A., A.S., or bachelor's degree will be designed to include: (1) the SUNY General Education Require-ment, with seven of ten areas and, 30 credits; and (2) a sufficient number of foundational major courses, as well as associated cognate courses for a bachelor's degree to be completed in two additional years of full-time study. Waivers will be approved for programs with exceptional requirements."

- "Each SUNY campus will grant credit to transfer students for successfully completing, as defined, at any SUNY campus: (1) SUNY General Education Requirement courses; and (2) transfer path foundational major courses, as well as associated cognate courses."

- "Each SUNY campus will limit its degree requirements to 64 credits for A.A., A.S., and A.A.S. degrees, and 126 credits for bachelor's degrees, unless there is a compelling justification for additional credits, and ensure that local graduation require-ments that exceed the SUNY General Education Requirement do not cause a student to exceed those credit limits."

In addition, campuses, with support from the SUNY Provost, were "to develop opportunities for students to successfully complete transfer path courses at other SUNY campuses when such courses were not offered at their home campus."[9] The last point referred to SUNY's new initiative in distance education, Open SUNY, which promised to more easily permit a student who was matriculating at one SUNY campus to register for courses offered by another.

The working relationship among the governance organizations began to break apart with this resolution, when it became apparent that the greatest curricular changes would fall on the community colleges, a realization that led the FCCC leadership to oppose the resolution strongly. The leadership of the University Faculty Senate, on the other hand, still supported both the concept of seamless transfer and the requirements of the resolution, offering assurances that its faculty and their programs would create pathways that would enable students who transferred with either an AA or AS degree, which now included a completed SUNY GER and disciplinary transfer path, to finish their degree program with 2 additional years of full-time study.

Finally, while a comprehensive review of national transfer policy is beyond the scope of this chapter, it is worth noting that SUNY's Seamless Transfer policy can be seen as part of a trend within the higher education sector to enact policies designed to support transfer students. Historically, the most common policies to address the challenges faced by transfer students have involved either encouraging voluntary or requiring mandatory articulation agreements between individual institutions or across public systems of higher education.[10] However, there is little evidence that, in and of themselves, articulation agreements are effective in supporting transfer student success.[11] As a response, as seen in the SUNY's Seamless Transfer initiative, some policymakers have begun to mandate more extensive changes to academic programs that regulate not only the acceptance of credit between institutions, but the actual content required in programs taken prior to transfer. In this way, advising and information gathering on the part of students are de-emphasized as curricular alignment ensures that transferrable coursework is embedded in academic programs.

System-wide general education programs are a notable policy development of this type that aim to address curricular alignment between institutions. To take a recent example, in 2004, the Tennessee Board of Regents system adopted a fully transferable general education core consisting of 41 credits in six subject areas or clusters. In 2010, this transferable core was extended to the University of Tennessee system as well. Though limited, recent research suggests that the approach is promising as it relates to student outcomes. Gorbunov, Doyle, and Wright examined the Tennessee general education core and demonstrated that completion of the entire core, or its individual components, at a 2-year institution led to increased graduation rates, increased GPAs, and decreased time to degree among transfer students.[12]

In addition to general education requirements across disciplines, recent policy efforts have also included aligning requirements within the major as well, as SUNY has done via its Transfer Paths. Aligning lower-and upper-division requirements across sectors and institutions provides students with clear guidance for transferring to bachelor degree programs. Ideally, this strategy better prepares students for upper-division coursework, while minimizing the number of credits lost in transfer. In addition, requiring students to complete a sequence of courses within a discipline encourages students to enter a specific field of study. Academic research shows that students entering a field of study (defined by taking three or more courses within an area of study) within the first 2 years are much more likely to attain a credential or transfer than students who do not complete these courses or complete them later in their college career.[13]

This strategy of identifying, aligning, and, in some cases, mandating common major requirements across sectors has been gaining traction within public higher education systems. For example, in Ohio, under directives from the state legislature, the Board of Regents established an initiative to develop "Transfer Assurance Guides" (TAGS) that identify courses that are guaranteed to satisfy program requirements in a given major across all sectors.[14] As of 2012, faculty groups had developed 42 TAGS in eight disciplines, which are mapped to over 3,500 approved individual courses across the state. In addition to SUNY's Seamless Transfer and Ohio's TAGS, similar initiatives have been developed or are underway in California, the City University of New York, Florida, Massachusetts, Tennessee, Texas, and Washington State. As with the general education programs, policymakers have seen the need to provide more structure and alignment within academic majors.

Excess credits have also begun to receive attention by policy makers—both those taken through student choice and, as with SUNY's policy, those embedded within academic program requirements. Several states and systems have begun to examine degree requirements at a system- or institution-level. Florida, Indiana, Louisiana, Minnesota, North Carolina, CUNY, and Texas have adopted policies that regulate the number of required credits in academic programs.[15] Of these states, North Carolina and Texas have adopted policies that both financially penalize students for excess credits taken and limit required program credits.

In sum, the arc of policies aimed at supporting transfer students in publicly supported system of higher education has moved from institutional level articulation agreements to more system-wide alignment of curricula in general education and in the major as well limitations in the number of credit hours required in academic programs. This policy trajectory can be seen as moving from the general strategy of encouraging articulation agreements between institutions to more particular requirements involving elements of individual academic programs. As has been the case with SUNY, policies have increasingly begun to regulate the content and structure of the first 2 years of academic programs in order to better align curricula between institutions with the final goal of supporting transfer student success.

Policy Implementation:
The Memorandum to Presidents

At SUNY, policy is implemented and guided through "Memoranda to Presidents" (MTPs), which address specific implementation issues such as communication, oversight, timelines, and assessment of the policy. Following the passage of the SUNY Board of Trustees' Resolution on December 17, 2012, the Office of the Provost began to develop the MTP, a process that spanned nearly 6 months. The seamless transfer policy had the potential to result in curricular revisions to many academic programs across SUNY; therefore, significant care had to be taken, to make certain that the implementation process was comprehensive. It had to adhere to both SUNY and New York State regulations, address accreditation needs across different disciplines, and finally, respect local campus culture. In addition, the implementation had to use a highly effective and organized communications stream, and ultimately seek/collect feedback that had the potential to be specific, timely, effective, and useful.

Initial drafts of the MTP were vetted by the staff in the Office of the Provost, and then distributed to a number of groups via email for feedback. Among the stakeholder groups, in addition to the Student Mobility Steering Committee, were campus Presidents, Chief Academic Officers, Chief Enrollment Officers, Registrars and Business officers, and faculty leadership from the 4-year and 2-year sectors (the President of the University Faculty Senate and the President of the Faculty Council of

Community Colleges, respectively). These groups were selected to receive the communication directly because of their leadership positions and their necessary roles in implementing the policy.

The email transmittals provided a brief overview of the purpose and development of the Seamless Transfer resolution, and a link to the draft MTP, which had been posted on a public SUNY webpage. Stakeholders were asked to review the draft MTP and submit feedback via email to a staff member in the Office of the Provost by April 19, 2013. Each campus and group was entrusted to collect and organize responses to the MTP under the direction of campus leadership and according to their local shared governance procedures.

From March 29 to April 19, 2013, feedback came in to the SUNY Office of the Provost from a variety of respondents, including campus administrative leaders, faculty governance bodies on the campus and system levels, and the Student Mobility Steering Committee (SMSC).[16] The SMSC submitted a formal set of 17 recommendations for revision. The SUNY Provost and senior staff then reviewed the summary of comments, organized by issues, and made final revisions to the MTP. The revision process emphasized achieving a balance between respect for local campuses (culture and autonomy) and maximizing the opportunities for transfer student success.

The final version of the MTP was published on June 13, 2013, and distributed widely across the system to the relevant groups and offices. Campuses faced a process requiring three steps in order to meet the implementation date of Fall 2015, beginning with an initial scan of programs to be completed by January 31, 2014 to determine the scope of work to be completed in the following two phases. Phase II identified and completed "minor" program revisions, which were defined as those that did not need approval from either the SUNY system administration or the NYS Department of Education. Essentially, campuses could complete these revisions locally by following local governance procedures for changing curricula. Phase III, the final phase, identified the programs that required "major revisions" to bring them into alignment with the transfer paths. These would require approval from entities outside the campus. With the publication of the MTP and its included timeline, the structure was created to implement one of the most extensive policy initiatives in SUNY's history.

When Provost David Lavallee retired in July 2013, it appeared that he had led the extraordinary effort that had created what other public systems could not: a Board- and administration-driven, but faculty-designated, set of transfer paths for nearly 40 academic disciplines. This achievement was tightly integrated into other SUNY initiatives, including Access to Success (A2S), Open SUNY, and degree completion at every level.

Fall 2014: Transfer Path Faculty Review

However, it soon became apparent that a crisis of shared governance threatened to disrupt and delay the planned implementation of Seamless Transfer. Once they returned for classes in the fall, faculty on campuses began to grasp the scope of the changes involved. The Transfer Paths, in particular, became a source of concern. The fact that the Transfer Paths completed by 2011 involved the participation of over 400 SUNY faculty members and included an extensive vetting period by the campuses was overlooked by many faculty members who had not directly been part of the process. Even those directly involved claimed they had been participating in the creation of *recommended* curricular paths, not curricular *requirements* for every program in SUNY.

Part of the faculty concern had been sparked by the faculty union's (UUP's) campaign against what it termed the "Canned Curriculum," a campaign that dramatized the recognition that the paths were not simply "recommendations" that supported transfer. In fact, the mandatory nature of the paths came as a surprise to many faculty members who had carefully read the language of the SUNY transfer website that implied they were recommendations for students and advisors. Seen in this light, many of the faculty who were examining the paths for their disciplines for the first time demanded that they should be reviewed and, if necessary, revised, *before* any curricular revisions could be made.

Faculty governance leadership, including the new President of the University Faculty Senate and the continuing President of the Faculty Council of Community Colleges, responded to the concerns from their constituents. The Faculty Council of Community Colleges took the lead against specific elements of the new policy, particularly the inclusion of the AOS and AAS degrees under the 64-credit cap for programs. At its Fall meeting, the organization passed a "Resolution in Opposition to a *De Facto* Core Curriculum" that called for the suspension of the implementation of the Board's Resolution,[17] a resolution that was supported in principle by the UFS at its plenary meeting later in the month.

Interim Provost Elizabeth Bringsjord, who had been responding to a growing number of complaints about the implementation of the policy since midsummer, quickly entered into serious discussions with the leaders of both governance organizations.[18] Out of these discussions emerged an imaginative, thorough faculty review process for each of the paths. Ultimately, this review process would engage more than 1,200 faculty members from across the SUNY system.

The proposed review would be confined to the contents of the Transfer Paths and would exclude both SUNY-GER or credit caps (64 credits for associate degrees and 126 credits for bachelor's degrees) issues. Newly empanelled disciplinary committees with representation from each campus offering a program in the discipline would review the substance of the specific courses in each path. By mid-November, every one of the major constituencies—as represented by the governance organizations, the academic administration of both the campuses and the System, and the SUNY Board of Trustees—had agreed to support the new process, one that would use technology to engage more than a thousand members of the faculty in discussion groups.

Winter–Spring 2015: Disciplinary Transfer Paths 2.0

One of the principal criticisms by SUNY faculty governance of the initial Transfer Path process was that it was not inclusive enough. Campuses with the greatest numbers of transfer students were included, but some campuses with programs in particular disciplines had not been invited to the table. To address this concern, the Office of the Provost, in consultation with faculty governance leaders and campus chief academic officers, planned to invite one faculty discipline-specific representative to participate in discussions from each SUNY campus that offered programs in that discipline. Accommodating the more inclusive model of shared governance in the disciplines required expanding faculty participation in the Transfer Path discussions far beyond what had been done previously, but the implementation date for the initiative remained Fall 2015.

However, it was immediately understood that the necessary size of the groups, the distances between campuses, and the time limits for faculty review posed genuine constraints on effective faculty review and revision of the paths. The task was daunting: How could the administrators in the Office of the Provost facilitate faculty discussions of curricula with potentially over a thousand SUNY faculty across 64 campuses? And how could these challenging dialogues reach full resolution, so that the entire project could be completed within 4 months?

Given the constraints, the Office of the Provost decided to use the online tools of the recently developed "SUNY Learning Commons" (SLC) to facilitate the faculty transfer path discussions. The SLC was launched in 2013 to support the formation of online communities of interest and practice. The website, built on open source Wordpress technology, offers password-protected access with a suite of online tools, including discussion boards, file sharing, wikis, and blogs. While the SLC satisfied the communication requirements of the project, the website itself was relatively unproven. Nevertheless, given the tight deadlines for implementing the policy, the SLC presented the best technology solution available, and the only conceivable way to overcome the barriers to timely completion of the entire agenda.

The discussions were organized with each disciplinary group being led by two faculty co-moderators, one each from a 2-year and 4-year campus. The role of the faculty moderators was to facilitate online discussions during the discussion period and provide a written summary of the advisory group's recommendations to the Office of the Provost of any changes that needed to be made to the Transfer Paths. The goal of the discussions was specific and clear: examine, discuss, and revise, if necessary, the specific disciplinary path for the first 2 years of study in the discipline. But there was a significant change from the original conception of the path. Rather than a strict focus on "courses," the participants were encouraged to think in terms of areas of knowledge, a small change, but one that would allow for significant variation within programs, yet achieve the goal of having all students acquire the knowledge and skills necessary for subsequent success in their chosen academic majors.

Within the discussion forum, "topics" were set up to help prompt and organize the faculty discussions. After they introduced themselves to one another and had an opportunity to talk about the process itself, they were to think in terms of:

- *The essentials.* Faculty members were asked to identify the essentials for students to complete by the end of their fourth full-time semester (2 years of full-time study).

- *Deletions.* The third topic, "Suggested Deletions," asked this question: "Are there any courses or content areas in the current transfer path that are not essential for students to complete by their fourth full-time semester?"

- *Additions.* The fourth topic, "Suggested Additions," posed this question: "Are there any courses or content areas that are essential to students completing by their fourth full-time semester that are missing from the current transfer path and need to be added?"

- *Additional Comments.* A final topic, "Additional Comments," was included for discussion that did not fit within any of the other threads.

These topics were designed to focus the group and keep the discussions targeted on possible revisions to the Transfer Path under review. However, participants were not limited to these discussion topics; any member of the group could start new topic threads. There were no limitations placed on participant contributions. In addition, the forum allowed each message to include file attachments. Participants could also upload files to shared folders within the "documents" tool.

To gather the contact information of faculty representatives, a request was emailed in December 2014 to campus Chief Academic Officers with an Excel file listing the Transfer Paths by discipline. Working through local shared governance procedures, campuses nominated one faculty representative for each Transfer Path discipline in which they offered academic programs. Often, these individuals were serving as department chairs, but the nominations extended to other faculty members as well. In addition, each campus was asked to select three disciplines in which they would like their representatives to serve as faculty moderators of the discussion groups. Moderators were chosen by system administration staff with consideration given to campus preference, coverage of the disciplines, and ensuring that each campus, where possible, had faculty in leadership roles.

The response was almost overwhelming. By early January 2014, campuses had submitted the names of 1,248 faculty representatives to participate in 37 disciplinary groups. Groups ranged in size from 10 representatives (Technology Education) to 55 representatives (Business), with an average group size of 35 representatives. Prior to the launch of the discussions, the faculty moderators were sent an introductory email communication containing background and instructional documents, and an invitation to a separate online discussion group within the SLC designed specifically for faculty moderators. In addition, a group conference call was held with the SUNY Interim Provost Elizabeth Bringsjord and Provost Office staff to answer questions about the Transfer Path review process.

The 2014 Transfer Path Faculty Review discussions were officially launched on January 17, 2014. Invitations were sent via email to 1,248 faculty representatives to join online discussion groups in their academic disciplines. The email contained a link to a webpage that hosted instructions, reference materials, and directions for accessing technical assistance. For technical reasons involving data security, each representative was sent an additional email with an invitation to participate in their discussion group in the SLC.

To be sure, technical problems plagued the process, especially at the beginning. For example, some campus email filter settings routed several email invitations directly to SPAM folders. Other users also had difficulty creating accounts, managing login credentials, navigating the SLC to find their groups, accessing the groups, and using the online tools. To assist faculty with technical issues, a Help Desk was established for the project. It was staffed by four individuals, who were available for phone and email support during business hours. A ticketing system was used to track issues and resolutions as they were submitted to the Help Desk, with the result that 225 tickets were submitted to the Help Desk and resolved during the project, with 44% of these submitted in the first 2 weeks. These data show the degree to which faculty representatives were willing to persist and work through technical issues, in order to participate in the disciplinary discussions.

Once faculty representatives created accounts, and successfully logged in to their discipline-specific groups in the SLC, they were brought to a welcome screen, containing notes and brief instructions. While there are several collaborative tools available within the SLC, the Transfer Path project primarily used the threaded discussion features of the "forum" and the document-sharing capabilities of the "documents" tool.

Overall, participation was high, though unevenly distributed. From January 17 through March 31, 2014 (the formal end of the discussion period), there were 2,772 individual posts to the discussion forum in 308 topic threads. Excluding the four fixed topic threads per group, as described above, representatives created 164 new topic threads during this period. The average number of posts per group was 77, with mathematics (367), biology (222), English (205), history (185), psychology (175), and business (171) among the most active discussion groups. Conversely, nutrition science (10), music industry (9), hospitality management (6), and technology education (1) had almost no discussion activity, perhaps a function of the small size of these groups. None was larger than 12.

In addition to the online activities, faculty moderators could request email surveys of the faculty discussion groups via Survey Monkey. Over the course of the project, 15 separate surveys were conducted in 12 disciplines (communication and computer science held multiple surveys), with 310 total responses. These are impressive response levels, given the time and technical constraints faced by the faculty participants.

While a detailed analysis of the surveys is beyond the scope of this chapter, they were most useful in determining the degree of consensus regarding specific issues identified in the discussions.

For example, Computer Science was an especially challenging discipline in which to achieve consensus. In fact, a faculty committee was convened during the first round of transfer path discussions in 2009–2010, and after the group could not come to agreement, it was disbanded. This time, participation was expanded from 10 to 43 campuses. Initially, many faculty members argued that there was little to no commonality regarding what should be taught in the introductory sequence of computer science courses (commonly referred to as Computer Science I, Computer Science II, and Data Structures). But, after the group used a survey to benchmark each campus's introductory courses against the curriculum advanced by their national disciplinary group, a high degree of consensus became apparent.[19] The learning outcomes used in the process later served as the basis for faculty representatives to craft course descriptions. While this was a laborious process, in the end the group was able to come to a consensus, and the SUNY Computer Science Transfer Pathways was completed.[20]

Following several months of electronic "discussion," the faculty co-moderators summarized the recommendations and submitted the proposed revisions of the transfer paths in a standardized document that became the disciplinary group's "Recommendations to the Provost." This document summarized the discussion, described any proposed changes to the transfer path, and provided explanatory notes that identified any deviations that were important for students and their advisors to be aware of. The summary included an overview of participation patterns, challenges, areas of disagreement, and resolutions. It concluded with any concerns with implementing the transfer path.

- Out of the 37 disciplinary groups, 32 submitted recommendations for revisions to their respective transfer paths.

- There were 232 total recommended revisions, including 22 tracks added to disciplines, 101 courses added, 55 courses deleted, 10 course title changes, 26 course descriptors created, and 18 advising notes added to the transfer paths.

The recommended revision documents were then posted in a password-protected webpage, and campus administrators and disciplinary faculty across the system were invited to review these summaries and provide feedback to the Office of the Provost before final approval. The purpose of this comment period was for additional campus administrators and faculty to identify courses or content areas that may be problematic to offer on their campus, and to note other concerns and questions regarding implementation. Due to the tight implementation deadlines, the comment period was short, extending from April 4 through April 14, 2014.

After compiling and reviewing the campus comments, the SUNY Provost and staff reviewed the recommended revisions to the Transfer Paths submitted by the faculty disciplinary groups. Of the 232 recommended revisions, 219 (94%) were approved. A relatively small number of the proposed revisions needed additional clarification to improve guidance for transfer students, while a very small number did not achieve the policy goals of the Seamless Transfer initiative.

For example, in the case of one discipline, the faculty did not specify any required courses, choosing instead to list any of four courses as recommended (optional). This poses an obvious problem when the goal of Seamless Transfer is for students to achieve rising junior status by the end of 2 years of full-time study, and in this case, the solution was clear: Students needed to choose any three of the four. The rationale for the change? While the number of courses required to achieve rising junior status varies widely by discipline, research has shown that students who completed at least three courses in a discipline in their first 2 years were much more likely to succeed in the major.[21] Therefore, the Office of the Provost did not approve any recommended revisions that did not specify at least three required courses.

On May 1, 2014, the Provost's Office posted the final versions of the approved Transfer Paths online for campus administrators and faculty and sent an email that gave an overview of the new requirements. More work remained: to update and publish the Transfer Paths website for students; to rebuild and remap the database of transfer path courses; and to revise academic programs by campuses to reflect both the policies of the Board of Trustees and the content of the Transfer Paths. Although this work required some adjustments within the implementation timelines specified in the MTP, the Transfer Path discussion project was completed in time to allow the final implementation goal of Fall 2015 to remain in place. A project that had looked to be nearly impossible at the outset was completed with maximum input, on time.

Lessons and Conclusions

For shared governance, several lessons can be drawn from this last phase of this project, in some ways the most innovative as it used electronic technologies that had not existed half a decade before to expand the number of faculty participants, close the geographical space, and move the project expeditiously. Other lessons include:

- **One size does not fit all.** Academic disciplines have distinctly unique cultures, and tend to have preferences in terms of communication styles and methods of collaboration. For example, some disciplinary groups, such as computer science, found email surveys useful for gathering feedback, while others, such as English, opposed using this method of communication. Therefore, *offering choices in the medium of communication is important to facilitate collaboration for faculty, both with their colleagues and administrators.*

- **Listen carefully and adjust to changing needs as discussions progress.** Although providing some structure is essential to ensure that goals for a particular project are understood, it is also important not to over-specify the process. If needed, administrators should have the flexibility to make adjustments to process on the fly, as long as the goals of the policies are being met. It can be often challenging for administrators, responsible for planning and executing shared governance projects to let go of control and trust the process. However, *listening to faculty concerns and demonstrating flexibility by making substantive changes as needed can build mutual trust and allow for compromise and consensus.*

- **Documentation is an essential component of transparency.** With complex discussions occurring over long periods of time, it can be difficult to demonstrate after the fact how degrees of consensus had been created. In the case of the transfer path discussions, the primary medium of communication—threaded online messages—provided a useful record that allowed for participants and administrators to track the ways that consensus were established. When some faculty members in the discipline-specific groups questioned the reported consensus, it was crucial that the records of online discussions remained. While other communication media, such as conference calls or in-person meetings, do not readily provide such detailed records, nonetheless *it is helpful to document and display records to participants in shared governance discussion, allowing participants, most of whom are volunteering their time, to see how their contributions are valued and included in the final outcome.*

In looking back over the longer period, almost a half-century, during which SUNY committed itself to "Seamless Transfer," several conclusions become apparent, especially as an examination of shared governance. First, this has been a process of genuinely shared governance, in which each of the major constituencies within the SUNY system played a necessary role: specifically, the numerous Boards of Trustees that adopted frequent resolutions reiterating the necessity for seamless transfer long before the issue had been part of the national discourse for publicly supported state systems; the SUNY system administrators, especially Chancellor and recent Provosts, who learned from the missteps during the SUNY-GER problems of 1999–2000 and who used great imagination and patience during the past decade to work through the difficulties of making real the Board's policy for SUNY students; the students who supported both the idea and who, when given the opportunity, raised the issue at the highest policy level; and the faculty governance groups (and unions) that worked with, and at times against, one another to create processes that would maintain faculty authority over the curriculum.

Second, several times we have referred to the problems with the SUNY-GER, both as a policy process and as a threat to shared governance. But at least one positive had emerged from that extraordinarily trying set of problems: A satisfactory solution to the implementation issues of the SUNY-GER rested on the SUNY administration ceding a good portion of the definitional control over the curricular content back to the faculty, replacing the locus of control in university-wide faculty representative groups rather than the campus-based faculty as tradition would dictate. The SUNY General Education requirements, then, in both their imposition and their implementation, strengthened the understanding of the crucial centrality of faculty to the creation and delivery of curriculum.

Finally, we believe SUNY has achieved what promises to be a unique accomplishment, a working, effective system of seamless transfer for the almost 30,000 students who move from one campus to another across SUNY's publicly supported campuses each year. And, it has been accomplished by the nation's largest university system without the legislative interference that has characterized the process for public systems in so many other states.

Notes

1. New York State. (1948). Report of the Temporary Commission on the Need for a State University New York.
2. Laving, M.W. (1986) *Current issues in transfer and articulation: Impact of general education requirements, joint admissions and service for transfer students.* A report support by the Donald M. Blinken Fellowship, Spring Semester (p. v).
3. Hartman, A. (2015). *A war for the soul of America: A history of the culture wars.* Chicago: University of Chicago Press.
4. The 12 categories include 10 content areas (Mathematics, Natural Sciences, Social Sciences, American History, Western Civilization, Other World Civilizations, Humanities, The Arts, and Foreign Languages) and two competencies (Critical Thinking and Information Management).
5. Rudnitski, R. SUNY and the promise of general education in American public higher education. *Faculty Senate Bulletin,* (Spring 2009), 14–15.
6. Memorandum to the presidents: Teacher education transfer status report, March 5, 2004. *State University of New York Master Plan, 2004–2008,* 106–108.
7. Dr. Bringsjord served as one of the SUNY staff assigned to the Commission.
8. New York State Commission on Higher Education. (2008). *Final Report, June 2008* (pp. 37–40).
9. State University of New York. (2012). Seamless transfer requirements (pp. 5–6). Retrieved from http://www.system.suny.edu/media/suny/content-assets/documents/academiic-affairs/Seamless-Transfer-Final2BOT-12-4-12.pdf
10. Ignash, J.M., & Townsend, B.K. (2000). Evaluating state-level articulation agreements according to good practice. *Community College Review, 28*(3), 1–21.
11. Anderson, G.M., Sun, J.C., & Alfonso, M. (2006). Effectiveness of statewide articulation agreements on the probability of transfer: A preliminary policy analysis. *The Review of Higher Education, 29,* 261–291.
12. Gorbunov, A., Doyle, W., & Wright, D. (2012). The effects of general education completion on transfer student success: A transcript study of Tennessee transfer students. Paper presented at the annual conference of *The Association for the Study of Higher Education.* Las Vegas, NV.
13. Jenkins, D., & Cho, S.W.C. (2012). Making the transition to four-year institutions: Academic preparation and transfer. CCRC Working Paper. *New York, Community College Research Center.*

14. Compton, P.K., et. al. (2013). Faculty determined course equivalency. In C.B. Kisker & R.L. Wagoner (Eds.), *Implementing transfer associate degrees: Perspectives from the states.* New Directions for Community Colleges. New York: Jossey-Bass.

15. SUNY Board of Trustees (2014). *SUNY's Associate in Applied Science (AAS) degree programs and Associate in Occupational Studies (AOS) degree programs* (Office of the Provost Report) (pp. 43). Albany, NY: State University of New York Board of Trustees.

16. The Student Mobility Steering Committee is advisory to the Provost.

17. Available online at http://www.fccc.suny.edu/resolutions/13_14/asa2_2013-2014_OpposeDeFactoCoreCurriculum.pdf

18. It is important to note that, while the SUNY faculty governance organizations were very involved in these discussions, the faculty union was not, as it was generally agreed that curricular matters were beyond the scope of the union's focus on the terms and conditions of professional staff employment.

19. See the Association for Computing Machinery/Institute for Electrical and Electronics Engineer (ACM/IEEE)'s Computer Science Curricula 2013 Guidelines for Undergraduate Degree Programs in Computer Science. Available online at http://www.acm.org/education/CS2013-final-report.pdf

20. A current list of SUNY's 50 Transfer Paths, including Computer Science, is available at http://www.suny.edu/attend/get-started/transfer-students/sunytransfer-paths/

21. See note 13.

7

Theorizing Open SUNY and Shared Governance

It's a Process

Tina Good

When asked to participate on the Open SUNY panel at the first SUNY Voices conference on shared governance in 2014, it seemed appropriate to discuss the Open SUNY initiative from a shared governance perspective. Indeed, the Open SUNY initiative manifested all the trappings of an initiative being implemented through a shared governance process; still, the process of implementing Open SUNY seemed to be floundering. For some reason, confusion—over (1) what Open SUNY actually was, (2) the responsibility of individual campuses in its implementation, and (3) the role of faculty and faculty governance in its development and maintenance—continued to persist.

The State University of New York (SUNY) has implemented other system-wide initiatives, so it seemed well positioned to tackle the challenge of expanding online opportunities, but a workable path to achieving the Chancellor's vision of Open SUNY seemed elusive. In order to discover the reason for what appeared to be system-wide confusion, I analyze how the beginnings of the Open SUNY initiative differed from other SUNY-wide initiatives, very specifically contrasting it with the SUNY Seamless Transfer initiative. In this chapter, I discuss how significant differences between the two initiatives can be found in the purpose and form of the authorizing board resolutions, and the processes for their development.

The lessons that can be learned from the analysis of these resolutions far exceed the initiatives themselves. A major outcome of these initiatives has been the development of multiple processes for resolution creation. These processes can either strengthen shared governance in higher education and position collaboration as a proactive means of effecting positive change within an institution, or they can undermine shared governance and threaten the institution's ability to build consensus and work toward a common goal.

Introduction

In January 2012, the Chancellor of the State University of New York (SUNY), Dr. Nancy Zimpher, announced in her State of the University Address that SUNY "would work to ensure access by developing a truly open path to accessing SUNY." It was clear from the context of her speech that the "truly open path to accessing SUNY" referred to SUNY's distance learning opportunities, in the form of a new initiative branded as "Open SUNY." Chancellor Zimpher announced that Open SUNY would launch in time for the fall 2013 semester and would have the following characteristics:

1. It would provide innovative and flexible education.

2. It would network students with faculty and peers from across the state and throughout the world and link them to the best in open educational resources.

3. There would be a combination of online courses, an expanded YouTube channel, and a newly created presence on iTunes U.

4. There would be an expansion of the SUNY Learning Network, the existing database and platform for campus-based online courses managed by SUNY System Administration.

5. There would also be a process for certifying prior work and learning experience.

This was the Chancellor's vision for Open SUNY initially, and, therefore, the beginning of the attempts to codify and implement the vision more specifically.

Unfortunately, as the months and years passed, as distance learning became online learning, as Massive Open Online Courses (MOOCs) became the newest fad in higher education, as technologies changed, as accrediting agencies tried to regulate online degrees, as public funds for higher education continued to decrease, the vision for Open SUNY became less clear to administrators and faculty at the campuses. It would be a mistake to name this confusion as resistance. While certainly resistance existed in the margins, the lack of policy, as well as the lack of a business plan, made it difficult for campuses to either support or resist the initiative in any definitive way. No doubt the rapid pace with which online learning was being transformed in higher education—and SUNY's desire to be a leader in innovation—contributed to the sense of the oft-heard phrase espoused in meeting after meeting: "We are building the plane as we're flying it."

So what is Open SUNY? The SUNY website describes it this way:

> At SUNY, we are transforming the landscape of online learning. Drawing on our rich history of innovation, we're placing the outstanding educational opportunities and talented faculty from our 64 campuses at your fingertips. . . . Open SUNY is a SUNY-wide collaboration that opens the door to world-class online-enabled learning opportunities. Open SUNY is not a new degree program or a new school; it's a seamless way for you to access the courses, degrees, professors, and rich academics of all 64 SUNY campuses flexibly—wherever and whenever you want. For the first time, SUNY is delivering its renowned high-quality education with an unprecedented breadth of tools, services, and supports designed to help you be successful. (http://open.suny.edu/about/what-is-open-suny/)

Sounds great, right? But as with any great initiative, to fall back on an old cliché, the devil is in the details. Enabling the Open SUNY vision—through both policy and infrastructure—became a real challenge for both the administrations and shared governance systems at the system and campus levels.

The Open SUNY initiative is not the first big initiative SUNY has launched. It is only one among many in just the last 15 years. Two additional major initiatives include the implementation of a system-wide SUNY General Education requirement for associate and baccalaureate degrees and the implementation of the system-wide seamless transfer mandate. All three of these prominent academic initiatives have fundamental similarities.

1. They integrally affect academic curricula and standards.

2. They seek a level of standardization across SUNY that privileges the autonomy of SUNY as a system rather than the autonomy of individual campuses within the system.

3. They seek to deal with the increasing reality that students amass credits from more than one institution, and sometimes several institutions, in order to achieve a degree.

4. Implementation of each initiative is labor intensive and tremendously bureaucratic.

5. Implementation of each initiative is authorized by the SUNY Board of Trustees.

With its history of implementing system-wide academic initiatives, SUNY should have been well positioned to implement the Chancellor's vision of Open SUNY. Yet, despite the resources and experts dedicated to the cause, confusion about the initiative was pervasive. Therefore, when I was invited to join the Open SUNY panel at the SUNY Voices first conference on shared governance, I sought to answer the following questions:

1. Why is the Open SUNY initiative floundering when SUNY has been able to implement other grand initiatives throughout the system?

2. How is Open SUNY different from other SUNY initiatives that seemed to move forward more deliberately?

At the time, I was the president of the Faculty Council of Community Colleges, the faculty governance group that represents the community college faculty across SUNY. As president, I also served as a nonvoting member of the SUNY Board that passed the Open SUNY resolution. Additionally, I served as a member of the Open SUNY task force. The access to information provided to me by serving in these many roles (along with a decade of experience working with the Faculty Council and SUNY) provide me with a unique opportunity to analyze and offer insights into the governance processes used to adopt and implement the Open SUNY resolution.

Although the SUNY general education and seamless transfer mandates are widely understood throughout the system, I do not mean to suggest either initiative was implemented without profound resistance. A tremendous amount of negotiation through shared governance processes was required to move these initiatives forward. My point, rather, is that at SUNY, we have processes and people in place for implementing system-wide academic mandates. So why was Open SUNY struggling to find its footing?

In determining how the process of implementing Open SUNY differed from the processes of implementing the other two initiatives, I examined the authorizing board resolutions, the processes by which those resolutions were developed, and SUNY communications to the campuses. Then, I looked carefully at the communication to and within the SUNY faculty governance groups throughout the development of the resolutions and the implementation thereafter. Although there were some differences in communication strategies that are worth investigating, the most significant difference manifested itself not in the vagueness of the initial visions of each initiative. Instead, the most significant difference was *the fundamental difference in form and purpose of the board resolution authorizing Open SUNY, as compared to the authorizing resolutions for the other two initiatives.*

For the sake of brevity and because the SUNY General Education and Seamless Transfer resolutions are similar in form and purpose, I will be comparing only the Open SUNY and seamless transfer resolutions in this discussion. At the end of this chapter, you will find the text for both resolutions. The "Seamless Transfer Requirements" resolution (hereafter referred to as the Seamless Transfer 2012 resolution), was passed by the SUNY Board in December 2012. The resolution, entitled "Growth of SUNY Online Instruction and Resources" (hereafter referred to as the Open SUNY resolution), was passed by the SUNY Board in March 2013, just 3 months later. The members of the SUNY Board were almost identical when these resolutions were passed. The people who held the positions of board chairperson, chancellor, and provost were the same. The presidents of the faculty governance groups (the Faculty Council of Community Colleges and the University Faculty Senate) were also the same. However, a comparative analysis of the two resolutions demonstrates significantly different understandings of the purpose and function of board resolutions.

I am going to forego the "whereas" clauses of the resolutions, and focus specifically on the "resolved" clauses for this analysis. For example, the resolved clause in the Seamless Transfer 2012 resolution states:

> <u>Resolved</u> that the following principles will guide undergradu-
> ate curricula within the State University to ensure seamless
> transfer. . . .

Then the clause goes on to state 10 principles that campuses are directed
to implement. Notice that the Seamless Transfer resolved clause establishes policy and is directed, for the most part, to the campuses for their
compliance.

In the Open SUNY resolution, the resolved clause reads as follows:

> <u>Resolved</u> that the following will guide the expansion of online
> education courses, degree programs and resources within the State
> University, under the name "Open SUNY."

The resolution then directs the SUNY Executive Vice Chancellor and
Provost to complete six tasks. Notice that unlike the Seamless Transfer
2012 resolution (which establishes policy and is directed to the campuses),
the Open SUNY resolution *does not establish policy* but, rather, *directs
the SUNY Provost to develop and explore* facets of online learning for
the purposes of expanding online offerings within SUNY. Rather than
establishing policy, the resolution is an *operational tool for communicating board demands to the SUNY Provost*. It can also be considered an
endorsement of expanding online learning within SUNY, without establishing policy for doing so.

Noticing this significant difference, I decided to research the typical
purpose of resolutions. Serving as a faculty governance leader for well
over a decade, it had long been my understanding that resolutions were
passed by boards *in order to articulate policy* and resolutions passed by
faculty governance groups were passed to *communicate to all stakeholders
and decision makers the group's position and recommendations on institutional policies*. It was also my understanding that the significant difference between resolutions and motions was in their development process.
The resolution process was a much more collaborative process than the
process for passing a motion from the floor.

But these understandings of mine came more from experience and
precedent than from any nationally understood definition. So, as any
seasoned governance leader would do, I conducted research within the
governance bible, *Robert's Rules of Order*, to seek the definitive purpose
for resolutions. *Robert's Rules* was authored by Colonel Henry Martyn
Roberts in 1876, and is now in its 11th edition. The text offers some
clarification when it states:

4. Motions and Resolutions. A motion is a proposal that the assembly take certain action, or that it express itself as holding certain views. . . . When a main motion is of such importance or length as to be in writing it is usually written in the form of a *resolution.* . . . A resolution is always a main motion. In assemblies with paid employees, instructions given to employees are called "orders" instead of "resolutions," and the enacting word, "Ordered" is used instead of "Resolved." (http://www.rob-ertsrules.org/rror-01.htm)

Let us assume the following:

- *Robert's Rules* are intended for use by governing bodies, such as a board of trustees, whose resolutions or motions *become law or policy or directives* that must be followed by those whom the body governs;

- that resolutions or motions can be adapted for use by governing groups whose resolutions and motions may not have the force of law or directive, such as many faculty governance groups;

- *Robert's Rules,* however, may not always apply to (or provide guidelines for) governance groups that contribute to institutional decision making, but who are not the primary governing body, such as many faculty governance groups.

What we can see through our analysis of the SUNY Board's resolutions, and *Robert's Rules,* is that the SUNY Board, if they were following *Robert's Rules,* could have made a mistake in calling the Open SUNY resolution a "resolution." More likely, it is an "order." It does not express an action to be taken by the assembly, but, instead, it "orders" or gives instructions to a paid employee—the SUNY Provost. Now, the question is, does this really matter? Who cares if it is a resolution or an order as long as the Board's intent is clear? The campus confusion that ensued about Open SUNY would suggest that clarifying orders from resolutions could matter very much.

To further understand why the distinction between resolutions and orders is important, it is valuable to first examine a traditional SUNY resolution, in this case, the Seamless Transfer 2012 resolution. In analyzing the Seamless Transfer 2012 resolution, it becomes clear that specific policies are put forth that demand compliance. For example, examine Principle #1 of the resolution:

Each curriculum leading to an A.A., A.S., and bachelor's degree *shall* enable students to complete *seven of ten* SUNY General Education Requirement academic areas (including mathematics and basic communication), two competency areas, and *30 credits* of SUNY General Education courses *within the first two years of full-time study* of the program (*or 60 credits*, whichever is greater), *unless a program-level waiver applies.* (Emphasis added)

The SUNY Board specifies that each SUNY undergraduate degree *must* allow students to complete 7 of the 10 SUNY General Education areas (including mathematics and basic communication) and 30 credits of SUNY General Education within the first 2 years of full-time study of the program unless the curriculum receives a waiver for doing so. The level of mandate to be interpreted from the words "shall enable" was certainly hotly debated, but, nevertheless, it is clear that the Board is establishing policy that *holds campuses accountable* for students' ability to fulfill certain requirements within the first 2 years of full-time study.

In contrast, compare the Open SUNY resolution to the Seamless Transfer 2012 resolution. As mentioned before, the bullet points of the Open SUNY resolution are *tasks* rather than *principles*; Task #1 is as follows:

Develop an implementation and financial *plan* for the recommendations of the Online Education Advisory Team and the related goals outlined in the 2013 State of the University presentation for the purposes of increasing System support to students and faculty in the expansion of online courses, degree programs and resources at all SUNY campuses. This plan *shall* address related business policies and practices and include, but not be limited to, an expansion of services delivered by the Office of Academic Technology and Instructional Support. This plan *shall* be developed in broad consultation with University constituencies, including campus leadership, the University Faculty Senate, the Faculty Council of Community Colleges and the Student Assembly. (Emphasis added)

The Board is requiring the SUNY Provost to develop a plan. The Open SUNY resolution does not require said plan to be submitted to the Board for approval.

The Board establishes guiding principles for developing and implementing the plan. The plan has to:

1. address related business policies and practices;

2. include the expansion of services delivered by the Office of Academic Technology and Instructional Support; and

3. be developed in broad consultation with University constituencies.

Therefore, the Board orders the Provost to develop a *plan* for Open SUNY but does not establish a policy for Open SUNY, itself, to which campuses must be in compliance. The rest of the bullet points in the resolution follow the same pattern of establishing guiding principles for the plan but *not actual policies* for Open SUNY. In fact, Task #4 further confuses matters when it states,

> Explore and implement, in conjunction with campus leadership and SUNY faculty, and in a manner consistent with campus governance practices, strategies that will promote academic excellence, encourage innovation and reduce cost barriers to education and research, including but not limited to . . .

In this task, the Board has actually called for more than a plan. It orders the Provost to implement strategies that adhere to a value statement but not a policy.

In other words, unlike the Seamless Transfer 2012 resolution that establishes policies for system-wide seamless transfer, the Open SUNY resolution offers no policies for Open SUNY, itself. Further, the resolution calls for the implementation of Open SUNY without requiring board approval of the plan, thereby, leaving policy setting for Open SUNY to the SUNY Provost.

There are probably very few, if any, faculty or administrators who would wish for anymore intrusion from their boards on academic matters than absolutely necessary. I would count myself among those who would argue that academic matters should be left to academic experts (faculty) to the fullest extent possible. However, if sound principles of academic shared governance are followed in developing policy, board resolutions can provide sound guidance and expectations for improving higher education opportunities.

It would probably surprise many of my colleagues to find me writing so favorably about the Seamless Transfer 2012 resolution. Most certainly, the implementation of the resolution has met with resistance, and I have argued on many occasions that it treads on fundamental principles of academic freedom and faculty purview over curriculum and standards. I do not intend to retract those statements here or argue that seamless transfer has been smoothly implemented as a result of a thoughtful policy. What I do argue is that as a result of the collaborative resolution creation and adoption process, there is very little confusion about the intent and the vision of the resolution.

The seamless transfer initiative has had a long and torrid history at SUNY, one not to be fully recounted here. However, some context is necessary. When SUNY began to consider seriously the enactment of a forty-year old policy on seamless transfer (defined then as 2-year degree to 4-year degree), the Faculty Council of Community Colleges, the University Faculty Senate (UFS), the Student Assembly, and SUNY System Administration formed a Joint Committee. This committee was guided by a board charge to "recommend a policy for implementing seamless transfer." (The Board charge to the committee did not take the form of a resolution.) The committee was co-chaired by Dr. Joe Hildreth (UFS) and me. The membership of this initial committee included faculty governance representatives, chief academic officers, and transfer counselors from 4-year and 2-year sectors as well as students and SUNY System Administration staff, including the Provost. Through months of negotiation, the Joint Committee passed a resolution with seamless transfer policy recommendations. The Joint Committee's resolution was subsequently endorsed by the Faculty Council, the UFS, and the Student Assembly. Eventually, the resolution was also adopted by the SUNY Board with very little change. (The resolution described here is *not* the Seamless Transfer 2012 resolution.)

The Joint Committee's resolution on seamless transfer was able to make the journey from committee through all four governance groups because the Committee coordinated collaboration with board members, the two faculty governance groups, the Student Assembly, campus administrative groups, and SUNY System Administration. By the time the resolution was passed by the Board (hereafter referred to as the Seamless Transfer 2009 resolution), stakeholders believed they understood not only the resolution, but the complexities of implementing seamless transfer.

Collaboration among the various constituencies and stakeholder groups required committee members to use consistent and redundant communication strategies, operating at all times within a strong shared governance infrastructure. Development of the Seamless Transfer 2009 resolution was not a "buy-in" process, but a representative and mediated process facilitated by people of good will who held passionate—and often conflicting—beliefs about what was best for SUNY, our students, and our faculty. This process created a resolution that all SUNY constituencies could embrace.

However, soon after the Seamless Transfer 2009 resolution was passed, there were significant changes in board membership. Also, a new chancellor and a new provost were appointed. Concurrently, the governance groups took on new leadership. The Chancellor and the Provost had their own ideas about how seamless transfer should work within SUNY, so the mechanisms for implementation of the Seamless Transfer 2009 resolution became uncertain. Therefore, it was decided that the Joint Committee would be reconstituted, and a new Memorandum of Understanding (MOU) signed by the Provost and the Presidents of the Faculty Council and the UFS, authorized a new charge for the Student Mobility Steering Committee (SMSC). The MOU authorized the committee to continue to make recommendations regarding seamless transfer. The membership (in terms of representation/roles) remained almost the same. Although the SMSC remained fairly constant, changes in System Administration philosophy and changes in ideas for implementing seamless transfer would result in the Seamless Transfer 2012 resolution, a revision of the Seamless Transfer 2009 resolution.

When the Seamless Transfer 2012 resolution was developed, it was developed through a much different process from the process used to develop the Seamless Transfer 2009 resolution. The new process foreshadowed a different role for shared governance in the development of academic policies at SUNY, culminating in the development of the Open SUNY resolution in 2013. Instead of being developed by the SMSC, the Seamless Transfer 2012 resolution was developed by the Provost and distributed for feedback. The SMSC was just another constituent group who could offer feedback on the new resolution. The Provost presented the concepts of the resolution through several PowerPoint presentations to constituent groups while distributing several drafts for feedback to those same groups.

If the success of a resolution process can be determined by the constituency groups' general support of the resolution, itself, the "feedback" process used to develop the Seamless Transfer 2012 resolution was not as successful as the committee process used to develop the Seamless Transfer 2009 resolution. The Seamless Transfer 2012 resolution was owned by the Provost rather than the committee; and at his discretion, the Provost chose to accept feedback or reject it. Consequently, the Seamless Transfer 2012 resolution received no endorsements from any of the governance groups, including the SMSC. The Board passed the resolution and the

Seamless Transfer 2012 resolution superseded the Seamless Transfer 2009 resolution.

While I have argued that the "feedback" model of resolution development was not as successful as the committee model, the feedback model still did allow for extensive discussion among the constituency groups. Even though there continues to be resistance to, and resentment of, the seamless transfer mandate, constituent groups still had the opportunity to engage in the resolution-development process and as a result learned about the complexities of seamless transfer and began preparing for its implementation. Because of the resolution processes used in both seamless transfer resolutions, general implementation could proceed deliberately. The plane was already built. Although its instruments and technology may have needed to be updated and pilots may have needed to be retrained, we could fly the seamless transfer plane without crashing it.

The Open SUNY resolution did not follow the path of development used in either seamless transfer resolution. Had the resolution been termed an order, it might have made sense that it not be subject to the collaborative process of a resolution. If the Board were using a corporate model, perhaps it would not be expected to vet its directives to a senior employee through other stakeholder groups before issuing them. But the Open SUNY initiative was issued as a resolution, suggesting that a policy on Open SUNY would be found within and that a collaborative process had been used in its creation. However, rather than benefitting from a collaborative or shared governance process, the Open SUNY resolution resulted from interaction between the SUNY Provost and the SUNY Board. The SUNY Provost presented the Open SUNY initiative to the Board in the meeting prior to the resolution's passage. The Provost wished to provide information to the Board about online learning and advocate for the adoption of the forthcoming Open SUNY resolution. The Provost then drafted the Open SUNY resolution and, at the following meeting, presented it to the Board for its adoption. The Board passed the resolution.

There was little, if any, opportunity for collaboration or feedback on the resolution prior to its passage. Instead, the collaboration and feedback was to come *as a result of* the resolution. Consultants were hired to work with the Provost's Office on the initiative. An Open SUNY task force was constituted to advise the Provost on how to operationalize Open SUNY. Task force members were confused about the role of the task force, the role of the consultants, the role of the Provost's Office, and the role of the campuses in implementing Open SUNY. Confusion persisted throughout the campuses as to exactly what Open SUNY was and how it was different from our previous online learning initiative, the SUNY Learning Network (SLN). Unlike with the seamless transfer resolutions, the Open SUNY resolution articulated no specific mandates to the campuses. Unlike with the seamless transfer resolutions, no Memorandum to Presidents was sent by the Provost to campuses to explain exactly how campuses were to come into compliance with the mandate. The avenues for developing Open SUNY policies through shared governance processes were unclear at best. Thus, the collaborative strategies that led to a shared vision of seamless transfer were supplanted by another set of strategies that were less transparent and less understood.

I must point out that there are some within SUNY who would challenge my premise that Open SUNY was/is floundering. There are some who would also dispute that seamless transfer now enjoys a shared vision within SUNY. But from a theoretical perspective, what concerns me most about this analysis of the two SUNY initiatives is the changing *purpose* of resolutions, themselves, within a shared governance system.

The *purpose of resolutions*, I think, is too often misunderstood within shared governance systems in higher education. Not long ago, a survey was posted on our Faculty Council listserv seeking information about how many faculty/campus governance groups passed resolutions. I was astounded by the question, but I was even more surprised by some of the answers. Of course, many governance groups did pass resolutions, but many did not. Some reported that their presidents "did not like" resolutions. Others responded that they never had passed resolutions, and did not understand the purpose of resolutions.

On another occasion, I was counseled by a SUNY administrator to stop the Faculty Counsel from passing so many resolutions; I was told that "no one read them, anyway" and they "just upset people." Another administrator stated that faculty governance resolutions "backed him up against a wall," and to comply with them would demonstrate weakness and a lack of leadership on his part. I have heard other perplexing statements from SUNY and campus administrators, but I have also heard them from faculty. Some faculty leaders have suggested that they must work backroom deals in order to get what they want, in order to allow their campus leaders to "save face." I have heard that academic senate resolutions are "only recommending," so they do not really matter. At the root of all these comments is a fundamental misunderstanding of the purpose of resolutions—and, more importantly, of shared governance, itself.

My work with campuses in developing and strengthening a shared governance culture has also suggested to me that even those academic senates that pass resolutions do not necessarily understand the need for a collaborative process in the development of resolutions. Too often, I worked with academic senates that (1) developed their resolutions in committee, without outreach to stakeholder groups, (2) submitted them to the senate for a vote, and then (3) presented them to the campus administration or board for their consideration, expecting implementation. Resolutions coming out of faculty senates are too often reactive rather than proactive, if they exist at all.

Robert's Rules does not really enable better understanding of how resolutions can and should work in a shared governance system. Too often, those of us in faculty governance (or on boards) are also "building the plane as we're flying it" when creating our resolutions, decreasing our ability to effect positive change.

One accusation frequently leveled against operating through a shared governance process is that "it takes too long." Certainly, that may be accurate at times; some academic senates may use delay tactics if they are opposed to an initiative. However, I would argue that as shared governance structures become more sophisticated, timelines become a part of the collaborative process. At its best, shared governance can streamline the process for building consensus. Implementing a resolution created through an effective shared governance process can be much more expeditious than initiatives developed through top-down strategies. For example, the SUNY Board gave the Joint Committee a deadline for submitting its recommendations. Not only did the committee meet that deadline, it garnered support from all stakeholder groups within the timeline.

As a participant/observer in the development and implementation of these SUNY initiatives, I have drawn the following conclusions:

- Governance groups (and administrators) need to understand the *purpose* of resolutions, and not confuse them with other mechanisms of communication.

- The process of developing resolutions should be collaborative and transparent.

- If a policy (or academic initiative) is going to be successful in effecting change, the development of a resolution can serve as a process for engaging others along the way. It can incorporate consensus-building, information gathering, and the education of stakeholder groups, resulting in an environment friendly to implementing the resolution itself, even if resistance continues to exist.

In the end, resolutions, and the processes used for their development and implementation, should lead to clarity rather than obfuscation, collaboration rather than antagonism, and negotiation among people of good will rather than authoritarian rule.

Part III

Personalized Reflections: Examination of Shared Governance Explorations and Solutions

8

Governance Leadership

A Journey

Kelley J. Donaghy

A personal reflection of a campus governance leader that probes the meaning of shared governance, its importance, and what it became over the 5 years she was Executive Chair. The challenges of leading while being untenured with little to no experience with shared governance, or the college, are explored. The chapter concludes with the Top 10 Things she wished she had known when she started.

Introduction

Shortly after arriving at the SUNY College of Environmental Science and Forestry (ESF) in the fall of 2006 as a new assistant professor, I was invited and encouraged to attend a college-wide faculty meeting. I had worked at two other institutions, one at which governance was negotiated by a body of the whole (with approximately 50 faculty members) and another that used a representative/senate model. Honestly, I never really understood the latter—it functioned outside my realm of interest at the time. In contrast, the former had been an interesting introduction to the world of academic politics, where all faculty members gathered, argued, and worked to create a community of united scholars.

Knowing that ESF's structure was a body of the whole, I expected the same feel—a place of vigorous, scholarly debate. Taking into account the size difference, I expected there would be more than twice the number of faculty as at my previous institution using a "body of the whole" format. Much to my surprise, however, there were fewer than a dozen faculty members, most of whom were present to be introduced. The total number present in the room was closer to 50—almost three times as many administrative personnel and staff members as faculty were in attendance.

The meeting began with the introduction of new faculty members and continued with a discussion of a proposed change to the bylaws. The change was a major one: to move from governance by a "body of the whole" to establishment of a senate, involving representatives of faculty and staff in a typical proportional model. This sounded similar to the situation at my previous institution, and I was concerned. There, I had observed that major decisions were made by a select group of faculty (not elected, but assigned by department chairs). These decisions were rarely communicated to the community as a whole for input, either before or after the decisions became policies. In most cases, policies just emerged, and the rest of us had to learn to live with them.

As the meeting continued, a division among people in the room was evident. Administrators and staff members supported the representative model, while faculty members expressed concern about the loss of something they considered to be their sovereignty. Other voices were heard. The president spoke out against the representative model; he wanted broad participation and agreed with keeping the model of a body of the whole. Although I was brand new, I felt compelled to share my experiences. I explained that I had observed that a representative body, like a senate, removes some of the faculty input; in my experience, a "body of the whole" offers everyone an opportunity to be heard directly. What I would come to learn is that in the bylaws under discussion, that in the current "body of a whole model," no one but faculty voted. At the end of the meeting, we were informed to expect two items in an upcoming campus mailing: ballots to vote on the bylaws revision via campus mail and ballots for elections of the coming year's officers and committee members.

The ballots arrived in our boxes within 7 days, and much to my surprise, my name was listed as a choice for one of the open positions! I did some investigation, and learned that, after just 1 month on campus, I had an enemy! I was to learn over the next few years that names could and did appear without the consent of the nominee. This was not the last time my name would appear on a governance ballot at ESF without my knowledge. Although I tried to decline the nomination, since my past experience had not included such a role, my efforts were unsuccessful. And thus I was elected.

In that first year, the day and time of faculty meetings were not predictably scheduled, making it difficult for all members to plan effectively.

When announced, meetings seemed to often take place at the end of a business day. While this time may have been convenient for some, it likely excluded many working parents with children in daycare. I was one of those people; my husband was working in Albany during the week, making me, essentially, a single mom to three children under 6. Timing and limited advance notice made it nearly impossible for me to attend. Therefore, despite my election, and the fact that my attendance at governance meetings at past institutions was nearly flawless, my participation in ESF's governance events was extremely minimal during my first year.

Despite my limited involvement, at the end of the first year, another ballot arrived in our boxes. Again, I was on it. I learned I was running for the position of University Faculty Senate Alternate. I could have turned it down, of course, but I have always, reliably, been the person who says, "If there's a job to do, I'll do it." The new Executive Chair promised that I would never have to travel (a near impossibility for a single parent) because the UFS senator from ESF would be attending all meetings. So I accepted the nomination, was elected, and only then learned that the position included a seat on the Executive Committee of ESF's Faculty Governance. I was amazed—I was nontenured faculty on campus no more than a year, and now I was a governance officer. This new position didn't fit with what I knew to be traditionally the case: that officer positions were held by some of the most venerable people at the university. But I decided to remain in the role to which I had been elected, presuming that my obligation would be limited to a few extra meetings each year.

I have found that not everything works out the way you expect. This was the case at the next turn in the road on my governance journey. Shortly after the start of the semester, the senator accepted a position at a new institution, and I was promoted from alternate to senator. I was able to attend only one UFS meeting that year, and as we had not elected a new alternate, ESF went largely unrepresented that year. Luckily, now that I was on the group responsible for the ballot, I quickly asked to be reassigned or removed from officer positions altogether. I was uncomfortable with my limited participation, and I wanted to return to what should have been my primary role: a faculty member working toward tenure. I stepped down from my position as USF senator. Much to my chagrin, however, I was nominated to run for a different senator position, this time to neighboring Syracuse University, where ESF holds two senate seats. Since this position required no travel, allowed me to remain an officer, gave me the chance to observe another governance structure, and thereby learn, I accepted the nomination and began my term that fall.

At the end of his first term, the Executive Chair informed us that he would not stand for reelection. We were not able to find someone willing to stand for election, and the ballots went out with a request for write-in suggestions. Several days after the ballots closed, my office phone rang, and the Executive Chair informed me that I'd been a write-in vote. He indicated that he'd worked through the other write-ins, but none of them would take it and I was the last name he had. He said his advice was not to take it. At the time I had been on campus only 4 years and was still 2 years from tenure.

After several days of thinking and reflecting, talking to my family and friends and department chair, all of whom counseled me to say no, I made a decision I was sure I would regret, I accepted the write-in and became Executive Chair of ESF's flagging faculty governance in May of 2010.

First Years as Executive Chair

My first months as Executive Chair were ineffective. I knew little, if anything, about being a leader. Immediately, I was thrust into many situations where I was easily intimidated. For example, agenda meetings (with the president and provost in attendance) would leave me shaky. A turning point came for me a year later when, in fall 2011, I met with the visiting Middle States Team for the scheduled 10-year review. One of the members of the visiting site team was concerned that an untenured faculty member was chairing the governing body. A member of the site team remained unsatisfied with a meeting with my executive committee, during which the committee members (without my asking) neatly deflected every question about my untenured state. The member invited me to a private lunch the next day. I did my research and realized that he'd been an advocate for faculty governance as a professor. Instead of being on the defensive about my junior faculty status, I chose to take the offensive, and I asked him if he thought governance was important. His response was telling: "As a faculty member I guess I did, but as a provost, not so much." It was then that I realized something very important: I needed to stop and think about what shared governance is, what role it serves on a typical campus, and then try to understand why it was in the state it was in at ESF where an untenured faculty member could be written in to be the Executive Chair. After I had thought all this through, I would, in good conscience, either become a leader in action as well as title, or get out.

What Is Shared Governance?

One of the first papers I encountered in my quest to educate myself on shared governance was entitled "Exactly What Is 'Shared Governance'?"[1] Olson asked and answered a lot of my questions. However, I found that the disparity of thought about the topic was a bit daunting. There are models in which shared governance is adversarial, pitting faculty and administration members against each other; models in which faculty are informed of decisions; and models in which consultation is another name for informing. One of the options is the model I think we all strive for: shared decision making within the context of administrative accountability. I was inspired by this view of governance, wherein faculty, staff, students, and administrators formed a plan together and created recommendations for decision making. This model incorporated focused feedback: Administrators were held accountable and expected to explain where and how recommendations were used. If recommendations were not used, an explanation was expected.

Naively, I endeavored to shape ESF's governance around the guiding principle of improving and strengthening communication across all campus groups, hoping to foster an environment of trust. In order to attain this ideal of shared governance, effective and broad communication was needed. I realized a subtle problem was occurring: The name of the body, Faculty Governance, was a deterrent to involvement by groups other than faculty members. If my goal was to create an inclusive body of people engaged with the academic mission of the college, that name was going to hold me back. Therefore, I stopped using the name Faculty Governance in my emails to the campus-wide listserv. I began instead using the more encompassing term, College Governance. I took another step to maximize involvement. With the help of our IT staff members, and with support of the president, we began to live-cast our meetings. This meant that community members who were traveling, or at remote campuses, or with schedules that precluded an end-of-day meeting could still "tune in." These steps might seem small, but I saw them as important paths toward increased visibility and creating governance synergy.

Working to broaden campus-wide participation and strengthen the campus community, we took a look at the committee structure. Committees at that time were composed solely of faculty members; administrative or staff input was at the discretion of the committee chair. Students were not committee members. At the time, there were only three committees:

Research, Outreach and Curriculum. On the plus side, it was a streamlined structure; however, many big topics fell outside the scope of these three committees. For example, one issue concerned the lack of time during the day to attend meetings. If you asked why someone was not at a governance meeting, inevitably you would be told that person had a class at that time. As Executive Chair, I wanted to eliminate that excuse; how could we achieve ideal shared governance if I couldn't communicate with my constituents? To do this, I needed a college hour (an hour a day when no classes could be scheduled), but immediately faced a problem: Which of the three committees would work on that matter?

When I took the matter to our provost, he suggested we consider a different committee structure. Recognizing that a college hour would affect all members of the campus community, including students, our first bylaws change was to create a Student Life Committee. This committee could have an overarching charge devoted to a variety of student life issues, but could also have a short-term charge to study the feasibility of creating a college hour. If such a special time was deemed workable, committee members could be involved in advocating for a schedule reset to reduce course conflicts. Committee members would include voting members from the ranks of faculty, staff, and students, as well as ex-officio, nonvoting members. Creation of this committee was our first attempt at increasing influence and asking opinions broadly. Their first charge was to create a college hour and to designate specific meetings during those college hours.

(Note: Two years after I first took office, with the support of both the provost and the registrar, our first faculty meeting was held during the college hour on September 19, 2012. Notice for the meeting was given well in advance. Attendance was 35% better than at any previous meeting. Now, 3 years later, our meetings are scheduled well in advance, always during the college hour. We routinely have 80 to 100 people in attendance—an order of magnitude better than when I started.)

Why Is It Important?

After my research, and after establishing a more engaged governance organization on campus, I had a better idea of what I wanted shared governance to look like at ESF. Next, I turned to the question: "Why is shared governance important?" If I was going to sell shared governance to others, I had to both understand and really buy into it. A rather dismaying commentary published in 2011 by John Lachs[2] rocked my idealistic boat. Lachs declared that shared governance is a myth, describing a world in which the university looks like corporate America. This means, to him, that faculty are employees, expendable if they don't want to do what the administration wants or don't share the ideals of the current administration. Part of the case he builds is based on the average length of tenure of top university officials at a single institution as less than a decade (The American Council on Education reported the average tenure to be 7 years in 2012.[3]). Thus, he concluded that the university enterprise is at risk of political whims and short-term managerial agendas. He predicts that scholarship will become "what product can we sell" rather than "what questions can be answered." An even more dangerous future is depicted for students: They will be trained for specific employment, rather than to become resilient thinkers who can adapt to a rapidly changing employment future.

Lachs's concluding question was essentially this: How can allowing these short-term administrative employees (with sole decision-making power) with no accountability to those on the front lines be a good idea? Lachs's point was compelling: Managers, no matter the level, seek the input of employees in a variety of ways. After the input is gathered, communication about how the work of a committee or the input given toward a problem and how it is used or discarded is essential or the idea of shared governance withers. Further, the community of scholars begins to look more and more like a business. Lachs's commentary suggested that perhaps it was time to look at shared governance realistically. His supposition was that, given the problems ahead, perhaps faculty should just step aside and give up committee work. Let the administration tell us what to do, and faculty can become like many Fortune 500 companies.

I think many busy faculty members might agree with that sentiment at face value. I can almost hear the conversation:

"Yes, please relieve me of my committee work. Give me more time for teaching and scholarship," says Professor X.

"Oh, you want to tell me what I should teach and how? OK, that's fine, as long as it means I have more time for scholarship," says Professor Y.

But how far can one push this scenario? Can we really push the envelope to include faculty members' creative endeavors? I can hear that discussion too:

"Now, wait, you are going to tell me what to do for my scholarship? Am I supposed to give up my projects and start working in this other area because you think it will bring in major funding?" queries Professor Z.

It is here that I think this business model would fail in academe. Faculty members are drawn to the Academy to investigate their own questions and their own interests, particularly in research and scholarship.[4] While I can see few faculty members lamenting the loss of committee work, perhaps more questioning a change in curriculum, I think it very likely that the research endeavor would create significant pushback by faculty members. The question I found myself asking was: "If we let go of committees and curriculum, how quickly will we lose ownership of our research agendas?"

Fast forward to 2014 for a moment, ESF started a strategic planning process. As Executive Chair, I had been heavily involved, mostly arguing for faculty input at all levels. I was utterly dismayed when many veteran faculty members privately asked me if I really think this will make a difference. They explained that their opinions didn't matter during the last strategic planning process, and they doubted they would matter now. Bottom line for them: As long as they could continue to do their research, nothing else mattered. Hallway conversations always returned to the same statement: "I don't really care what happens as long as I can do my research."

After so many of these conversations, I finally came to question the basic fundamentals of these broad assumptions. Is perhaps the importance of a strong shared governance structure to ensure academic freedom? But can we do that if we cede the committee work to the managers? How long before administrators, not faculty, start to affect curriculum and even to determine research endeavor?

Shared Governance at ESF

By the fall of 2011, midway through my second 2-year term, I had an idea of what I wanted shared governance to look like, and I had a reason for making it a priority for myself, my executive committee, and the rest of the college. But I had several hurdles to overcome. In spite of increased attendance at our governance meetings, I recognized that there was low campus-wide interest and participation in governance, general apathy, and a popular, benevolent president. I needed to understand how the campus had arrived at this point. Senior faculty would often reminisce about the "good old days," when governance meetings would fill the 154-seat auditorium where the meetings were held; members would argue for hours about curriculum issues. These faculty members told me that they missed having the big conversations—about where the college was headed. They thought nostalgically about how to structure a specific course (economics was a favorite) and how to determine what was important and necessary.

Listening to them made me ask myself "What was the turning point? When did governance begin to fail at ESF?" I wondered where and how I could get the answers to these questions. I asked as faculty members, professional staff, and administrators to tell me about the history of shared governance at ESF. Always, the story sounded the same: "We were strong, and faculty loved to attend meetings until . . ." There was great disparity in what followed after "until," but three explanations were the most common:

1. the committees stopped bringing the conversations to the floor;

2. the Bray Hall effect (Bray Hall houses our administrative units)—all decisions are made at Bray, and nothing others say is considered; and

3. we don't have the kinds of professors who are interested in governance (implying that science professors don't engage in policy writing).

After listening to many individuals, I realized that I needed more than stories. Although I might find that there was nothing I could fix easily, I decided to go back to the primary sources. I turned to the governance meeting minutes. I opted for the meeting minutes that were available digitized, dating back to 2000 (about 6 years before I arrived). Although these gave me more information than the conversations had, they did not point toward solutions. They painted a picture of a faculty that was slowly growing disinterested in governing itself, where the committees functioned to promote the agenda of the administrative units. For example, at a 2005 meeting, the ability to make curriculum and course recommendations was delegated solely to the Committee on Instruction. By then, the Committee on Research (although possessing a healthy charge) carried out only the administrative programs of the Office of Research. The Committee on Public Service and Outreach was rumored to be responsible only for picking the lunch menu for conferences on teaching and learning, but had little input into the conferences' content. Truth or fiction, these meeting minutes painted a story of faculty committees serving as extensions of administrative offices. Faculty were being pressured to do more research, continue to excel at teaching, and then were asked to do what they saw as the work of the administration through committees. I understood now how service had become unappealing and distasteful. The bigger question for me was, "How would this type of service in shared governance protect and underscore academic freedom?"

In December 2011, I delivered my first set of opening remarks intended to communicate to my constituents what I'd come to understand:

- fundamentally, we had a lot to lose if we sat back and didn't engage with shared governance;

- the university, if run as a business, could mean a loss of the autonomy of research; and

- ultimately, we might fail to control our own scholarship.

The ideal of shared governance that I envisioned was fully based on superior communication, so that's where I started. I felt that to be successful I had to start at the top, which meant communicating effectively with the key administrators.

Our president at the time was a people person. He did not remain aloof; he walked among us and talked to us. He knew us on a first name basis—and probably knew our spouses' and children's names, too. He fought for our campus, and was heavily involved in the budget battles with SUNY. I knew he was already my personal supporter, but I felt that I needed another ally, one who might have more time for a fledgling leader.

I scheduled an appointment with the "new" provost. He and I had arrived on campus within a year of each other. We'd both come from much larger institutions, and had witnessed very different governance structures than we were seeing at ESF. Neither of us wanted to exactly replicate those at ESF, but we did know that what we currently had at ESF wasn't going to stand the test of time. The status quo was particularly vulnerable if a different administrative group was established. During that first meeting, we found we had a lot in common with regard to our hopes for shared governance at ESF.

As described at the beginning of this chapter, the recent attempt to create a senate body at ESF just as we arrived on campus (with faculty, staff, administrators, and students as voting members) had failed. We decided that we needed to move slowly, but methodically, in order to go forward. Our goals—from very different perspectives—were shared: to create a body that would be effective, do meaningful work, and be strong enough to endure the challenges of administrative change. We wanted the evolved shared governance organization to be inclusive. That first meeting set the stage for a partnership that would last for 5 productive years. During those years, we would often argue, vent to each other, and eventually compromise. In the end, ESF's governance structure is stronger for the partnership we formed.

In the early years, however, we started with three ideas:

1. increase faculty attendance at meetings,

2. create meaningful work for faculty committees beyond administrative agendas, and

3. write bylaws that populated committees effectively and began to include the broader campus community.

Our president at the time, at an Executive Committee meeting, suggested that if we offered adult beverages at our meetings we'd draw a crowd. We capitalized on that idea, and also on the fact that the campus liked to hear directly from the president about the state of the campus. As a result of our president's participation, and our changed refreshments, our attendance rose steadily. So, I had my audience—now I had to sell the idea of academic freedom and faculty responsibility.

The summer before I officially took office, Academic Council, a taskforce on promotion and tenure, and the provost had crafted a set of college-wide promotion and tenure (P&T) procedures. While there were loose ideas across departments about how this was to be done, there were few if any cross-campus checks for faculty undergoing review. This was an item of business that would interest even the most apathetic faculty member. Together, the provost, the chair of the taskforce charged with reviewing the P&T materials, and I brought the idea to the governance meeting for faculty review and comment. It was the beginning of meaningful work.

Middle Years as Executive Chair

With tenure came a little less stress, and a lot more responsibility. Now I had no excuse for shying away from the big issues. It was at this time that faculty governance started to become more of a partnership, with administration, faculty, staff, and students working more closely to achieve important goals. In December 2012, our beloved president announced at a governance meeting that he was stepping down, presenting me with a new challenge. After being pulled in several different directions by the administration, concerning the composition of the search committee, we found the Guidelines for Presidential Searches on the Board of Trustees website.[5] Even with these guidelines, populating the committee was not going to be easy. The Executive Committee and members from the entire campus wanted to ensure diversity; however, with only three female full professors, choosing from just the highest ranked among us (a common practice) would not ensure diversity. An open call for nominations was held, and 19 candidates were put forth, including seven women (two full professors, four associate professors, and one tenured assistant professor). With careful attention to rank and gender, required for a voting process intended to force diversity, a faculty group of six, consisting of four women and two men, was elected. Three of the members held the rank of professor, and three held the associate professor rank. After a whirlwind search, our new president took the reins of ESF and ushered in a new era on January 2014, just 12 months after the public announcement of the search. This experience taught me the importance of bylaws, guidelines, policies, and procedures. Without the SUNY Board of Trustees guidelines, I would have been informed of who would be on the committee, not consulted. As a result, I believe it would have been highly unlikely that there would have been elections.

Progress Since 2010

What follows are the improvements and actions we have taken since I became Executive Chair in 2010 to improve and strengthen participation of all of the constituents on campus in shared governance. We focused on bylaws and membership, academic policy, and communication.

Bylaws

Within months of taking office in 2010, I noticed that something was amiss with our current bylaws. Faculty members with significant institutional history at ESF regaled me with stories about well-attended meetings and hotly contested curriculum proposals. They lamented having changed the bylaws to allow committees to make decisions on their behalf. On a cold and snowy Friday afternoon, in 2010, I finally uncovered the problem. I had searched through our bylaws for the clause in the bylaws that said that all decisions were made at the committee level. On that snowy day, I realized that we had one set of bylaws that had been amended in 2010 to add an awards committee, but that version did not include the changes made to move things from the faculty floor to committee with no campus-wide vetting in 2006. We had pieces of two separate versions of bylaws under which we had been functioning. This realization forced me to actually read and fix the bylaws—something I had steadfastly tried to avoid up to this point.

Once I made this discovery, I realized that, at the very least, we had to pull the two versions back together. At the same time, when introducing the issue to the faculty, it became apparent that they did not want to simply bring the two versions together; rather, many wanted to return some of the decision making to the floor of governance meetings. It took us several years, and many iterations, to make this happen. Learning from the failed senate attempt in the fall of 2006, but still being committed to an organizational structure that would be more inclusive of the greater campus, we needed to take baby steps.

Without changing the bylaws immediately, I worked with the executive committee to create opportunities for professional staff to have a voice without seeming to threaten faculty provenance. I started with recommending that we incorporate professional staff as voting members of standing committees. After that, provision was made so that all voting members were eligible to chair committees. Each chair also serves and votes on the executive committee. At the same time, I worked with department chairs to develop a rotation system for smaller departments to populate committees, so that they were not overburdened. Two or more departments would share a seat and rotate in and out of the committee every 2 years. Moving the election of committee members to the departments instead of relying on votes by the faculty of the whole allowed us to completely fill our committees every year. This was something that had not happened previously. We left it up to each department to decide how they would fill their open positions. Some departments elect, others appoint or volunteer, but we have effectively spread out the work of the group. At this time I believe we are approaching the "many hands make light work" system we set out to create.

We also expanded our committee system to try and capture the wide range of issues that might arise. We went from three overburdened and ineffective committees to eight: curriculum, instructional quality/academic standards, research, honors and awards, student life, promotion and tenure, library, and technology. Currently, the executive committee acts as the budget committee. With each committee needing between 7 and 10 members, we now have almost 80 people heavily involved with the work. These members are therefore vested in attending meetings, and keeping up with campus developments.

In 2015, we decided to make a bold change to our bylaws: We moved away from allowing only faculty members the right to vote. We proposed changing the name of the group from Faculty Governance to Academic Governance, and created a membership to expand and more clearly define voting members. Our membership includes all faculty as defined by the SUNY Board of Trustees, 30 professional staff members, a minimum of two students, and the presidents of the Undergraduate Student Association and the Graduate Student Associations. Twelve other students who actively participate on one of our governance committees also have a vote.

Bylaws are meant to keep order and should be adhered to whenever possible, but they also need to have a significant amount of flexibility in order to change with the college. I am reasonably confident that our new policies will readily adapt to changes quickly, and yet include the necessary checks and balances needed to maintain an orderly and fair organization.

Academic Policy

As governance started to function more effectively, I realized that we still had a problem to be addressed: We had no way of effectively making decisions as a campus. For many years, it was the wild, wild West: If you wanted more resources, a better classroom, new software for your research, or a release to do a special project, you took your request to the highest-ranking administrator (usually the president), and it would be done. Or, if a policy needed to be developed, the administration crafted it. Campus members were then expected to follow the policy, whether they knew about it or not. Policies were largely unwritten, not well communicated, and there was no official procedure for policy to actually be made. A strong believer that solid, vetted, reasonable policies are like good fences, and they make good neighbors—or, in this case, solid working relationships—I set out trying to determine how we could most easily go about writing, vetting, and communicating policy.

The first thing we needed to understand was how to actually make things happen. Resolutions were not common at ESF, and when one would come up, we didn't really know what to do with it. The officers and I created a flowchart and a resolution template to help make things more obvious to our members and to get things going. This started to stem the tide of individuals coming forth, asking me (as Executive Chair) to act on their individual requests. Now, given the governance structure we had in place, we had a way to ask for faculty consensus, something we'd not been doing. Some departments and individuals were still rogue, and continued to take things to the administration directly, without really gathering consensus. We were pleased to observe that members of the administration started to use governance more effectively as well: Administrators asked us to help vet ideas before they were put into operation.

The next test of governance occurred when several administrators issued a policy on visual media production and intellectual property. Although we thought we were making progress, this policy appeared seemingly out of the blue. It was not well communicated, and had not been vetted by faculty. In spite of these failings, it would be enforced. Response to the new policy was swift and harsh. Specifically, the technology committee raised concerns about the absence of guidelines for implementation. Whether or not the policy was sound, the bigger issue for governance was how policy is created and announced. Particular difficulty was anticipated, since the policy crossed administrative silos. I heard concerns from many faculty members across campus.

I was able to build on my experiences to address this situation in a new way by drawing on the partnership I had established with Provost Bruce Bongarten. Together, we helped smooth over this issue and planned ahead for the future. Jointly, we created a set of procedures for making college policy. To do this, we examined the kinds of policies likely to be made, and then identified how and when governance could and should have a voice. After that, we crafted a way to communicate policy that had to be made, but did not necessarily involve governance. For example, a policy on how media on scholarship is distributed should have significant governance input, whereas a policy on vacation leave during the holidays should not.

We also realized there would be times when urgent policy was passed down to campuses by SUNY system administration. We proposed a way to implement these policy mandates, followed by our campus review. Most important, we clarified how to broadly communicate all of these changes, as well as new policies, going forward.

While the provost and I were clearly the leads on this initiative, it would not have happened without the input of the executive committee, the president, and several other vice presidents. This was one of the biggest challenges we'd had, and it took true shared governance with all of the people at the table to make it happen.

These new procedures have been in place for a while now, and have been very successful. They allow us the flexibility that we need to keep campus running while addressing new policies. Now we have a strategy to make sure that all policies are communicated at governance meetings as well as on the governance website. We ensure that those requiring governance review are reviewed by the executive committee, remanded to committee, and then brought before the full body of academic governance. This procedure on policymaking was the first time that all sides of the administrative house came together with faculty and staff to write a procedure for how policy would be made. It was a victory for governance, but it would not have been possible without the strong and trusting partnership I had forged with Provost Bongarten. The importance of trust and partnership in governance should never be underestimated.

Communication

In the course of my tenure as Executive Chair, the SUNY system worked through many "systemness" initiatives (otherwise known as Shared Services, Seamless Transfer, Open SUNY initiatives, and START-UP NY). In implementing each one, the key was communication. Taking the time to attend University Faculty Senate Plenaries was vital to making sure that when these items came to ESF I was informed and could speak about them intelligently. Further, I wasn't always reacting to something: Sometimes, because of attending a plenary, I was bringing information about a new initiation to my administration. Hearing information first-hand, without an ESF filter, gave me a chance to process it with input from my colleagues in the University Faculty Senate.

The SUNY structure, because many decisions are made and implemented system-wide, can generate dismay among campus community members left to implement a new initiative, many unfunded. As in most statewide systems, presidents at each campus have specific, but limited, decision-making powers, while the chancellor has the authority and responsibility for the entire system. This can create a stressful dynamic on campuses, since the faculty and staff recognize their ability to make changes in system-wide policy is often negligible. The gray areas where academics may or may not be involved are less troublesome. However, any encroachment into the curriculum (such as Seamless Transfer and Applied Learning) are areas that have sometimes devolved to battlegrounds.

As my journey winds down, I find that I prefer diplomacy to antagonism whenever possible. And when diplomacy fails, well, there are always resolutions!

Where Is ESF Today?

In the 5 years of my tenure as a campus governance leader, I believe ESF's governance structure has come a long way. We now have a set of procedures for how policy on campus can be made, we have a set of bylaws that include the professional staff and student voice in full-body votes, and we have a functioning set of standing rules that can be easily updated to accommodate institutional change. To be more inclusive, we've changed the name from Faculty Governance to Academic Governance, and we've established a relationship with the administration that is not antagonistic. By now, the mentoring between and among governance leaders and administration has started to gain momentum and is helping the institution find its way.

What am I most worried about? The leadership vacuum! I realize, now, that we have not developed a plan for succession—that is, figuring out who the leaders in the wings will be. It disturbs me that I've run uncontested for the last two elections. No one has yet expressed interest in taking the reins. As occurs on many campuses where someone has been in office successfully for a while, the status quo becomes the norm. Without nurturing the next generation of leaders, members of the campus become happy to let the leader do the work for as long as the leader will do it.

By announcing my decision well ahead of time, I am hopeful that one or more campus members will express interest in taking on the challenge. I realize that I may have to explicitly seek out people who I think have the potential to take on the role, and meet with them to discuss what is involved. In working with the administration, we've been able to make the position more attractive via a 25% administrative workload adjustment (the equivalent of a course release each semester). Although the work has increased significantly since I first took office, I continue to believe that the opportunities to learn and grow within the position make it an exceptionally worthwhile professional experience.

Was It Worth It?

Am I glad I did this? Should I have listened to the naysayers when I was first written onto the ballot? I think everyone asks these kinds of questions, and every leader asks, "What impact did I have?" I have no doubt that some colleagues would say that I've wasted my time, or ask, "What do you have to show for 5 years of hard work?" Such colleagues have missed all that I've gained, and perhaps to them it is not important. But to me, all I have gained is huge.

Invaluable to me are the friendships outside my own field and department, my partnerships with administrators, and, because of my work on the University Faculty Senate, the friends and acquaintances I now have across SUNY. True, I've made some enemies along the way, but I see that as inevitable. For me, the real value has been to meet so many people for whom service is a core value, for whom keeping the faculty and staff voice in all things academics, matter. I've had some amazing role models along the way, and I am most appreciative of their influence on my leadership. As a minority in my department and field, I think that being visible outside of my building has greatly contributed to my professional job satisfaction, as well as to my self-esteem.

Additionally, I've learned a lot about myself. To be a leader is to see yourself reflected in the eyes of those you lead. I've learned how to listen, when to act and when to wait. Inaction is a lot harder than one might think. When you choose not to do something about an issue or a topic, significant care must be taken; it is essential to explain your rationale for your choice. Many times, it is easier to adopt someone's ideas than to reject them. The same attention needs to be paid to "seeking input;" when you ask for people to provide an opinion, you don't have to follow their suggestions, but you are best served if you explain to them—in a timely way—why you strayed from their advice. Not doing so is extremely costly on the trust scale. Leaders cannot afford to lose the trust of their constituents if they hope to be able to influence them. I've often said that I've justified myself more as a governance leader than at my doctoral defense and all the years after as a practicing chemist! As a result, I have changed. I find myself to be a stronger researcher. I have become a more reflective scholar. I'm definitely a better manager of people.

Finally, I have learned a great deal about higher education generally, and the SUNY system and ESF in particular. I don't know how I will use this knowledge in the future, but I'm sure I will. I like understanding how decisions are made, and how the outcome can be influenced by the process. I've enjoyed the challenge of getting broad buy-in and input for a cause. I hope that I will continue to serve in some capacity as a governance leader at ESF or within SUNY, as I've found the work fascinating. Although I never considered myself much of a leader, I've stood at the helm for 5 years. With 1 final year to go, I look forward to the challenges of not being the "go to" person any longer, and spending more time with my graduate and undergraduate students. It has been a great ride, and while I absolutely think it was worth the "blood, toil, tears and sweat," it is time to step down and let someone else take the reins. It is time to let ESF "go forward with our united strength."[6]

Advice to Others

Here is my top 10 list of things I wish I'd known before I started:

Know why you are doing what you are doing. Too often, governance seeks to insert itself in places where it has no role. A case in point is whether or not to be included in the president's cabinet meetings. Members of the governance executive committee thought that being present would help with two-way communication. Our presence could allow us to have more influence. After several requests, a compromise was struck: The governance Executive Chair meets biweekly with the president, provost, and chief of staff; in this way, the discussion can focus simply on what is governance related.

Develop goals and be flexible in achieving them. Over the years I've learned that getting where you want to go isn't going to be a straight line. Negotiation is a lot like sailing—as a faculty member you'll be going into the wind a lot, so you'll need to be ready at all times to tack to make any forward progress. Being able to go back and forth in the boardroom is essential. If, however, you don't know what or where the target is, you won't be able to reach it. Have a clear vision, write out a draft plan whenever possible, and then be prepared to your modify plan. You will need to be adaptable to achieve your vision of the goals of your constituents.

Committees need clear goals and meaningful work. This was the biggest challenge. We had committees, but too often they would spin their wheels or be asked to do things that were simply not meaningful to the people on the committee. I found that having a fall planning meeting the first week before the semester started was essential. At this meeting, we made sure each committee had specific and important goals and plans.

In all honesty, some years, I just had to give up on a committee. No matter how hard I tried, a committee just wouldn't accomplish very much. After investing many hours in trying to mentor some committee chairs, I found that waiting out the leadership was often the only way to make changes. Patience is often the key when you have committees that are not functioning. I made an effort to seek out people to serve as chairs. Many new chairs turned a previously lackluster group into a sought-after committee. Also, be on the lookout for when a committee is no longer needed, and then let it go.

Not everything needs action. This was very hard in the first years. At first I tried to solve every problem that arose. I had to learn that, although I wasn't tenured, sometimes, I had to say no. I could listen and empathize, but if an isolated complaint came up that I didn't think would have broad buy-in, I simply had to pass on it.

With tenure, I could stop walking on eggshells. I had increased freedom to simply say, "I'll take that under advisement," or "Can I think about it?" Sometimes I would say, "Write a resolution, and I'll take it to faculty for the collective opinion." I wish I'd had these phrases in my vocabulary the first 2 years, as they've made the middle years so much better.

Achieving consensus among faculty is difficult. One of the biggest complaints you will hear about governance, particularly from administration, is that it is slow. It doesn't have to be, but you have to accept that fewer than 100% of your constituents will be happy with a decision. Faculty members, in particular, are highly critical; nothing will satisfy all of them all of the time. If faculty decisions take too long, or things end up in nondecisions, that's when administration must step in and make the call. I learned this quickly, but it would have been great to have understood it on day 1!

Realize that you won't be able to go against the tide. Sometimes there are simply too many who won't allow something to move forward. It took me time to learn the old adage that you can't please everyone all of the time.

Shared governance MUST be a partnership. Faculty can organize themselves all they want, but they need the buy-in of the administration to actually make things work. Actually, names of the organization aside, it is shared governance that we are trying to achieve. Unless communication goes in all directions, it won't work. All parties involved need to know what their roles and commitments are to each other for it to work. Presidents (freshly minted or well seasoned), provosts, and academic leaders need to understand what they want from each other, and all groups need to work together to figure out how to harness the power of faculty, professional staff, and students to help the institution in a meaningful way.

Listening is the first step. It's a vital skill, and one at which I've only recently developed proficiency. It took me time and effort, but now I really understand what good listening looks and feels like.

Consultation—what it is and what to do when it is poor. There is a big difference between (dialogue) consultation and (one-way communication) informing. I think most of us recognize the difference, and know it when one or the other is used. The problems occur when we try to lead without doing both, or deciding what to do when we feel we've not been consulted appropriately. Recently, a change in administrative leadership occurred. The consultation went a little like this: Individuals were called in for private consultation meetings. The opening gambit was, "I want to know who you think should take the position, I'm thinking about X person."

Only afterward could I label that question as "informing" rather than consulting. The moment the person of choice was revealed, I was on the defensive. In retrospect, the individual meetings left us all wondering who had agreed that the choice of X was a good one. We doubted that anyone had.

Consultation needs to be open discourse, with large and small groups. It takes time; it's not something that can be done in a day or two. It also needs follow-up. Those consulted need to know why you didn't take their advice; they need to know you listened to them. I wish I'd known this much, much earlier, because—reflecting back today—I would have definitely been more outspoken when I felt we were being informed, but there was the presumption that we were being consulted. If I had learned how to do this with the small issues, perhaps I could have handled the bigger issues better.

Shared governance creates a strong work culture. When functioning at its best, effective shared governance creates a strong harmonious campus, one where all constituents feel valued. When the people in the trenches (faculty, professional staff, students) feel that they have opportunities for significant input into decisions, and that they have been heard, they can feel invested in the work and will support it. When something is handed down from on high, without buy-in, it creates resentment. No one likes to be told what to do; even well-intentioned, well-crafted plans can be thwarted. This is especially likely if splinter groups oppose the decisions. The stronger the communication between all members of a campus, the more easily the campus will adapt to change when it comes.

Attend university faculty senate meetings. In the early years I didn't think I needed to go to the meetings. I couldn't foresee what I would gain. In later years, I realized that without attending those meetings I would not have been nearly as successful. As ESF transitioned to a new president, I talked with others who were going through—or had recently gone through—the same things. Having a resource group of people (from campuses throughout SUNY) who were struggling with challenges I could relate to was incredibly helpful. Over the years, the campus governance leaders (CGLs) of UFS have explored compensation for CGLs (which is why I finally took the course release the provost offered). We've also looked at administrative searches, presidential review, influenced Seamless Transfer and Excels, and generally helped shaped the idea of consultation. We've leaned on each other, and learned from each other. If you are a SUNY CGL, attend the UFS meetings! If you can't or don't attend, I recommend that you find a support group—you'll need it at some point!

Enjoyment is a bonus outcome of being a governance leader. Serving as a governance leader has been an interesting ride. It was often hard to keep enough adult beverages in the house during the early years. As I began to wear the mantle more comfortably, I began to see the good I was doing. I've increased faculty attendance and involvement by an order of magnitude, and professional staff and students now have an official voice. I've searched for a president and made a campus-wide procedure for vetting and communicating policy.

I didn't do everything right, but I'm leaving office having come a long way personally—in learning how to listen and to keep my mind open, in learning how and when to assert myself, in learning the value of not revealing my opinion so that I can hear what others have to say. Mostly, I've learned that leading, while difficult, can have a huge impact when done well. I like to think that while not perfect, I've led well. There is more to do, but I'm content now. I can honestly say I enjoyed it, and that I will miss the work, the people, the influence. I am glad I refused to listen to the naysayers and stepped up when there was a need. I've benefitted, and I hope that others have too.

Acknowledgments

The successes outlined in this journey would not have been possible without the support and encouragement of Provost Bruce Bongarten. We both believed that if the work could be spread out to many, it would mean less work for all and a broader set of opinions would and should be gathered. And while not perfect, governance at ESF is getting there. I am thankful for Bruce's patience with me as I learned how to lead. He has been a great example of calm under fire! Bruce was the recipient of the first-ever ESF Friends of Governance (FOG) award in May 2015.

Notes

1. Olson, G.A. (2009). Exactly what is 'shared governance'? *The Chronicle of Higher Education.* Retrieved from http://chronicle.com/article/Exactly-What-Is-Shared/47065

2. Lachs, J. (2011). Shared governance is a myth. *The Chronicle of Higher Education.* Retrieved from http://chronicle.com/article/ Shared-Governance-Is-a-Myth/126245

3. Cook, B.J. (2012). The American college president study: Key findings and take-aways. *American Council on Education.* Retrieved from http://www.acenet.edu/the-presidency/columns-and-features/Pages/The-American-College-President-Study.aspx

4. Shared governance in colleges and universities. A statement by the Higher Education Program and Policy Council. *AFT Higher Education.* Retrieved from http://facultysenate.tamu.edu/Quick_Links/Shared_Governance_in_Colleges_and_Universities.pdf

5. The State University of New York Guide to Presidential Searches at State-Operated Institutions, 2012. Retrieved from http://system.suny.edu/media/suny/content-assets/documents/faculty-senate/GUIDELINESFOR PRESIDENTIALSEARCHESFinal.pdf

6. In these two sentences, both quotes are from Winston Churchill, speech to the House of Commons on May 13, 1940.

9

Diversifying Shared Governance

Intentional Strategies and Best Practices

Noelle Chaddock and Beth Hinderliter

Approaches to diversifying higher education often focus on how best to include underrepresented voices on campus. The well-intended efforts to attract and retain faculty who bring diversity, in particular race, ethnicity, nationality, gender, and sexual orientation, often produce little movement. This essay looks at the inverse possibility: What practices are we engaged in that restrict and block diversity? By highlighting barriers to the diversification of shared governance and issues that jeopardize the retention of diverse faculty, we promote strategies for gaining equitably balanced shared governance systems and campuses, more broadly.

Introduction

The culture of shared governance is changing. Previously, its membership drew from a population of dedicated, tenured, demographically homogenous, senior experts who often have built and maintained the structures and policies of governance. Now, governance participants have begun to reflect a more heterogeneous constituency. There is increased need for the intentional implementation of inclusive practices within all levels of governance.

Progress can be noted—and celebrated—in regard to the diversity that shared governance organizations have experienced around gender, generational representation, discipline, and institutional differences. However, it would seem that, despite such advances, leaders and member of shared governance organizations still struggle with inclusion around race, class, gender, ability, LGBTQAI, and professional staff representation. The problem does not appear to be unique to the State University of New York (SUNY) University Faculty Senate (UFS). Under the committed efforts of recent UFS leadership and "minority pioneers" in the senate, the conversation about diversifying shared governance has led to the beginning of a deeper examination of both the best practices and the major challenges in reaching the goal of a richly diverse institutional and systemic governance bodies.

First, we might mention that both of us came to shared governance through a committee structure that allowed non-senators to participate in issues of governance. For committee members, this is often a first experience with governance, the state system offices, and the ideas and foci of governance bodies. For new members, especially those with marginalized identities, it becomes very clear, very quickly, at annual committee meetings that racial and ethnic diversity is minimal to the point of tokenization. One can then quickly understand the room as lacking *out* LGBTQAI diversity, and thus assume other areas of diversity are probably lacking, too. New research in diversity initiatives have pointed to how *visible* diversity (most often racial and ethnic diversity) on campus is an indicator of increased forms of other diversity that are often invisible or indiscernible without knowledge of individuals background, experiences, and identity. An inclusive atmosphere only grows.

In the words of the current UFS president at the January 2013 plenary: "We are a room full of old white guys." One might ask, "Why is that a problem?" Color and gender aside for the moment, the room is full of very dedicated people, some of whom have given upward of 40 years of service to governance in higher education. However, the "room full of old white guys" *is* a problem—according to past presidents Carl Wiezalis and Ken O'Brien, both of whom pioneered the UFS efforts around diversity—in that we have a governance body that is not capitalizing on the richness of diversity that higher education has to offer. Our governance also does not reflect the composition of SUNY. As one of the chapter authors in this volume observed: "I am often startled when I offer a perspective that someone with 25 years of governance experience has simply never thought of how incorporating diversity of lived experience, perspective, and framing into governance makes it better. Period."

This chapter is intended to be a starting point, an invitation to our colleagues to think about the importance of diversifying shared governance at every level. Shared governance is a leadership pipeline that requires strategic cultivation and intentional examination in order to remain relevant, attractive to new membership, and impactful in its function.

One key area is how, and with whom, governance bodies are populated. The matters of faculty (along with administration, staff, students, and other institutional considerations) need to be represented via leadership, and so do the concerns of faculty, professional staff, students, and future members of those populations. A good place to start the conversation is to ask you, our reader, to look at the constituting members of a shared governance body and ask questions like these:

"Does our governing body represent our institution's demographic population accurately?"

"Has the configuration of this body shifted over time in direct relation with the institution's shifts?"

"Why has the body failed to evolve, such that it is no longer truly representative of the diversity of the campus or system it represents?"

This examination of composition is of great importance. Please understand—we are not advocating quantity over quality. Instead we are suggesting that quality requires diversity and metrics to evaluate diversity. The data that come out of such an examination allow leadership to hypothesize how effective the body might be in responding to, and also steering, governance issues that are relevant to the full population it serves.

Challenges: The Real and Perceived

When governance leaders are asked why a governance body is homogenous or very low in diversity, the most consistent response is "we try." The chapter authors, and members of the UFS Diversity Committee, are familiar with multiple versions of this response, as well as other coded equivalents. In the end, what members of campuses explain is that they try to recruit diversity members onto their governance bodies, but the members are either not available, not interested, or (even when they join) don't stay.

Unfortunately, these responses are not often a starting point to strategically and intentionally rectifying the issue: Instead, they are frequently the very reasons recruitment and concerns about a diverse body have been abandoned. It is imperative that we do not accept these explanations: We cannot afford to leave our pipeline to the tomes of "we tried that." We *must* do the work of making strategic and intentional strides to cultivate a diverse pipeline for governance, and governance leadership.

There is evidence that most campuses make well-intended efforts to attract and retain faculty who bring diversity—in particular, gender, race, ethnicity, and nationality—to join the campus community. However, these efforts regularly seem to produce little movement in campus governance. This is reflected up through the larger governance leadership body, the SUNY University Faculty Senate. Of equal concern are the ways that recruitment efforts focused on diversity can be fraught with the very stereotypes and mythological thinking, the very concepts that these initiatives set out to oppose.

We invite our committed campuses to problematize diversity recruitment efforts. Rather than looking at what is done to increase diversity, especially in areas of governance and campus leadership, we recommend campus members identify what might be taking place that inhibits its advancement.

First, appraise campus leadership. Is the shared governance body demographically representative of your current faculty and staff population? Is the shared governance body reflective of your current and future student population?

Second, give governance participants the opportunity to think about how and if those populations differ. This becomes a governance issue to consider. Part of this consideration might be to decide how your "demographic" is understood. Who is being identified and by what measures?

Promoting diversity within shared governance is essential for many reasons. First, shared governance is meant to be *representative*, a body through which our leaders are called on to voice the plurality of opinions, experiences, and positions within our larger population. Second, the notion of *sharing* within shared governance suggests an implicit openness, yet junior faculty, women, racial and ethnic minorities, the LGBTQAI community, differently abled people, veterans, international faculty/staff, and other groups are often underrepresented. The reasons behind the reality of homogenous, nonrepresentative governance are complex and the challenges to change are numerous. What might be accessible and effective in your governance committees is an understanding of the climates and practices that function as barriers, regardless of other attributes of shared governance.

What current practices restrict and block diversity? Often, it is assumed that *obstacles* put in the path of diversification are the main challenge, and we respond by keeping our eyes on the prize. Yet, there are alternatives, within which we examine both the path and the speed of our travel toward a fully diverse governance body. Study of these alternatives is needed, especially if the process of change includes a continual becoming and improving. Starting from this question—"What current practices restrict and block diversity?"—the Diversity in Shared Governance presentation at the 2014 SUNY Shared Voices conference (from which this chapter emerges) sought to identify opinions or mindsets, leadership practices, and other institutional structures that block diversity. Such barriers could include stagnation in leadership, tokenization, timeliness of diversity initiatives, and campus readiness for change.

The Elevator Conversation

In order to articulate barriers to diverse leadership, ask yourself this question: "Have I followed up with those who have refused an invitation to join, or have left, a governance body?" Following up will likely surprise you, by giving you detailed information about your institution. Asking the question will also demonstrate and promote the importance of communication and sharing on campus.

As Kerry Ann Rocquemore, President of the National Center for Faculty Development and Diversity, detailed in her keynote speech for the SUNY Making Diversity Count: Ensuring Equity, Inclusion, Access, and Impact conference on November 12–13, 2014, many people who are marginalized and end up leaving their institutions to go elsewhere feel as if they had little opportunity or choice in their departure. Often, these professionals would have preferred to stay at their original institution as their decision to leave may have been a particularly painful one.

Whether or not individuals left for another position, or remain on your campus in a position of limited engagement, reaching out to them to ask their perspectives can elicit insightful and often surprising information about campus climate. The information that you can gain will help you shape structures on campus and your institutional climate.

Tokenization

We cannot assume that every diverse candidate for a governance position will be a diversity advocate. Assuming a female scholar wants to represent issues of gender equity on campus tokenizes her and reduces her expertise to mere symbolism. Ensure that candidates are recruited for their expertise rather than for the purpose of filling a quota. For diversity initiatives to work, they must be more than just surface treatment or creating multi-cultural "optics." By realizing how stereotypes cause alienation and marginalization among those who are the target of unfair generalizations, we recognize the potential danger of what Steele and Aronson (1995) called "stereotype threat" and the hostile environments that it creates.

One self-fulfilling myth about diversity in shared governance is that every diversity candidate is already overloaded with service requirements representing diversity on numerous committees across campus and will be unable to commit to additional service activities. This perception can be the worst form of tokenization, due to its perpetuation of invisibility. In spite of what sociologist Tiffany Joseph identified as a pattern of "race, gender and cultural taxation," which exists within many institutions (Joseph & Hirshfield, 2013), the answer is not institutional censorship or quashing of diversity initiatives. Rather, we must be deliberate and persistent in crafting our approaches to diversity, so that no such unfair or unequal taxation can continue to exist in the future.

If diversity candidates are not invited to participate in shared governance, it is impossible to know how specific individuals view their current schedule and workload. Without the invitation to governance, the risk exists that these individuals will be assigned to numerous service activities, but that these other activities may not offer the same exposure to positions of campus leadership. Not asking puts the campus at risk of stasis in leadership, in which the next leader is always predictable, the "heir apparent." There is an inherent problem in succession planning that is viewed as exclusive. Not asking perpetuates a tautology of "coming up through the ranks" as issues of access and equity are overlooked. Not asking assumes that said candidates cannot answer or prioritize for themselves. Ask. Let individuals tell you what they can/will or cannot/don't wish to do.

Speed

How can authentic collaboration be promoted? How is it possible to make room for new people in a timely fashion? The question of speed has persistently haunted the process of creating equitable and diverse educational institutions. From *Brown v. Board of Education*'s (1954) specifically vague language that schools will integrate with "all deliberate speed" to contemporary discussions of the "white fatigue" sapping the momentum of diversity initiatives (Flynn, 2014), speed has been a central yet ambiguous component of diversity. Even when there is agreement over the necessity of promoting diversity, speed is relative: too fast for some, stagnant for others.

Change needs to occur. We often hear that once positions of majoritarian privilege and power are increasingly held by minority candidates, then conversations will change and attitudes and environments will change with them. "We cannot wait," Martin Luther King Jr. once asserted. "We will not wait," R.D. Kelley recently advised in light of the racial profiling and unjust social dynamics taking place in American cities (Kelley, 2014).

When is the time for our conversations to change? How can change be measured? As Cornel West recently decried in an interview on CNN, sometimes a change of faces in power doesn't upset the status quo. Are diversity initiatives in higher education any different? A change of faces without a transformation in campus climate can defeat well-intentioned attempts to promote diversity and ensure inclusion. This is a reminder: The urgency of our diversity efforts cannot be put on pause for "people to come up through the ranks."

This discussion has been designed to be a starting point for continued diversity conversations based on the original conference presentation. The authors have taken advantage of the opportunity to stimulate further outreach of the ideas shared at the conference, in the hope that readers from many governance bodies will discuss these ideas with their colleagues and constituents. We invite you to sit down and grapple with each of the following questions:

Do we *want* to diversify our shared governance body?

Do you *need* to diversify our shared governance body?

Can we articulate the *want* and *need* around diversification?

Can we create space where existing members of our governance body will see the value added for them as people as well as the body and the process of governance through diversification?

What will we *gain* from diversifying governance spaces?

What will we *lose* if we don't make intentional efforts to diversify governance in higher education?

And, last, what are the significant actions and ideologies that function as barriers to diversifying your campus/system governance body?

Conversations about diversity and diversification are not easy to begin, and certainly not easy to sustain. Often, you might feel stuck in the same conversation over and over with the same array of actors on campus. There are many barriers facing the diversification of campuses today—from fatigue with diversity conversations, the perpetuation of structural discriminations without reflection or ownership of problems, to out-and-out hostility to the collapse of white privilege. We know that without numerous conversations, some of them difficult, we would not be able to articulate the importance and framing of diversity in governance. Every governance body has its own work to do. Start by asking yourself: Everyone brings diversity to the table, but who is at the table?

References

Flynn, J. (2014). *White fatigue and the myth of a post-racial America*. Unpublished manuscript presented at SUNY Buffalo State, February 24, 2015.

Joseph, T.D., & Hirshfield, L. (2013). "Why don't you get somebody new to do it?" Race, gender, and identity taxation. In M. Chesler & A. A. Young, Jr. (Eds.), *Faculty Social Identity and the Challenges of Diverse Classrooms in a Historically White University* (pp. 153–169). Boulder, CO: Paradigm Press.

Kelley, R.D. (2014). Why we won't wait. *Counterpunch*. Retrieved from http://www.counterpunch.org/2014/11/25/why-we-wont-wait

Steele, C.M., & Aronson, J. (1995). Stereotype threat and the intellectual test performance of African Americans. *Journal of Personality and Social Psychology*, 69(5), 797–811. http://dx.doi.org/10.1037/0022-3514.69.5.797

10

A Self-Critique of Shared Governance at Medgar Evers College

The Recent Protest Years, 2009–2013

Sallie M. Cuffee, Owen Brown, and Evelyn Maggio

Founded in 1970, Medgar Evers's history has been marked by a period of conflict with top-level administrative leadership appointed over the College by the City University of New York (CUNY). Appropriating this respected academic tradition, College stakeholders have sponsored a series of votes of "no confidence" to indicate the severity of the impasses. From any careful review, shared-governance for this College, with a core constituency of people of African descent, has been difficult to actualize in its over 40-year history. Subsequently, we will analyze some of the internal and external constraints that have contributed to truncating shared governance at Medgar Evers College, giving specific attention to the "recent protest years," 2009–2013. We conclude with recommendations in going forward to employ best practices in the progressive development of shared governance at this Predominantly Black Institution (PBI) in the CUNY system.

Introduction

Since its founding in 1970, Medgar Evers College's historical annals have been filled with protest rhetoric of gaining equal access and opportunity to the academic resources of the City University of New York (CUNY). The College was established in response to the "1960s project to democratize higher education through open admissions, remediation and affirmative action," as written in the abridged history by Florence Tager and Zala Highsmith-Taylor (2008, p. viii). In step with the changing times, Mayor

John Lindsay hailed Medgar Evers as "a model for the whole nation." While there was much to celebrate in the groundbreaking event, heralding the start of Medgar Evers College, the College was far from being simply one of the long-range priorities of the City University of New York. Across racial barriers, this College evolved as the brainchild of a number of radical equal rights activists consisting of elected officials, community leaders, educators, and parents. As grassroots historians have noted, this 42-year institution emerged out of "a community struggle" as well as the "racial conflicts" being waged in New York City at the time. Given the College's close ties to the community that helped to give birth to its existence, this "communiversity" (as it is fondly called by longtime professors and community leaders) was to serve a twofold institutional purpose: It would educate an underserved and disfranchised African American, Caribbean, and Latino population, and would participate in anchoring the economic, political, and social development of a burgeoning Central Brooklyn community.

Thus, from its very inception, Medgar Evers College has represented lofty and transformative goals. In particular, its history attests to its academic innovation when "it tried to redefine the relationship between town and gown, the relationship between the community that it would serve and the academy" (2008, p. 5). From then to now, its protest legacy continues to have currency in the College's ongoing interactions with students, faculty, and other key stakeholders' demands for greater transparency and accountability, as well as managing its external relations with the CUNY power system.

Although the College has had a stellar historical development, it has not been without its own internal challenges. Specifically, an ongoing challenge has been to develop an effective shared governance process to sustain its growth and longevity. In what follows we will focus on the constraints (primarily internal) that have truncated shared governance at Medgar Evers College during the most recent period of the protest years: 2009–2013. We focus on this recent period because we were both intimately involved and have firsthand account of these years. This historical account is written from that perspective, and is an extension of that trajectory. Throughout Medgar Evers's history, protest has been an important form of communication to make visible and vocal controversial positions and conditions at the College to vested stakeholders. Such protest is the founding cornerstone in the development of this institution, reinforcing its mainstay in the Brooklyn community.

We will focus substantive attention on external dynamics subordinating Medgar Evers' governance effectiveness. Consideration to both internal and external power dynamics is important because the College has not operated independently from a powerful university system that asserts pressure as necessary to drive its own short- and long-term priorities. We conclude with recommendations for going forward to employ best practices, as they relate to shared governance, monitoring, and development at a predominantly black college within the CUNY system.

A Sketch of Shared Governance

Admittedly, no substantive critique can be done on shared governance at Medgar Evers College without situating it in the larger discourse on nationwide trends in governance. That is to say, the governance trajectory of Medgar Evers did not evolve in isolation. Throughout academic institutions, institutional forces were at work infringing on the development of shared governance in educational settings, as seen up to the present time. Past President of the American Association of University Professors Gary Rhoades made the following points in his provocative article "We Are All Contingent: Reorganizing Higher Education and Society," in *AFT on Campus*, which discloses grimly that "over the past four decades, a systematic deterioration in the structure and working conditions of the professoriate has occurred. This has coincided with a systemic disinvestment in public higher education and, in particular, in instruction" (2014, p. 2). These systemic changes were underway concurrent with the birth of Medgar Evers College—the institution transition from a 1960s dream to a 1970s brick and mortar institution. On one level, it would have been difficult for Medgar Evers to escape the changes occurring nationwide; via restructuring, academic institutions were morphing into alignment with a corporate model of administrative management. A dramatic example of this type of transformation occurred for the College, because shortly after opening the Medgar Evers College doors, a 1975–76 fiscal exigency gripped CUNY. Most drastically, what this meant is that the college would receive long-term "inadequate funding that often resulted in inferior physical conditions, a lack of technology, and an increase in the number of adjunct faculty" (2008, p. 100).

Amid this austerity, Medgar Evers was hit particularly hard in the demand to restructure its senior college status to community college.

This period lasted from 1976 through 1990. During this time, the public rhetoric was not about the corporatization model, as we now know it. However, the fiscal exigency anticipated what would become full-blown in the following decades, in the second-tier funding of Medgar Evers and its truncation into community college status. Until 1991, it was underresourced and underserved. Only after 1991 did the College regain its senior college status, but it has yet to receive the corresponding funding status.

Rhoades's trenchant reading of the de-professionalization of faculty in his article gives further elucidation to the corporate model. He explains that, at the systemic level, there was an "emerging restructuring transpiring in colleges and universities nationwide" (p. 2). In the academic community, it is rhetoricized today as the full-scale emergence of the corporate business model, which trends toward directing institutional resources to "maximize institutional revenues and minimize investment in instructions," with this leading to faculty having a "declining influence in the various realms of academic and educational decision-making." In Rhoades's assessment, administrators have "increased their exercise of 'strategic' managerial discretion. That discretion has involved applying the logic of the market to academic decision-making, thereby reducing—and not uncommonly, overriding and replacing—the role and plans of faculty in various academic and educational matters" (p. 2). The over-arching concern is that these academic and educational priorities are not limited to administrative agendas but are "invading faculty controlled curricula matters" (p. 2). In hindsight, this [invasion of faculty-controlled curricula matters] may very well account for some of the contentious relationships between faculty and administrators within American colleges and universities.

The battle for control of colleges' and universities' curricula has been the basis of many struggles played out within the context of shared governance. For example, faculty members have tried to assert their control over the curricula, but they have not succeeded: college presidents and their administrations have largely gained the upper hand. Administrators have succeeded in controlling the process because they often engineer the support of trustees and/or state legislators. The result has been to undermine (at best) or truncate (at worst) faculty control over colleges and universities curricula.

A recent example is the introduction and imposition of Pathways on CUNY units by the Board of Trustees, engendering a bloodied exchange among local college units, the University Faculty Senate (UFS), and the university's administration. In this scrimmage, the loss of faculty control of curricula, which had been a time-honored tradition at CUNY, led to a highly politicized and publicized legal battle. Ultimately, the case was brought before Judge Anil Singh on February 21, 2011. The case was decided ·n favor of the UFS/PSC. However, the legal crossfire did not end there. The litigation involving Pathways was brought before the New York State Appeals Court, where the original decision was reversed, and the Court found in favor of the university/CUNY.

In the future, whether conflicts over curricula matters will require a legal course of action for resolution is uncertain. Just to note, some CUNY units remain in noncompliance with the Appeals ruling. Benjamin Ginsberg, author of *The Fall of the Faculty: The Rise of the All-Administrative University*, projects gloom and doom in his article "Power Shift" in *AFT On Campus*. According to him, "this shift in power within the university from academic professional to administrators" portends to be "an unmitigated disaster for higher education," (2014, p. 5).

Historical Sketch of Shared Governance at Medgar Evers College

From the limited body of literature addressing shared governance practices on black campuses, a general consensus prevails that such practices have been under-researched and have yet to receive the qualitative and quantitative attention necessary. The body of research literature is growing, though, since the publication of James Minor's 2005 article, "Discerning Facts about Faculty Governance at HBCUs." In his constructive piece, Minor argues that much of the perspective on governance at historically black colleges and universities (HBCU) is based on "isolated incidents; anecdotes rule the discourse" (2005, pp. 34–35). His article argues for "accurately gauge[d] perceptions about the quality of shared governance" on HBCU. Although Medgar Evers is not technically an HBCU, like many land grant black colleges it shares similar characteristics in historic mission and leadership style to HBCUs.

In principle, we have no dispute with what Minor observes about the anecdotal nature of the research of black college campuses, for he raises an important point that demands critical redress and analysis. However, until we can conduct enough of the data-driven studies he requires, faculty in their analyses must rely on the body of research and reflection readily available to advance best practices of shared governance on black college campuses. Indeed, there is research value in the descriptive, qualitative narratives of what is transpiring on such campuses. As we teach our students in the social and behavioral sciences, observation is one of the first steps in research and an important step in validating and/or invalidating perceptions.

Furthermore, stories related to votes of no confidence are no fictional tales. This highly regarded academic practice occurs at black and white institutions as a referendum on the effectiveness of administrative leadership. In the recent past of the CUNY system, Medgar Evers was not the only College hosting a vote of no confidence at the university. The College of Staten Island (CUNY) also called for a vote of no confidence during this time. Other colleges in the New York City area during this period such as New York University and St. John's College also took advantage of this long-respected practice. About this time, nationwide cries of no confidence were heard at the University of Virginia and at Idaho State University. When such an event happens, it usually indicates a breach in the institutional mechanism of college governance. A vote of no confidence signals the final breakdown in what should have been a participatory process, a breakdown that most faculty had hoped to avoid.

In my experience at Medgar Evers, the vast majority of faculty members had concluded that the College president was totally against oppositional voices. Because students, faculty, and community stakeholders' repeated calls for constitutive dialogues were largely ignored and/or dismissed, they initiated coordinated campaigns for a change in the College's leadership.

Since the tumultuous days of its founding, Medgar Evers has been navigating its own precipitous climb toward shared governance. In its over 40-year history, the College has had five presidents: Dr. Richard Trent (1970–1982), Dr. Jay Carrington Chunn, II (1984–1987), Dr. Edison O. Jackson (1989–2009), Dr. William L. Pollard (2009–2013), and Dr. Rudy Crew, appointed in 2013. It has also had one interim administrator, Dr. Dennis Paul (1982–1984), and an acting president, Dr. Leo A. Corbie (1987–1989). Three of the presidents—Trent, Chunn, and Pollard—allegedly left the college under the cloud of votes of no confidence. Reasons for their removal remain uncannily similar: Presidents were accused of "making" deals with the power structure to "administrative build-up" and ultimately "ignoring" the needs of students:

The vision and energy evident in the first few years of the College became compromised during the 1975–1976 economic and political crisis in CUNY. Perhaps, the greatest betrayal . . . was that the President had accepted community college status. Even though the College was allowed to keep its Baccalaureate programs, this change in status was a betrayal of the many years of struggle by the community for a senior college (Tager & Highsmith-Taylor, 2008, p. 100).

In particular, during Trent's administration, much of the rhetoric bantered about was the language of "compromise" and "betrayal." He was cast as "selling out the College and the Community" and "fostering" his own personal "self-interest" instead of "the founders' dream of a four year community controlled college." The tenure of the College's second president, Jay Carrington Chunn, was short-lived, as recorded by Tager and Highsmith-Taylor. Within 3 years, Chun was asked to resign, and Corbie was appointed to serve as acting president until 1989.

During the Pollard years, shortly after his appointment as president in 2009, a fulcrum of dissent arose at Medgar Evers when College constituencies, including faculty, staff, students, elected officials, and some community stakeholders, began to voice their concerns about the state of the College. Pollard's administration saw a growing culture of unilateral decision making, as reflected in his policies: a reduction in student services, a drop in enrollment, departure from the historic mission of the College, unprecedented attacks on women in leadership at the College, and unerring complaints about the administrative and consultant build-up. Much of this was reminiscent of earlier decades in the College's history under President Trent.

Out of this growing discontent between the college community and Pollard's administrative leadership, the first vote of no confidence was called by disparate College constituencies in December 2010. Once this action was taken by what was established as the Committee for the Whole, it sealed the cleavage in governance leadership. In the first round of voting, the consensus showed an obvious and growing disaffection on campus. The vote of no confidence was gaining momentum. However, the Faculty Senate did not lead this first round of vote, and CUNY Central questioned the legitimacy of the vote, intimating that perhaps it did not accurately signal the will of the faculty. The Faculty Senate addressed this when we led the 2012 vote of no confidence. With its unprecedented turnout, the will of the faculty was made overwhelmingly evident.

More than questioning the legitimacy of the process, as CUNY was doing, concerned faculty members were convinced that CUNY had its own reasons for desiring the Pollard administration to remain in leadership at the College. The suspicions swirling around the campus during the recent protest years differ little from the protest cries heard through the decades. As was alleged now and then, there was a CUNY agenda for Medgar Evers, and students and faculty alike were persuaded that this agenda did not support the historic mission of the College as an open-admission campus. News articles circulated that opinion throughout the community in *Our Time Press* and *Amsterdam News*. In the background, reservations about gentrification coming to Central Brooklyn were vocal. By extension, a query was bantered about: Does Medgar Evers need to have the persona of a black college any longer?

It is important to understand that during these protest years the campus was not on one accord. To suggest otherwise is to paint an inaccurate canvas of the power politics at play. Not only that, President Pollard had his own advocates and defenders who stood before the Board of Trustees and other judicatory bodies to argue the efficacy of his administration. The campus was polarized, but the overwhelming consensus was against the administration. One hundred and thirty-seven voted "no confidence," and 13 voted "confidence." In the final analysis, how people's particular histories intersected with the power politics occurring on campus factionalized the campus, and loyalties were split.

In the heat of battle, no faculty member could be questioned about his or her motives. Indeed the campus would have turned into a battleground of no return. Taking the long view, the Faculty Senate leadership knew that after this "no confidence" conflict was over, we had to work together in the forward movement of the College. Also, to be fair, those from the 1970s days and thereafter, who had orchestrated votes of no confidence against Dr. Trent and Dr. Chunn, were tired of the negative animus bred by such volatile actions. In the second decade of the 21st century, these "warhorse" faculty members wanted a different culture to distinguish the College's future.

The Imposed Governance State

Since June of 2013, Medgar Evers College (MEC) had been stripped of its governance. An imposed governance plan was ratified at the Board of Trustees' meeting. During the course of this imposed governance plan, President Rudolph Crew called together a committee to craft a new governance plan. The committee charged with developing the College's governance is composed of members of the College Council, Student Government, and the College President's appointees. The majority of the committee members are chosen from the ranks of the College's faculty. Eventually, the plan will be submitted to the College Council for ratification, and then sent on to CUNY's Board of Trustees for finalizing. During this process, the governance document has met unexpected resistance from faculty, although the document attempts to address some of those sticky areas of shared governance that have destabilized Medgar Evers over the decades. For instance, the role of administrators on governing bodies such as the College Council and the College-wide Personnel & Budget (P&B) Committee is addressed.

In our opinions, the version being crafted by the selected College constituencies is a more participatory document. It leads in empowering the collective body of the College without being heavily administrative driven. This is one article from the governance document reviewed during academic year 2014–2015:

ARTICLE 6—THE EXECUTIVE BOARD OF THE
COLLEGE COUNCIL

Section 1. Members. The Executive Board of the College Council shall have the following Members:

a. The President, who shall serve as Chairperson of the Executive Board. The President shall preside at all meetings of the Executive Board.

b. The duly elected Vice Chairperson of the College Council.

c. The duly elected Secretary of the College Council, who shall serve as the Secretary of the Executive Board.

d. The Provost and two Deans designated by the President.

e. Four faculty Members elected by and from the faculty Members of the College Council at its first meeting of the academic year.

f. The President of the Student Government Association

Other key areas that reinforce shared decision making in academic matters addressed in the governance plan, such as department chairs, standing committees, deans' election, protection of junior faculty, a transparent budgetary process, and faculty control over curriculum can only enhance shared governance at the College.

Since President Crew's arrival in fall 2013, his posture has been to give the charge of developing the new governance to the committee. Those faculty members who are participating and those observing believe that this proposed new governance is actually critical to the College's stabilization and movement in the direction of shared governance. It would appear also that the findings of the Collaborative on Academic Careers in Higher Education, known as the COACHE Report, substantiate much of what faculty has identified as important issues in shared governance.

Difficult Dialogues

Medgar Evers weathered the 2012 no confidence vote and an ousted president. Junior faculty's voices are encouraged to rejoin the governance process. Rather than intensify a culture of blame, punishment, or ostracism, the Faculty Senate on campus has proceeded from the position that a great deal of relationship building and healing should be the priority. This we learned: When past schisms are allowed to fester because of hurt feelings or injustices, imagined or real, the internal development of the campus is placed in jeopardy.

As we attend meetings at the College, often we hear objections from faculty about the lack of communication. They believe that insufficient communication ensues from the chairs, deans, and/or administrative officers. The point being raised is that without opportunities for sustained, transparent dialogues, old patterns reassert themselves to undermine shared governance and make it more elusive. At the administrative level, to facilitate infrastructure building as it relates to communication, President Crew institutionalized an annual leadership retreat to create a space for difficult dialogues to be engaged. The president must be commended for his forward thinking. This space responds to the need for communication to flow from the bottom up as well as top down. The College Council is another space that has been accessed for shared dialogues. It is the space where elected leaders vote on the business of the College. The Faculty Senate should be another. Perhaps there is no one space. Difficult dialogues, however, do anticipate a place of transparency for communication. It cannot be guaranteed that it is always a safe space.

For years, the budget at Medgar Evers has been a contentious issue. Recently, the Faculty Senate and other constituent groups asked the president how to make the budgetary process accessible, transparent, and inclusive.

The complaints heard at Medgar Evers are certainly not unusual. As Professor Ivory Phillips notes in his article "Shared Governance on Black College Campuses," "the budget is considered to be outside the purview of the faculty and the faculty senate" (2002, p. 53). When faculty members are not allowed to weigh in on the budget, we see hires at the College making corporate salaries but who do not meet expectations in their job performance. An excerpt from Ginsberg helps explain some of the animus of the protest politics at Medgar Evers:

> Everywhere, it seems, legions of administrators, including many who have never taught a class, are engaged in strategic planning, endlessly rewriting the school mission statement and 'rebranding' their campus. All these activities waste enormous amounts of time, require hiring thousands of new, "deanlets"—administrators who are not of the faculty—and, more often than not, involve the services of expensive consultants. (2014, p. 5)

These words are insightful in deconstructing why colleges cannot move forward because of the layers of consultants and administrators, often-times with faculty who are underpaid having to show administrators the way. This places an undue burden on those who make less but must lend their academic and scholarly expertise to train those who benefit the most. Here is a passage from Ginsberg's critical reading of this "superstructure" on college campuses:

> External cost drivers such as federal or state mandates are far less important than internal or voluntary factors, particularly growth in administrative spending, in explaining rising costs on college campuses. Schools have chosen, not been forced, to spend more, and what they have chosen to spend money on is the administrative superstructure, not the education of students. (2014, p. 6)

In other words, the budget, rather than the academic mission, often drives the priorities of the College.

On black or white campuses, in interpreting Rhoades, the corporate model serves the institutions but does "a disservice to a large portion of our student populations, particularly the growing number of [the] low-income, underserved population [who] are seeking education opportunities" (2014, p. 2). For instance, whether one believes that shared governance is an issue or not, seemingly something as innocuous as classroom size has implications for the academic mission of the college. If classes are ballooned for financial reasons, and yet the pedagogy being employed does not accommodate large classrooms, student learning is jeopardized, as well as teaching effectiveness. Faculty lines, course offerings, upper-level courses, in which class sizes are inordinately small or outsized large, the availability of particular majors or programs, and the nature of faculty appointments are also affected. These are budgetary issues that impact on governance, whether at the department level or college wide.

Recently, a campaign against a ROTC program was led by a junior faculty member. It was refreshing to see that level of engagement and passion in the College Council about an issue that had implications for the whole campus. The ROTC program would have helped financial matters at the college, but at whose expense? These matters that appear to be so innocuous are in fact not. They affect the educational and academic culture and environment of the institution, with a direct correlation to students' retention and graduation rates.

The 2015 COACHE Report

The recent findings of the Collaborative on Academic Careers in Higher Education (COACHE) Survey regarding the level of job satisfaction of the faculty at Medgar Evers College substantiate the arguments set forth in this chapter. Several of its findings buttressed our argument that there is a significant need for college leadership to renew its commitment to shared governance. The COACHE Survey is administered by the Harvard University Graduate School of Education. Since 2003, the survey has been used to assist colleges and universities to pinpoint problem areas and to assess how they compare to other institutions that share their demographic profiles.

In 2014–2015, Medgar Evers College participated in the COACHE Faculty Job Satisfaction Survey. Its cohort institutions included John Jay College, the College of Staten Island, York College, and the New Jersey City University. Of the 157 faculty members, 58 responded to the COACHE Survey. In the area of shared governance, the College was rated as very ineffective when compared to its cohort institutions (COACHE, 2015a, p. 2). In specific terms, when asked in the survey the question, "If a candidate for a position asked you about your department as a place to work would you . . . ," over 25% of respondents answered they would not recommend their department as a place to work (Job Survey Provost Report, p. 17). Finally, in 75% of the indicators of job satisfaction, MEC faculty scores were below that of its cohort institutions (COACHE, 2015b, pp. 21–23).

From just this brief summary of the COACHE Report, the indicators are clear that a governance overhaul is in order at Medgar Evers College. An important step is faculty involvement in the ratification of a participatory governance plan, which is already underway; however, leadership at the top, such as in the Office of Academic Affairs, is also necessary. Surprisingly, the report suggests that greater leadership is required at the departmental level, as well. A significant number of faculty members indicated that leadership in the departments was in need of improvement.

Of significance, the ineffective performance of Medgar Evers on the COACHE Report is not placed at the door of the current senior administrative leadership alone. What the administrators decide to do with these preliminary findings will indicate their level of political will toward securing effective governance in the College's forward movement. Finally, the COACHE Survey indicates that a self-critique in this case requires looking at administrators as much as faculty.

Recommendations

First, at Medgar Evers College, faculty leaders must work harder to ensure the involvement of junior faculty members in governance structures. Their involvement is important for their own professional development and benefits the institution in that faculty members who feel included and empowered are easier to retain. Unlike passive junior professors, assertive new faculty members also make excellent role models for students and are more likely to become courageous, engaged senior faculty.

Second, another area of concern is evaluation. This is why surveys such as the COACHE Survey are so important for faculty to participate in, because at Medgar Evers a mechanism has not been in place for the college's routine evaluation of our administrators—chairs, deans, vice presidents, and presidents. Nor do we have access to evaluation results and the assurance that those results will influence administrators' compensation or future employment. Such lack of evaluation sends a clear message that the boards and the presidents—not the faculty, staff, or students—are responsible for all administrators. It also conveys the message that administrators need not be concerned about the opinions of faculty, staff, or students, nor be responsive to them. This kind of atmosphere most certainly undercuts the concept of shared governance and destroys its effectiveness.

Third, internal data collected at the College and CUNY Central should be used to determine best practice for improving students' success and identifying the academic priorities of the College. Students are the life blood of all institutions. To address the need to increase students' success, students' performance data should be used to increase students' persistence and graduation rates. These decisions include effective pedagogy and the use of technology to better prepare students for the world of work.

Fourth, administrative leadership should not pander to professors' vestige interests that are not aligned with student success. Far too often, influential professors have exercised undue influences over the decisions of academic departments and what is best for students' success. While this has promoted the short-term interests of career-centered professors, it has done precious little to advance student success. Open, honest dialogue among faculty, students, and administrators will ultimately advance student success and the commitment of the College to preparing students for life after college.

Last, Medgar Evers College should promote leadership that is student centered and use data to deliver the best educational product that empowers students to become agents of change in their communities. College presidents and faculty should use the accreditation process to seriously evaluate whether a college remains true to its core mission (Middle States Commission on Higher Education, 2006, pp. 21–22). Key college stakeholders must insist on open dialogue, sometimes difficult dialogue, to ensure that the college's resources are being used efficiently to improve student success. Equally important, these key stakeholders' dialogues should buttress and promote shared governance and academic freedom.

Conclusion

Medgar Evers College remains one of the cornerstone institutions within the CUNY University systems because of its core mission to provide educational services to the underserved residents of the Central Brooklyn community and beyond those circumscribed borders. Its core mission is as relevant today as it was at the time of the founding of the institution in the early 1970s. Regrettably, critics often cite the College's low retention and graduation rates as reasons why Medgar Evers College is a failed institution in need of change. What they choose to overlook is that the students that Medgar Evers serves are typically ignored by other colleges and universities (driven by the corporate model) because most of them are poor and underprepared for college. To its credit, Medgar Evers began as an open-enrollment institution and remains so, targeting students who were failed by the New York City public school system.

While many of Medgar Evers's faculty members agree that there are several problems regarding curricula, students' academic progression, graduation rates, and fiscal control that need to be addressed, these problems cannot be resolved without the input and involvement of a key constituency: the College faculty. If nothing else, the COACHE Survey results provide quantitative evidence that many faculty members of Medgar Evers College feel demoralized and devalued. Without shared governance, how do we move forward effectively?

Finally, without the valuing of shared governance by the College and CUNY's Board of Trustees, the Medgar Evers faculty, students, and community cannot hope to achieve its founders' vision and continue their intended trajectory. Subsequently, for Medgar Evers College to advance in shared governance, there must be mandate supported and encouraged by the president's office. The desired end result is not to tie the president's hands, as some might suggest; rather, the intent is to see that a clear vision and committed political will exists at the highest office in the institution down through the ranks to secure an effective process going forward into building the future of the College.

Last words: It is important to note that while Medgar Evers has its own unique trajectory of protest and politics in its historical development, it shares some of the same grievances and challenges, losses and opportunities as other academic institutions. In other words, the College is not an anomaly. To paint such a canvas would be a breach of trust on our part. Under-resourced, with enormous expectations to do the impossible, the College has survived and thrived. But when will we actualize the full potential of this institution? What could this College evolve into if it became a strategic priority of the university system, with resources to achieve its end goal? The next chapter in Medgar Evers College's illustrious history waits to be written.

References

COACHE (2015a). *COACHE Faculty Job Satisfaction Survey Governance and Leadership Medgar Evers College.* Cambridge, MA: Harvard Graduate School of Education.

COACHE (2015b). *COACHE Faculty Job Satisfaction Survey Provost's Report Medgar Evers College.* Cambridge, MA: Harvard Graduate School of Education.

Ginsberg, Benjamin. (2014). Power shift. *ATF on Campus, 33*(4), 5–6.

Middle States Commission on Higher Education (2006). *Characteristics of excellence in higher education.* Philadelphia: MSCHE.

Minor, J.T. (2005). Discerning facts about faculty governance at HBCUs. *Academe, 91*(3), 34–38.

Phillips, I. (2002). Shared governance on black college campuses. *Academe, 88*(4), 5–55.

Rhoades, Gary. (S 2014). We are all contingent. *ATF on Campus, 33*(4), 2–4.

Tager, F., & Highsmith-Taylor, Z. (2008). *Medgar Evers College: The pursuit of a community's dream.* New York: Caribbean Diaspora Press.

11

Conclusion

Working Together
to Share Governance

Norman Goodman

In this final word in the volume, I detail answers to the two questions posed to the panelist for the wrap-up session of the conference: (1) What do you take away as the single most important message you have heard at the conference? (2) Looking forward to the future of shared governance, how can—or should—it be best achieved as universities continue to evolve in this first part of the 21st century?

The answer to question 1 involves developing a strategy to engage and retain faculty, staff, and students to work with sympathetic administrators in a process of shared governance. That means identifying appropriate faculty, staff, and students and demonstrating the alignment of their goals with those of shared governance. It also involves agreeing on a reasonable timeframe for action, as well as clarity as to what will be expected of them. Finally, it is important to follow up the results of shared governance action to allow necessary adjustments to unanticipated consequences of these actions.

The answer to question 2 involves fostering a sense of trust and mutual respect among participants. Participants need to be empathic, taking into account differences in conceptions of the university and the roles played by the different participants. Additionally, the process involved in a shared governance action, the information necessary to accomplish the task, and the results of the activity need to be transparent.

Finally, faculty, staff, and students need to realize that they have leverage to affect administrative decisions because of their knowledge, expertise, and experience—as well as their necessary involvement in implementing campus policies and programs.

For the final wrap-up session of the "SUNY Voices Conference on Shared Governance for Institutions of Higher Education in the 21st Century: Beyond Stereotypes," a panel was asked to sum up the activities of the conference. The moderator of this session, who was also the co-organizer of the conference, Peter Knuepfer, President of the SUNY University Faculty Senate, asked the panelists to respond to two questions: (1) What do you take away as the single most important message you have heard at the conference? (2) Looking forward to the future of shared governance, how can—or should—it be best achieved as universities continue to evolve in this first part of the 21st century?

The following is an illustration of the response of one panelist, based on attendance at many of the concurrent sessions and his multi-decade experience in shared governance.

What do you take away as the single most important message you have heard at the conference?

It is important to develop a strategy to engage and retain faculty, staff, and students in a process of shared governance, and to bring governance members together with administrators who see the benefits of shared governance.

Align Individual and Governance Goals

In order to encourage faculty, staff, and students to get involved in shared governance, it is necessary to demonstrate that many of their personal and professional goals and aims have a direct connection to the current and long-term goals of the governance organization. Governance bodies are generally composed of working committees that focus on different campus functions (e.g., budget, curriculum, academic standing, promotion and tenure, student life). Many campus individuals (faculty, staff, and students) have interests, knowledge, and experience in areas in which these committees operate. Governance bodies need to identify and then recruit these individuals. Outreach to them should be individualized and emphasize the fact that their involvement in these committees will not only be useful to a well-functioning campus, but to meeting their own goals as well. For one example, faculty, staff, and students who are interested in the details of the academic programs that will be required of students should be encouraged to get involved in the campus' curriculum committee. Participation of interested and knowledgeable people enhance the expertise of the committee and serve the campus as well.

For administrators, it is necessary to demonstrate that there are faculty and staff (and, in some cases, students) who have the relevant knowledge, expertise, and experience that is useful in the development of university policy and programs. Consequently, their involvement can contribute to policies and programs that would be better with their participation than without it. Equally important is the consideration of the implementation of new policies and programs. Generally, faculty and staff are charged with the responsibility of carrying out new policies and programs. Therefore, their involvement in establishing these policies and programs will increase the likelihood of the acceptance of them by faculty and staff—and also lead to a greater commitment by these groups to making them work successfully.

Agree on a Reasonable Timeframe for Governance Action

This is an important issue for faculty, staff, and students as well as administrators. There needs to be an agreement of a reasonable amount of time to devote to an issue to bring it to some measure of conclusion. Most faculty, staff, and students need to see some "light at the end of the tunnel"—that is, the possibility of obtaining a sense of accomplishment for a task completed that is generally measured by a semester or academic year. Beyond that, many (and most especially students, whose involvement with the campus is generally of a much shorter duration than most faculty and staff) will lose momentum—and possibly interest—for working on a specific governance activity. Also, change in governance leadership and committee membership from one year to the next can create difficulties in moving some activities forward.

On the other hand, administrators are often responsible for making decisions rather rapidly. Due to pressure from above, or from general administrative schedules, their timeframe for action is generally shorter than those for faculty and staff. Consequently, from their point of view, speed of action is desired in a matter of weeks or months rather than semesters or academic years. Thus, there needs to be an early discussion and a clear agreement on a timeframe for any necessary governance action. The conclusion reached regarding the deadline for action needs (to the extent possible) to fit the time requirements of the administrators as well as to take into consideration input from the governance body. Governance leaders need to determine an appropriate amount of time that would be adequate to consider the action involved. Ideally, consensus between the administration and the governance body should be reached before there is a commitment to work on the activity involved.

Establish Clear "Rules of Engagement" for Those Involved in Governance Activities

If faculty, staff, and students are to be encouraged to play a role in governance activities, they need to know exactly what will be required of them.

- Perhaps the most important requirement is time. They need to know the time commitment that they are being asked to make in advance of actually making that commitment to serve.
  - Specifically, they need to be informed of how many meetings are required, and on what schedule (weekly, biweekly, monthly).
  - They should be informed of the overall timeline of the effort, as well as any expectations that they will be asked to contribute during times when classes are not in session.
  - They need to clearly understand what will be required of them between meetings.
- They also need to be given some sense of the *actual activities* that are likely to be required of them if they join a particular governance activity.
  - For example, will they be asked to obtain and analyze relevant documents?
  - Will they need to interview campus officials, members of other campus constituencies, or contact other institutions?
  - Will they be required to provide oral and/or written reports of their work to the committee?

Sharing this information, along with a clear charge for the work to be accomplished, can go a long way toward involving people who know what they are getting into prior to agreeing to serve. Consequently, any potential resentment about the scope of their obligations can be greatly minimized and accomplishments can be maximized.

Close the Loop

It is important for all parties to review the results of the action(s) agreed on through shared governance. Following up the results of a new policy or program after a reasonable period of time will allow parties to assess if the results expected from their collaboration has in fact occurred. In effect, this follow-up is similar to "midcourse corrections" that are typical in space flights. Similarly, it has become routine that when a new computer program is developed and put into practice, "bug fixes," or necessary adjustments, are expected. A similar practice is often useful in following up on actions taken through shared governance since the establishment of new policies or program may well have unanticipated results for which adjustments will be necessary.

This follow-up is also essential to give faculty, staff, and students a sense that their efforts have had some consequence. Too often, faculty, staff, and students do not have any evidence that the time, thought, and effort that they put into a shared governance project have had any effect. If they conclude that their contributions were negligible or ignored, they are less likely to continue participating in shared governance. It is far better to illustrate to them that their participation was consequential so that they will continue to be engaged in shared governance and to encourage their colleagues to become involved as well. Showing the continued viability of their work serves this purpose.

Looking forward to the future of shared governance: How can—or should—it be best achieved as universities continue to evolve in the first part of the 21st century?

Engender Trust and Mutual Respect

The answer to this question was best approached by two key leaders of SUNY: H. Carl McCall, the chairman of the SUNY Board of Trustees, and Nancy Zimpher, the chancellor of the State University of New York. In his remarks opening the conference, McCall said that "shared governance is not a part of corporate or military organizations, but it is an essential part of institutions of higher education." He emphasized the importance of trust and mutual respect on the part of various constituencies of the university. Zimpher, for her part, emphasized the importance of collaboration among the various stakeholders of institutions of higher education. She linked this directly to McCall's point about the importance of trust by stating that "collaboration moves at the speed of trust."

Trust and mutual respect are essential. Administrators differ from faculty, staff, and students in terms of their roles and sets of responsibilities within the institution. It is an article of faith in my discipline of sociology that people who occupy a different status and play a different role perceive and interpret things differently. This may result in the members of each group having different goals for the organization or believing in different means to attain even agreed-upon common goals. Their perceptions of a situation differ and, thus, the actions that they see as necessary will also likely differ.

Take into Account the Fact That There Are Different Conceptions of the University—Collegial and Bureaucratic

Part of the difference between administrators and faculty is rooted in the fact that, in general, faculty (and, to some extent, staff and students) tend to see the university as a "collegial" institution. Collegial refers to "colleagues [who] are . . . explicitly united in a common purpose and respecting each other's abilities to work toward that purpose [Wikipedia] . . . [and] relating to or involving shared responsibility, as among a group of colleagues" [Oxford Dictionaries].

Administrators, on the other hand, tend to view the university as a bureaucratic organization. This view stresses (1) the importance of hierarchical authority in decision making, (2) following a set of relatively rigid and consistent rules, and (3) the necessity of maintaining formal written documentation of actions.

These different perceptions of the nature of the university, and the different roles that administrators, faculty, staff, and students play in it, are often the basis of some of the difficulties of their cooperating in shared governance. This is why trust and mutual respect—based on in-depth understanding of and empathy for the "other"—are essential.

Be Empathic

To work together effectively, each group must be able to "take the role of the other" (to be empathic) in order to understand how their partners in a shared venture see the situation. To be empathic doesn't necessarily require agreement with the other; it does, however, involve understanding that the different perceptions and interpretations of the other need to be taken into account in order to arrive at a common agreement on any issue at hand. Mutual understanding is an essential element in arriving at a compromise that respects the core views and responsibilities of each of the participants.

Years ago, I had an idea that I thought might well increase understanding, empathy, and trust among faculty and administers. I suggested to a previous campus president that a mutually beneficial policy to this end could be established by the practice of routinely appointing several faculty who had recently received tenure to a short-term (2 to 3 years) administrative assignment (e.g., Assistant Dean, Assistant Provost, Assistant Vice President). There could be several benefits as a result: (1) This experience could allow these faculty to better understand the administrative perspective and responsibilities, including the limitations on administrators; many faculty are generally unaware that there constraints on administrators as a consequence of state and federal regulations as well as system policies; (2) at the same time, rotating faculty into short-term administrative assignments would ensure that administrators have ongoing contact with these faculty whose perceptions might well differ from theirs; (3) the result of such a program might well provide the opportunity for administrators and faculty to better understand the role of the other, which would facilitate their ability to make the necessary compromises that are at the heart of collaborative action; and (4) it might serve to recruit faculty to extended administrative assignments.

Ensure Transparency

Another element that was identified as important for shared governance in today's world was the issue of transparency. The lack of transparency breeds suspicion and can undermine any effort for fruitful collaboration. It also hinders effective collective action.

Transparency is important so that governance members not only believe that they have all the necessary information to be able to play a significant and knowledgeable role in an activity of shared governance, but that is in fact the case. This is especially important for faculty, staff, and students, whose involvement in governance is understood to be advisory and not determinative. As an example of required transparency, if faculty, staff, and students are to participate in a proposal to create a new academic department/school/college, they need to know the resources (human, financial, capital) that will be devoted to the new venture, where those resources are coming from, and what effect the establishment of this unit will have on other elements of the campus. Ideally, all of the participants in this shared governance process would agree that transparency has the potential for beneficial outcomes and would, consequently, be less reluctant to share all necessary information.

Concluding Comments

One of the lessons learned from the various presentations at this conference is that though faculty, staff, and students are only "advisory" in the governance of the university, they do have significant leverage to influence policy and actions. Their knowledge and expertise—as well as their necessary involvement in carrying out policies and programs—give them persuasive influence if not actual power in determining university policies and programs.

Equally important, working together through a process of shared governance often results in each of the campus constituencies developing a much more nuanced view of each other than they originally had—with greater potential to increase trust and mutual respect. This more nuanced view of the other will make it more likely that the different perspectives, skills, and experience of the participants will be considered seriously. Consequently, it can facilitate necessary collaboration that is more likely to produce a satisfying result that generally will engender greater acceptance of new programs and policies by the various campus constituencies.

Finally, a cautionary note: The success of this conference was a result of numerous examples of shared governance on particular campuses that could be seen as potential models elsewhere. However, the conference had the feel of "preaching to the choir." Frequent stumbling blocks to shared governance are administrators who do not necessarily value the input of faculty, staff, or students in developing campus policies and programs. Rather, they tend to see shared governance as an intrusion on their authority. The success of future conferences on shared governance will require the involvement of administrators who are not adequately convinced that they need to seriously include these other constituencies in the establishment of campus policies and programs. These individuals—who might automatically dismiss the value of attending such a conference— are the very people who need exposure to the positive effects of shared governance that was evident in the various sessions of this conference. Had they attended, they might have been surprised by the level of overt support for shared governance by the SUNY leadership—the chairman of the SUNY Board of Trustees and the SUNY chancellor, both of whom have espoused and practiced shared governance, as well as some of their fellow administrators—to make the campuses of SUNY the kind of collegial organization that should be the hallmark of institutions of higher education. In the future, it is hoped that the leadership of SUNY would use their persuasive abilities to increase the number of administrative participants to this conference.

Contributors

Oluwadamisi Atanda recently completed a master's degree at Columbia University. His research focused on the role of human rights in U.S. Foreign Policy, particularly as it relates to the distribution of foreign aid to the Middle East. He served as Foreign Affairs Fellow with the U.S. Department of State and has completed internships with both the federal and state governments in between his studies. He holds a bachelor's degree in political science and public policy from the City College of New York, where he was a Colin Powell Community Engagement Fellow and graduated valedictorian.

Minna S. Barrett is a Distinguished Service Professor in the State University of New York, College at Old Westbury. She began teaching in 1975 as a founder of a program in psychology. Dr. Barrett received a BA (1969) and PhD (1978) in psychology from the State University of New York at Stony Brook. She is the author of a variety of articles and book chapters on language development, education in the People's Republic of China during the Cultural Revolution, adolescent socialization, women's microfinancing, environmental exposures and migrant farm worker health, mental health treatment modalities for women with breast cancer, treatment approaches for complicated grief and disaster related PTSD, impacts of environmental exposures on first responders, and women and breast cancer. She has received numerous awards for psychology in the public interest, including the Sarah J. Haley Award from the International Society for Traumatic Stress Studies, a NYSUT Service Award, a U.S. Congressional Citation in the Congressional Record, and a Henri Dunant Humanitarian Award from the American Red Cross. She garnered millions of dollars for disaster mental health program design and delivery and is a member of the American Red Cross Disaster Human Resources System. She traveled to the People's Republic of China during the Cultural Revolution in 1973 to study the organization of science research and education; the Republic of Kenya in the 1980's for the UN Decade for Women; Brazil for the UN Conference on Environment and Development in 1992; and numerous other countries over the last decade to discuss mental health interventions to natural and human-caused disasters. She has worked on local, regional, state, and federal government committees and boards for environmental oversight, environmental justice, and women's and children's health. She received the rank of Distinguished Service Professor in 2009 for a career-long engagement in professional service in the public interest and continuous service to the governance committees of her campus and, currently to SUNY. She is and has been an ardent supporter of high-quality public higher education.

Elizabeth L. Bringsjord is Vice Chancellor for Academic Affairs and Vice Provost at SUNY System Administration. Over the course of her 17-year tenure at SUNY, Dr. Bringsjord has led numerous system-wide initiatives focused on academic quality, strategic planning, accountability and transparency, and data-driven policy- and decision making. She currently oversees SUNY Excels, the University's performance system, which calls for system-wide commitment to continuous improvement toward excellence in key mission-critical areas. Notable among her accomplishments, she served as SUNY's Interim Provost between 2013 and 2014, and was instrumental in finalizing SUNY's seamless transfer initiative, the largest such effort in the country. She was co-convener of SUNY's Innovative Instruction Team, which led to the launch of Open SUNY, one of the largest online and instructional technology support networks in the nation. As Principal Investigator of TeachNY, she supports its Advisory Council's work on developing bold, forward-thinking policy recommendations for teacher preparation and development. Dr. Bringsjord is an expert in program evaluation and assessment. She spearheaded the restructuring of SUNY's process for reviewing and approving academic programs across the System, to ensure alignment with the evolving needs of the state workforce, along with best practices for student completion and success. She has supervised the preparation of numerous SUNY policies and guidance documents, as well as the university's three most recent master plans. A strong proponent of shared governance, Dr. Bringsjord has served on the Executive Committee of the University Faculty Senate, and currently sits on the Chancellor's Cabinet and executive team. In recognition of her outstanding dedication and service, Dr. Bringsjord is a recipient of the Chancellor's Award for Excellence in Professional Service, and holds a

PhD and MS in educational psychology and statistics from the University at Albany, a Master's in nursing from the University of Pennsylvania, and a BS in nursing from Boston University.

Owen Brown received his doctorate from Binghamton University Department of Sociology. Dr. Brown's area of specialization is Economic-Sociology. Currently, he is a tenured Associate Professor and Chairperson of the Department of Social and Behavioral Sciences at Medgar Evers College. Medgar Evers College is a Senior College of the City University of New York. Dr. Brown has served on the U.S. Departments of Labor and Education Nation School-to-Work Board. As a contractor, he organized a national conference aimed at the management and distribution a $33 million dollar H-1B Training initiative for the United States Department of Labor. He has written grants that have generated over $7 million dollars for Medgar Evers College and the City University of New York Research Foundation. He is currently working on a book for publication in 2016 titled *President Barack Obama and the Myth of Black Progress in America: A Study in White Supremacy, Historical Capital, and the African American Experience.*

Noelle Chaddock is Associate Dean of Academic Affairs for Diversity and Inclusivity at Rhodes College, working with faculty around issues of equity and inclusion in and outside the classroom. After 8 years in the SUNY System (the last 2 of which as the SUNY Cortland Chief Diversity Officer), Dr. Chaddock contributed to the system-wide cultivation of inclusive leadership. For 3 years, Chaddock served as chair of the University Faculty Senate Committee on Equity, Inclusion, and Diversity. Chaddock also served on the Chancellor's Diversity Task Force and on the planning committee of the first annual SUNY System Diversity Conference. Chaddock has presented to (and provided diversity training for) the University Faculty Senate, SUNY Environmental Science and Forestry (ESF), SUNY Morrisville, Stonybrook University, and community partners in the public and private sectors, including the Binghamton Police Department. Chaddock received her doctorate in Philosophy from Binghamton University and focuses her scholarship on and through critical race and critical mixed race frameworks and theory.

Sharon F. Cramer, a SUNY Distinguished Service Professor at Buffalo State College, was a faculty member from 1985 to 2011. During her career she served as an academic leader in roles that included department chair (1995–1999), chair of the College Senate (2007–2010), and chair of the Governance Committee of the SUNY University Faculty Senate (2007–2010). She was an officer, on the Board of Directors, of four professional and governance organizations, and received the highest award from each of them. From the SUNY University Faculty Senate, she received the Ram Chugh award in 2011 and the Senator Emerita award in 2015. From 2011 until 2017, she served as Parliamentarian for the SUNY University Faculty Senate.

Dr. Cramer has given over 100 presentations and keynotes in 23 states and two provinces in Canada. She completed her PhD studies at New York University, and earned an MAT degree from Harvard University and a BA from Tufts University. Her publication record includes 3 books (one co-authored with Jan Stivers), 26 scholarly articles, 22 reflective, personal articles in the *Buffalo News*, and 7 chapters. She is listed in *Who's Who in America* (2006–present), *Who's Who in American Education* (2006–present), and *Who's Who in American Women* (2008–present).

Sallie M. Cuffee holds a PhD in Christian Ethics from Union Theological Seminary in New York City. She is Professor in the Department of Social and Behavioral Sciences at Medgar Evers College/City University of New York. She served as an adjunct professor in the Doctor of Ministry and Master of Divinity degree programs at New York Theological Seminary. Dr. Cuffee founded the National African American Clergywomen Oral History Project and the Brooklyn African American Clergywomen Oral History Project. These oral history projects received modest support from the American Academy of Religion and the Professional Staff Congress–City University of New York.

Dr. Cuffee has published extensively, including "The Moral Agency of Black Church Women Matters: Constructing a Womanist Discourse of Sexual Resistance," "Medgar Evers College: CUNY's Last Colony in Shared Governance," and *Manchild Dying in the Promised Land*. Her first book was the study guide to Elsa Tamez's *Jesus and Courageous Women*. Her book *Women's Power in the Pulpit: Stories of Trial and Triumph of African American Clergywomen in Leadership* is forthcoming.

Dr. Cuffee has broad experience in the areas of human rights, women's rights, environmental issues, and racial justice. As a United Nations' liaison for Church World Service, she served as one of the organizing representatives at all international preparatory meetings for the 2001 World Conference against Racism, Racial Discrimination, Xenophobia, and Related Intolerance, at Durban, South Africa, and co-convened the Commission on Religious Intolerance. Her duties included leading a delegation, hosting a special session with the U.N. Special Rapporteur in the field of religious freedom and tolerance, as well as moderating a session on gender and religion, with regional follow-up leadership meetings funded by the Ford Foundation. Her commitment to social justice has been recognized with a number of awards, among them the Martin Luther King, Jr. Award.

Rob Deemer is Associate Professor of Music Composition, State University of New York at Fredonia, and was a 2016–2017 ACE (American Council on Education) Fellow. Dr. Deemer's compositional career has seen his music performed at Weill Recital Hall at Carnegie Hall, the Kennedy Center, the Cannes Film Festival, the Edinburgh Fringe Festival, Joe's Pub in New York City, The Jazz Showcase in Chicago, the 50-yard line of Ralph Wilson Stadium, and the steps of the United States Capitol. As an author and new music advocate, Deemer has become well known for his essays for NewMusicBox.org, Sequenza21.com and the *New York Times*. In addition to being the Head of Composition in the School of Music at the State University of New York at Fredonia, he also serves on the composition faculty at the Interlochen Summer Arts Camp. His work with pre-college composers has included being a founding member of the National Association for Music Education Composition Council, the chair of the New York State School Music Association Composition/Improvisation committee, and a member of the National Coalition for Core Arts Standards Composition/Theory Standards Subcommittee. His work in governance at the State University of New York at Fredonia has included 4 years as the chair of their University Senate and 3 years as the chair of their Faculty and Professional Affairs Committee. He holds the following degrees and certificates: DMA, Music Composition, University of Texas, 2005; MM, Music Composition, Northern Illinois University, 2001; Performers Certificate, Orchestral & Wind Conducting, Northern Illinois University, 2001; Advanced Certificate, Scoring for Motion Pictures and Television, University of Southern California, 1996; and BM, Music Education, Northern Illinois University, 1994.

Kelley J. Donaghy is Associate Professor of inorganic chemistry at the State University of New York College of Environmental Science and Forestry (ESF). She has been serving as Executive Chair of Academic Governance (formerly Faculty Governance) at ESF since 2010. She is also the Director of the Environmental Scholars Program which is funded by the National Science Foundation Scholarships in Science, Technology, Engineering and Math Program. Her main focus of research is creating educational materials for teaching and learning chemistry for majors and nonmajors, and synthetic boron hydride chemistry. In addition she runs one of the few service-learning courses in chemistry in the country, which serves about 100 students every year and more than 10 local organizations in the Syracuse area with chemistry related projects. Students engaged in this service-learning course routinely perform close to 3,000 community service hours each spring and are credited with preserving one of Onondaga Counties few fish hatcheries. After stepping down from the Executive Chair position she plans to create a Community Engagement and Environmental Leadership Institute (CEELI) at ESF. In 2008, Donaghy received three awards: the Distinguished teaching professor award from the ESF Undergraduate Student Association, the ESF President's Award for Community Service (for her work on campus), and the ESF President's Public Service Award for her service-learning course and community service through her professional organization, the American Chemical Society. Kelley received her BS from Syracuse University and her PhD from the University of Pennsylvania. In 2014 she was awarded the SUNY Chancellor's Award for Faculty Service. In 2016, Donaghy received the Chugh/University Faculty Senate Outstanding Service Award, which is conferred by the UFS Faculty Executive Committee to a person who has achieved a reputation for outstanding service in the area of faculty governance at the system and campus levels for a minimum of 5 years.

Tina Good is Professor of English at Suffolk County Community College and served as President of the SUNY Faculty Council of Community Colleges from 2009 to 2015. As president of the Faculty Council, Dr. Good was also appointed an *ex officio* member of the SUNY Board of Trustees and also served as Chair of the Community College Committee.

During her 15-year tenure with the Faculty Council, she served on many SUNY task forces and steering committees, including the Open SUNY Advisory Committee and the Power of SUNY Strategic Planning Steering Committee. She co-chaired the SUNY General Education Assessment Review (GEAR) Group and the SUNY Joint Committee for Transfer and Articulation and currently serves as Chair of the SUNY Steering Committee on Student Mobility. Working with SUNY System Administration, the University Faculty Senate, the Student Assembly, and the Faculty Council, Good worked to establish the strategic planning initiative known as SUNY Voices, a collaborative effort designed to strengthen shared governance throughout the State University of New York. Dr. Good served as the President of the Ammerman Campus Faculty Senate at Suffolk County

Community College for 5 years and has chaired the College's Curriculum Committee for over 15 years.

She is the co-editor of *In Our Own Voice, Graduate Students Teach Writing* and co-authored the article, "A Cautionary Tale About System-wide Assessment in the State University of New York: Why and How Faculty Voices Can and Must Unite," which appears in *Literary Study, Measurement, and the Sublime: Disciplinary Assessment*. Dr. Good received her BA and MA in English from California State University, Fresno. She received her PhD in English from State University of New York at Stony Brook.

Norman Goodman is SUNY Distinguished Teaching Professor and SUNY Distinguished Service Professor of Sociology at Stony Brook University, the first person in New York State to be awarded two distinguished professorships. He is an accomplished scholar as author or editor of nine books and over 20 articles in professional journals and book chapters. He has also presented papers at major disciplinary conferences. His academic specialties are in social psychology (especially issues of identity and socialization) and marriage and family life.

Dr. Goodman has extensive governance experience. He was chair of his department for 20 years and, at Stony Brook University, was president of the Arts and Sciences Senate and twice president of the University Senate. He has served as a member or chair of most of the standing committees of these two governance organizations. Goodman also worked collaboratively with administrators at Stony Brook University to establish, maintain, and teach in a number of interdisciplinary undergraduate programs He has also been involved in statewide governance since 1990. He was Vice-President/Secretary of the SUNY University Faculty Senate for 6 years and, a member of its governance, student life, graduate and research, and undergraduate academic policies and programs committees, serving twice as chair of the last one. He edits the SUNY University Senate Bulletin, as he has done for more than a decade. He was named the first SUNY University Faculty Senate Fellow, now called the Carl P. Wiezalis/ SUNY University Faculty Senate Fellow.

Beth Hinderliter is Associate Professor of Art History and coordinator of African and African American studies at SUNY Buffalo State. She received her doctorate from Columbia University. Her recent publications appear in *African and Black Diaspora, NKA: Journal of Contemporary African Art* and *Journal of Postcolonial Writing*. She has served on the

SUNY University Faculty Senate Committee on Diversity and Cultural Competence and has received the Muriel A. Howard Presidential Award in Equity and Diversity at Buffalo State.

Síocháin Hughes is an artist working with a diversity of materials including camera, paint, sculpture, installation, and digital media. The recipient of a Fulbright Fellowship, she studied at the University of the Arts, Berlin, Germany. She has exhibited internationally at forums including the Musée Carnavalet and the Galerie Lambert in Paris, France; the Kultur Senat Roloff-Momin, the Galerie Am Scheunenviertel and the Amerika Haus Gallery, in Berlin, Germany; the Henry Street Settlement and White Columns in New York City; and several east coast universities. Her work is in the collection of the Musée Carnavalet and numerous private collections. Ms. Hughes taught at Hunter College CUNY from 1995 to 2013. She maintains her studio in New Jersey and teaches as an adjunct at local area colleges.

Daniel J. Knox is the Director of Student Mobility at SUNY System Administration. He holds a BA in English Language and Literature from the University of Chicago and an MS in Educational Administration and Policy Studies from the University at Albany, SUNY, where he is currently pursuing a PhD in Educational Administration and Policy Studies. As the Director of Student Mobility, Daniel oversees the implementation of several university-wide student success initiatives, including seamless transfer and reverse transfer, and provides program direction for SUNY's Degree Planning and Audit program (Degree Works). Prior to working at SUNY, Daniel taught 8th grade English Language Arts in New York City as a member of Teach for America and Earth Science at a residential psychiatric treatment center in Chicago.

Peter L.K. Knuepfer is Associate Professor of Geological Sciences and Environmental Studies at Binghamton University and President of the Faculty Senate. He joined the SUNY Board of Trustees July 1, 2013. Professor Knuepfer received his BS and MS degrees in geology from Stanford University and his PhD in geosciences from the University of Arizona. A member of Binghamton's faculty since 1986, he specializes in the study of processes operating at the Earth's surface, particularly rivers and flood hazards. He has taught undergraduate courses in environmental studies and both undergraduate and graduate courses in geology, as well as courses in the Binghamton Scholars program and freshmen seminars. He has been principal advisor to 11 Masters and four PhD students, as well as serving on numerous Masters and Doctoral committees.

Professor Knuepfer has served Binghamton, SUNY, and the public in many ways during his time at Binghamton. He served as director of the Environmental Studies Program at BU for more than a decade, has chaired several committees on campus, been a member of a number of senior administrative search committees, and a member of SUNY-wide committees on system-wide assessment as well as University Faculty Senate committees on undergraduate education, graduate education and research, and academic integrity. He has also presented several talks to groups in the Binghamton area on flood hazards and assessment, and has been a member of the advisory board to the Union-Endicott Educational Foundation. He also serves as a church musician. He received the Chancellor's Award for Excellence in Faculty Service in 2005.

Dr. Knuepfer's research has ranged from the study of earthquake hazards (including part of a team that assessed earthquake potential for the proposed Yucca Mountain nuclear waste repository), to analysis of mountain growth in Taiwan and New Zealand, to the glacial history of New York, to the assessment of past and potential future flooding in the Susquehanna River basin. He has authored or co-authored more than 40 scientific papers and 100 professional presentations, and has co-edited three books. His current project focuses on the magnitude and frequency of pre-historic flooding of the Susquehanna River as well as changes in the frequency of large flooding throughout the Northeast United States in recent decades. He has received many federal grants in support of his research.

David Lavallee served as Provost and Executive Vice Chancellor of the SUNY system from 2009 to 2013. Prior to his position as system Provost, he served for 10 years as Provost and Vice President for Academic Affairs at SUNY New Paltz and at the City College of New York for the previous 5 years. As Executive Vice Chancellor and Provost, his responsibilities spanned academic and operational aspects of the nation's largest integrated system of higher education, including student mobility and success initiatives, the OPEN SUNY on-line degree initiative, shared services among campuses and presidential searches and leadership development. As University Professor and Senior Advisor to the Chancellor, he now conducts leadership training for new presidents and provost in the system and for staff and faculty at the New Paltz campus. He is developing and coordinating science and mathematics content courses for the state-wide master teacher initiative that is being conducted on nine SUNY campuses and in New York City.

Dr. Lavallee's research in bio-inorganic chemistry has produced more than 60 peer-reviewed articles, two books, and two patents. He has been awarded more than $5 million in research and training grants from the National Science Foundation, National Institutes of Health and several other agencies and foundations. He has been an invited speaker at more than 125 universities and research centers in 11 countries and was a Fulbright senior research fellow in Paris in 1986. Dr. Lavallee has also served as a research collaborator or consultant at several national laboratories, including Argonne in Chicago, Brookhaven in Upton, New York, and Los Alamos in Los Alamos, New Mexico. His teaching and curriculum work has led to the Catalyst Award, a national award for chemistry teachers, major grants from the Department of Education for science preparation for teachers and from the National Science Foundation for high school technology education. Dr. Lavallee earned his BS in Chemistry from St. Bonaventure University and his MS and PhD in Chemistry from the University of Chicago.

Evelyn Maggio is Chair of the Department of Business at Medgar Evers College-CUNY and has been a professor of Business Law since 1998. Professor Maggio obtained her BS in Accounting from Bernard M. Baruch College and her JD from Seton Hall University School of Law. She is currently completing her LLM in Taxation. Professor Maggio has served as Vice-Chair of the MEC Faculty Senate from 2011–2012 and as its Parliamentarian from 2011 to 2014. She is also legal counsel to the Chair of the Governance Committee at Medgar Evers College. Prior to her academic position, Professor Maggio was Law Clerk at McCarter English, Newark New Jersey and Law Clerk to the Honorable Edmund Bernhard, Superior Court of New Jersey, Hunterdon County. She also served as counsel with Thompkins, McGuire, Wachenfeld in Newark, New Jersey, and as Tax Counsel with Price Waterhouse. Professor Maggio and her family reside in New Jersey and North Carolina. Professor Maggio has published in the areas of Business Law, Auditing and Taxation.

T. John McCune is Director of Technology Support Services, State University of New York at Fredonia. From 2013 to 2015, he served as the Governance Officer at Fredonia during the time Fredonia was recognized with the first ever SUNY Shared Governance Award. His research interests include human-computer interaction, governance, learning environments, and multimedia. In 2013, he was honored with being selected as a member of the inaugural Educause Breakthrough Models Academy. In 2015, he was recognized by the SUNY Educational Technology Officer's Association (EdTOA) through receiving their Outstanding Service Award. He has a BS in Communication from SUNY Fredonia, a MSM in Information Technology Management from Colorado Technical University, and an Ed. S. in Computing Technology in Education from Nova Southeastern University. Currently, he is a PhD candidate in Computing Technology in Education at Nova Southeastern University.

Rochelle Mozlin graduated from the New England College of Optometry in 1981. In 1982, she completed the Residency in Vision Training at the State University of New York, State College of Optometry, where she has remained a member of the faculty and is currently an Associate Clinical Professor. In May 2003, she completed a master's degree in Public Health at New York Medical College's School of Public Health. In 2005, Dr. Mozlin became involved in SUNY's University Faculty Senate when she was elected Faculty Senator. She served on the UFS Executive Committee as the elected representative of the Health Science sector and as the appointed Chair of the Governance Committee. She was also a member of the steering committee that developed SUNY Voices Orientation/Leadership Conference for faculty and student governance leaders across the university. In 2014, she received the prestigious Chugh Award from the UFS for outstanding faculty service. Dr. Mozlin is a Fellow of the American Academy of Optometry and the College of Optometrists in Vision Development. She has lectured extensively and published many articles on vision development, optometric education and public health.

Kenneth P. O'Brien is the Immediate Past President of the University Faculty Senate and is currently a Faculty Fellow in the SUNY Provost's Office. He came to the State University of New York College at Brockport in 1970, and has served as history department Chair, Director of the College Honors Program, and Director of Transfer Articulation. From 1985 to 1987, he was a member of the Motion Picture Association of America's Ratings Board and has served on the New York State Historical Records Advisory Board for more than a decade. The recipient of an NEH College Teachers in Residence Fellowship and both the SUNY Chancellor's Award for Excellence in Teaching (1981) and Excellence in Faculty Service

(2005), his major publications include *The Home-Front War*, co-edited with Lynn Hudson Parsons, *SUNY at 60*, co-edited with John Clark and W. Bruce Leslie, "The United States and War in the Twentieth Century," in *The Cambridge Companion to Modern American Culture*, and "Education Markets in English and American Universities," with co-author John Halsey, in Sarah Pickard, ed. *Higher Education in the UK and the US*. His most recent publication is *Sixty-Four Campuses—One University: The Story of SUNY*, co-authored with W. Bruce Leslie. He received his PhD in American history from Northwestern University.

Duncan Quarless is Professor of Chemistry at State University of New York College at Old Westbury. His research interests and scholarship are mainly associated with inorganic chemistry that has its scientific relevance in understanding metal/metalloid chalcogenate chemistry in biology, medicine and the environment. The nature of this work involves synthetic models and materials, which provide insight for such things as, spin states, structural coordination modes, redox states and mechanistic reactivity. His curricular and co-curricular activities include work directing state- and federally funded STEM Education programs on the SUNY Old Westbury campus. Professor Quarless has served on the Executive Committee of the SUNY Old Westbury Faculty Senate and is the immediate past chair. SUNY's Research Foundation recognized him for his record of extramural funding in support of his scholarship and contributions to science education (Research and Scholarship Award, 2006). Subsequently, he received the SUNY Chancellor's Award for Excellence in Teaching (2007). Quarless received his BS in Biochemistry from the City University of NY College of Staten Island, and his MS and PhD in Inorganic Chemistry from the State University of NY at Stony Brook.

Daniel Ryan currently serves as Director of the offices of Veteran Services and of Off-Campus Student Services at the University of Buffalo. Prior to this appointment, Dr. Ryan was Director of Career Services at the University at Buffalo. Dr. Ryan currently serves on the Board of the International Town/ Gown Association in Buffalo. He has also served on the Boards of the Association on Higher Education and Disability; the Eastern Association of Colleges; and Region II of the National Association of Student Personnel Administrators. Dr. Ryan is the author of *Job Search Handbook for People with Disabilities*, now in its third edition. He received his BA and MS from Canisius College, and his PhD from the University at Buffalo.

Bruce Simon is Associate Professor of English and Chairperson of the English Department, State University of New York at Fredonia. Dr. Simon is Fredonia's representative on SUNY's University Faculty Senate, Officer for Contingents for the Fredonia Chapter of United University Professions, a former Chair of Fredonia's University Senate, and a former Co-General Editor of *Workplace: A Journal for Academic Labor*. At Fredonia, he teaches courses in American, African American, and world literature, literary theory, and popular culture. His essays can be found in *The Politics of Information* (eds. Marc Bousquet and Katherine Willis), *Postcolonial Theory and the United States: Race, Ethnicity, and Literature* (eds. Amritjit Singh and Peter Schmidt), *Race Consciousness: African-American Studies for the New Century* (eds. Judith Jackson Fossett and Jeffrey Tucker), and *The Social Construction of Race and Ethnicity in the United States* (eds. Joan Ferrante and Prince Brown, Jr.). He received an AB in English and mathematics from Hamilton College, an MA and PhD in English from Princeton University, a certificate from the School of Criticism and Theory (then at Dartmouth College), and a Fulbright Lecturing Grant in American Studies (where he taught at Kyushu University, Seinan Gakuin University, and Fukuoka University in Fukuoka, Japan).

Emily Sohmer Tai (PhD Harvard University, 1996) is an associate professor of History at Queensborough Community College of the City University of New York (CUNY), where she teaches the history of Western Civilization, the History of Religion, and the History of Women, and specializes in the history of the medieval Mediterranean. Professor Tai has also been active in faculty governance, serving variously, over the last decade, on the Steering Committee of Queensborough's Academic Senate as Secretary, Vice-Chair, and Chair. Since 2010, Professor Tai has also served on the Executive Committee of CUNY's University Faculty Senate (UFS), acting as Editor for the UFS's main publication, the UFS Blog (formerly *The Senate Digest*). In addition to various publications relevant to her field of scholarly specialty, Professor Tai has written extensively about governance and academic professional issues. Her work on these subjects has appeared in *The Community College Humanist*, a publication of the Community College Humanities Association, for which she serves as Contributing Editor; *Perspectives on History*, the newsmagazine of the American Historical Association, on whose Editorial Board she served from 2003 until 2015; *The Journal of Higher Education Outreach and Engagement*; and *NWSA Journal*.

Index